Mathematics 11–14

Elevate

David Baker
Lynn Byrd
Paul Hogan
Simon Longman
Graham Macphail
Kathryn Scott

levels 5–6

Text © Paul Hogan, David Baker, Graham Macphail, Kathryn Scott, Lynn Byrd, Simon Longman, 2008
Original illustrations © Nelson Thornes Ltd 2008

The right of Paul Hogan, David Baker, Graham Macphail, Kathryn Scott, Lynn Byrd and Simon Longman to be identified as authors of this work have been asserted by them in accordance with the Copyright, Designs and Patents Act 1988.

All rights reserved. No part of this publication may be reproduced or transmitted in any form or by any means, electronic or mechanical, including photocopy, recording or any information storage and retrieval system, without permission in writing from the publisher or under licence from the Copyright Licensing Agency Limited, of Saffron House, 6-10 Kirby Street, London EC1N 8TS.

Any person who commits any unauthorised act in relation to this publication may be liable to criminal prosecution and civil claims for damages.

Published in 2008 by:
Nelson Thornes Ltd
Delta Place
27 Bath Road
CHELTENHAM
GL53 7TH
United Kingdom

08 09 10 11 12 / 10 9 8 7 6 5 4 3 2 1

A catalogue record for this book is available from the British Library

ISBN 978 0 7487 9913 8

Illustrations by Roger Penwill and Harry Venning
Cover photograph: girl in red jumper - Alamy
Page make-up by Tech-Set Ltd

Printed and bound in Great Britain by Scotprint

Acknowledgements

The authors and publishers would like to thank Amanda Miles and Nicola Morgan for their contributions. The authors would also like to thank: Clodagh Burke, Geoff Covey, Linda Harvie, Olivia Ironside, Jonathan Litton, David Mantovani, Jeff Nosbaum, Nick Taylor, Natalie Williams, Amanda Wilson.

The publishers would also like to thank the following for permission to reproduce copyright material:
p. 19 – Fotolia; p. 22 – First Great Western; p.26 – iStock, Fotolia, Rex Features, Corbis; p. 54 – Alamy; p.80 – Fotolia; p. 90 – Tatton Park; p.99 – Sarah & Anna Burke; p121 – Science Photo Library, Fotolia; p.133 – Fotolia; p.195 – Fotolia; p.230 – Rex Features; p.233 – Fotolia; p.244 – Alamy; p.255 – Empics; p.257 – iStock; p.258 – Alamy; p.264 – Alamy; p269 – Fotolia; p.309 – iStock; p.315 – Yorkshire Television

The publishers have made every effort to contact copyright holders but apologise if any have been overlooked.

Introduction

We hope that you will enjoy using this book. It has been designed to help you learn and understand mathematics. These are the features you will find inside:

Chapter opening page

This book has 18 chapters. Each chapter has an opening page like this:

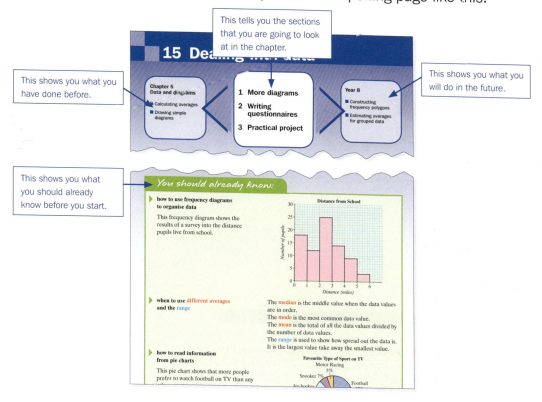

Start of section page

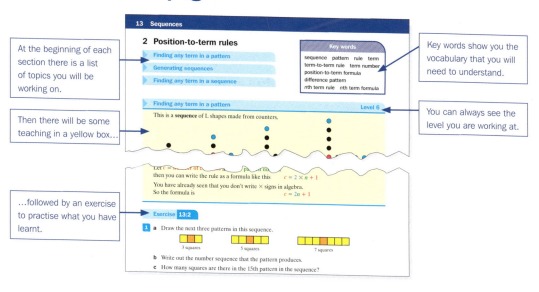

Introduction

Special features

Look out for these at the end of each chapter:

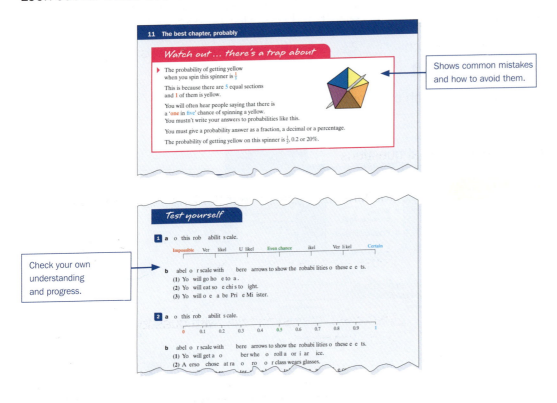

Shows common mistakes and how to avoid them.

Check your own understanding and progress.

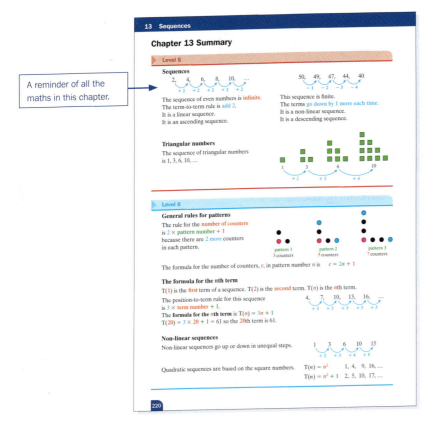

A reminder of all the maths in this chapter.

Icons and special questions

Look out for these icons...

S This is for a SAT question

This is a Real World question

⚠ This is when a question is more challenging!

🖩 This shows when you should use a calculator...

🚫 ...and this shows when you shouldn't

... and look out for these special questions

Think on! — You'll need to use all your thinking skills for these!

Explore — These are mini investigations.

Facts to figure — These are interesting facts with questions to make you think.

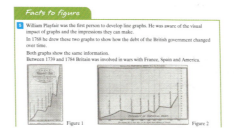

Break Away and Functional Maths

Have fun with the **Break Away** and **Functional Maths** pages! These are mini projects and interesting tasks at the back of the book.

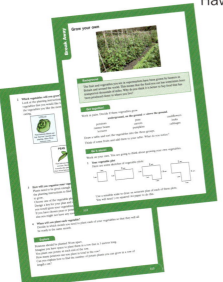
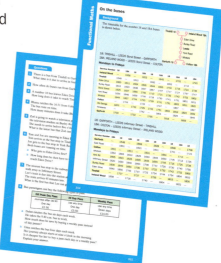

Contents

	Introduction	iii
1	The language of algebra	1
2	Multiplying and dividing	15
3	Coordinates and symmetry	35
4	Types of numbers	53
5	Data and diagrams	69
6	Formulae and algebraic operations	87
7	2-D and 3-D shapes	101
8	Decimals, fractions and percentages	115
9	Equations	137
10	Angles – on the turn	153
11	The best chapter, probably	171
12	More fractions and percentages	181
13	Sequences	203
14	Area, volume and measures	221
15	Dealing with data	237
16	Ratio and proportion	253
17	Algebraic graphs	273
18	Transformations	289
	Break Away Water	310
	Break Away Grow your own	312
	Functional maths On the buses	314
	Test Yourself Answers	316
	Index	341

1 The language of algebra

Year 6
- Multiplication tables up to 10 × 10
- Adding, subtracting, multiplying and dividing whole numbers mentally

1. Algebraic notation
2. Like terms and brackets

Chapter 6 Formulae and algebraic operations
- Constructing and using formulae
- Inverse operations
- Substituting into expressions and formulae

Chapter 9 Equations

Solving equations

You should already know:

▶ multiplication facts up to 10 × 10 = 100 and related division facts

×	1	2	3	4	5	6	7	8	9	10
1	1	2	3	4	5	6	7	8	9	10
2	2	4	6	8	10	12	14	16	18	20
3	3	6	9	12	15	18	21	24	27	30
4	4	8	12	16	20	24	28	32	36	40
5	5	10	15	20	25	30	35	40	45	50
6	6	12	18	24	30	36	42	48	54	60
7	7	14	21	28	35	42	49	56	63	70
8	8	16	24	32	40	48	56	64	72	80
9	9	18	27	36	45	54	63	72	81	90
10	10	20	30	40	50	60	70	80	90	100

$6 \times 7 = 42$ is a multiplication fact.

$42 \div 6 = 7$ and $42 \div 7 = 6$ are related division facts.

▶ that you use letters for unknowns in algebra

If $n + 6 = 8$
then $n = 2$

1 The language of algebra

1 Algebraic notation

▶ **Using correct algebraic notation**

▶ **Doing algebraic operations in the right order**

Key words	
expression	variable
term	equals (=)
equation	brackets

Using correct algebraic notation — Level 5

$n + 8$ is an **expression**. An expression can contain letters and numbers. The letter n is called a **variable**.

If you start with a number n you need to know how to write expressions that are linked to n.

Adding 8 to the number or **8 more than the number** $n + 8$ or $8 + n$

Subtracting 3 from the number or **3 less than the number** $n - 3$

Subtracting the number from 10 $10 - n$

Multiplying the number by 5 which you should write as . $n \times 5$ or $5 \times n$
$5n$ and **not** $n5$

Dividing the number by 3 which you should write as $n \div 3$
$\frac{n}{3}$

Dividing 12 by the number which you should write as $12 \div n$
$\frac{12}{n}$

Multiplying the number by itself which you should write as $n \times n$
n^2

Adding the number to itself is the same as **multiplying the number by 2** $n + n$
$2n$

$n + n$ is **not** the same as $n \times n$
So $2n$ is **not** the same as n^2

Multiplying the number by 3 and then **adding 4** $n \times 3 + 4 = 3n + 4$

Adding 2 to a number and then **multiplying the answer by 5** $(n + 2) \times 5 = 5(n + 2)$

Never write $1n$. Just write n for the number itself.

Each part of an expression is called a **term**.
In the expression $3n - 4$ there are two terms. $3n$ is one term and -4 is the other term.
There is no **equals** sign in an expression.

An **equation** contains an equals sign. Equations can be written in different orders.
If $a = b$ then $b = a$. If $c = a + b$ then $c = b + a$, $a + b = c$ and $b + a = c$.

Exercise 1:1

1 Write an algebraic expression for each of these.

a add 4 to a
b 12 more than b
c subtract 5 from c
d subtract d from 29
e multiply e by 21
f multiply 8 by f
g divide 32 by g
h divide h by 12
i multiply i by itself
j half of j
k 7 more than twice k
l 3 less than twice l
m 7 more than four times m
n 6 more than a quarter of n
o the product of r and s
⚠ p 5 times the value of 3 less than n
⚠ q three times the sum of p and q
⚠ r the square of the sum of u and v
⚠ s the sum of t squared and 5
⚠ t the product of 6 and the square of w

2 a $n + n + n$ is 3 lots of n. This is the same as the simplified expression $3n$.
  Simplify the expression in each part.
  (1) $n + n + n + n$ (2) $g + g + g + g + g + g$ (3) $a + a + a + a + a$

b $n + n + m + m + m$ is 2 lots of n plus 3 lots of m. This is the same as $2n + 3m$.
  Simplify the expression in each part.
  (1) $n + n + m + m + m + m$
  (2) $y + y + y + y + z + z + z$
  (3) $a + a + a + a + a + b + b + b$
  (4) $k + k + l + l + l + l + m + m$
  (5) $b + c + b + c + b + b + c + b + c + b$
  (6) $j + k + l + k + l + j + j + l + k + j$

⚠ **c** $n \times n \times n$ is the same as n^3.
  Simplify the expression in each part.
  (1) $n \times n \times n \times n$ (2) $r \times r \times r \times r \times r$ (3) $b \times b \times b \times b \times b \times b$

⚠ **d** $m \times m \times n \times n \times n$ is m^2 multiplied by n^3. This is the same as $m^2 n^3$.
  Simplify the expression in each part.
  (1) $m \times m \times m \times n \times n$
  (2) $r \times r \times r \times r \times s \times s \times s$
  (3) $a \times a \times b \times b \times b \times b$
  (4) $d \times e \times e \times e \times e$
  (5) $p \times q \times p \times p \times q \times q \times p$
  (6) $m \times n \times p \times n \times p \times p \times n \times p \times p$

3 Write an algebraic expression for each of these.
Write each expression as simply as you can.

a multiply m by 3 then add 8
b multiply n by 12 then subtract 9
c divide p by 2 then subtract 6
d divide g by 3 then add 13
e add 4 to y then multiply by 6
f subtract 2 from x then multiply by 9
g add 6 to q then divide by 5
h subtract 2 from r then divide by 7

4 Explain why the two expressions in each part are different.

a $4n$ and $n + 4$
b $8 - n$ and $n - 8$
c $2n$ and n^2
d $5(n + 1)$ and $5n + 1$
e $n^2 + 4$ and $(n + 4)^2$
f $2n^2$ and $(2n)^2$

1 The language of algebra

5 In the expression 6m − 2n there are two terms. 6m is one term and − 2n is the other term.
Write down all the terms in each of these expressions.

a 3n + 5
b 8x + 7y − 2
c 2x − 6y + 8k
d 4x − y − 2w + 3
e b^2 + 3a
f $2c^2$ − 3d + 2

6 A teacher has **5 full packets** of mints and **6 single** mints.
The number of mints inside each packet is the same.

The teacher tells the class,

'**Write an expression** to show **how many mints** there are **altogether**. Call the number of mints inside each packet y.'

Here are some expressions that the pupils write:

5 + 6 + y   5y6   5y + 6

6 + 5y   5 + 6y   (5 + 6) × y

a Write down **two** expressions that are correct.

b A pupil says, 'I think the teacher has a total of **56 mints**.'
Could the pupil be correct? Explain how you know.

7 a It is Tina's birthday. We do not know how old Tina is.
Call **Tina's age**, in years, n.
The expressions below compare Tina's age to some other people's ages.
Use words to compare their ages. The first one is done for you.

Tina's age	n
Ann's age	n + 3

Ann is 3 years older than Tina.

Tina's age	n
Barry's age	n − 1

Barry is ....

Tina's age	n
Carol's age	2n

Carol is ....

b In one year's time Tina's age will be **n + 1**.
Write **simplified expressions** to show the ages of the other people in one year's time.

	Tina	Ann	Barry	Carol
Age now	n	n + 3	n − 1	2n
Age in one year's time	n + 1			

8 The equation $x = y$ can be written as $y = x$.
Write down another equation that you know is true in each part.

- **a** $p = q$
- **b** $h = 2g$
- **c** $r = t + w$
- **d** $a + f = k$
- **e** $d - e = j$
- **f** $x^2 = y^2 - z^2$

Think on!

9 Sort the expressions on these cards into groups.
Each group should contain cards that show equivalent expressions.

7 more than n	$n - 7$	$7 - n$	n subtract 7
7 subtract n	7 less than n	$7n + 7$	n more than 7
	$7 + 7n$	$n + 7$	n less than 7
	multiply n by 7 then add 7	$7 + n$	

Doing algebraic operations in the right order   Level 5

You must do multiplications and divisions **before** you do additions and subtractions.

The expression **5n + 2** means that you need to **multiply n by 5** before **adding 2**.
The expression $2 + 5n$ is the same as $5n + 2$.
So $2 + 5n$ also means that you need to **multiply n by 5** before **adding 2**.

You have to do anything in **brackets** first.

So **5(n + 2)** means that you have to **add 2 to n** before **multiplying the answer by 5**.

The expression **7(n − 6) + 3** means that you **take 6 away from n**
before you **multiply the answer by 7** and then **add 3**.

Exercise 1:2

1 The expression **4n + 2** means **multiply n by 4** and then **add 2**.
Write a sentence to explain the order of the operations in each part.

- **a** $6n + 5$
- **b** $7n - 1$
- **c** $\dfrac{n}{2} + 4$
- **d** $\dfrac{n}{9} - 3$
- **e** $\dfrac{12}{n} + 5$
- **f** $\dfrac{n + 7}{5}$
- **g** $\dfrac{n - 2}{4}$
- **h** $4(n + 2)$
- **i** $6(n - 8)$

1 The language of algebra

2 Look at the pupil's statement in each part and say whether it's **True** or **False**. Explain each of your answers.

   a Lucy: 'The expression $a + b$ is different from the expression $b + a$.'

   b Amber: 'The expression ab means the same as the expression ba and they both mean the same thing as $a \times b$.'

   c Louis: 'The expression $a + (b + c)$ has the same value as the expression $(a + b) + c$ and they both have the same value as $a + b + c$.'

   d Declan: 'The expression $a \times (b \times c)$ is different from the expression $(a \times b) \times c$.'

3 The expression $21 - 3n$ means **multiply n by 3** and then **subtract the answer from 21**. Write a sentence to explain the order of the operations in each part.

   a $15 - 2n$ **b** $12 - 6n$ **c** $20 - \dfrac{n}{4}$ **d** $8(3 - n)$

4 Each part contains two expressions that are different. Explain the difference between the two expressions in each part.

   a $5n - 2$ and $5(n - 2)$ **c** $n - 7$ and $7 - n$

   b $\dfrac{n}{4}$ and $\dfrac{4}{n}$ **d** $\dfrac{n}{3} + 2$ and $\dfrac{n + 2}{3}$

5 Stephen has m computer games.
Dai has twice as many as Stephen.
Liam has two more than Dai.
Jamie has two more than Stephen.
Nick has twice as many as Jamie.

Write an expression for the number of computer games that each person has.

Stephen   Dai   Liam   Jamie   Nick

6 Write a sentence to explain the order of the operations in each part.

   a $5(n - 1) + 6$ **b** $3 + 2(n + 7)$ **c** $30 - 8(n + 1)$

7 Copy these and fill them in.

   a $2 + 3 = \ldots$ $4 + 5 = \ldots$ $7 + 3 = \ldots$ $a + b = \ldots + \ldots$
       $3 + 2 = \ldots$ $5 + 4 = \ldots$ $3 + 7 = \ldots$

   b $2 \times 3 = \ldots$ $4 \times 5 = \ldots$ $7 \times 3 = \ldots$ $a \times b = \ldots \times \ldots$
       $3 \times 2 = \ldots$ $5 \times 4 = \ldots$ $3 \times 7 = \ldots$ $ab = \ldots$

   c $2 + (3 + 4) = \ldots$ $5 + (2 + 1) = \ldots$ $a + (b + c) = (\ldots + \ldots) + \ldots$
       $(2 + 3) + 4 = \ldots$ $(5 + 2) + 1 = \ldots$

   d $2 \times (3 \times 4) = \ldots$ $5 \times (2 \times 4) = \ldots$ $a \times (b \times c) = (\ldots \times \ldots) \times \ldots$
       $(2 \times 3) \times 4 = \ldots$ $(5 \times 2) \times 4 = \ldots$ $a(bc) = (\ldots)\ldots$

2 Like terms and brackets

▶ **Collecting like terms**

▶ **Multiplying out an expression in brackets**

Key words
like terms   simplify
collect like terms   multiply out
brackets

▶ **Collecting like terms**   Level 5

Like terms have an identical combination of letters in them.

So $3x$ and $5x$ are like terms.
They are both x terms.

$2y$ and $4y$ are like terms.
They are both y terms.

$4xy$ and $6xy$ are like terms.
They are both xy terms.

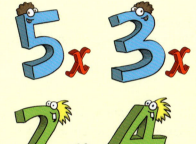

$2p^2q$ and $7qp^2$ are like terms.
p^2q means $p \times p \times q$ and qp^2 means $q \times p \times p$.
But $p \times p \times q = q \times p \times p$ so p^2q means the same as qp^2.
You should write letter combinations in alphabetical order so the terms are both p^2q terms.

$3rs$ and $3st$ are **not** like terms. $r \times s$ isn't the same as $s \times t$.
$5x^2y$ and $5xy^2$ are **not** like terms. $x^2y = x \times x \times y$ but $xy^2 = x \times y \times y$.

You can **simplify** expressions by **collecting like terms**.

If you have ordinary numbers you can collect them together too.

You collect like terms by adding and subtracting them like this:

$2d + 7d = 9d$ $11xy - 3xy = 8xy$ $3p^2q + 11p^2q = 14p^2q$

$5g + 3k + 2g + k = 7g + 4k$ $4y^2z + 8 + 5zy^2 - 2 = 9y^2z + 6$

Exercise 1:3

1 Simplify these expressions by collecting like terms.

a $3g + 4g$
b $9v - 2v$
c $5ab + 3ab$
d $9rs - 3sr$
e $5a^2b - 3a^2b$
f $3d + 6e + 5d + 2e$
g $11w + x - 5w + x$
h $3xy + 3gh + 5yx + 4hg$
i $9pq + 2st - pq + ts$
j $6uv + 15 - 3vu - 7$
k $5mn + 9 - 4nm - 4$
l $7kl + 5lm + 2kl - 3ml$
m $4p^2q + 7p^2q$
n $8y^2z + 5zy^2$
o $4r^2s - 3sr^2$

1 The language of algebra

2 Write each expression in its simplest form.

   a $7 + 2t + 3t$ **b** $b + 7 + 2b + 10$

3 Simplify these expressions.

   a $5k + 7 + 3k$ **b** $k + 1 + k + 4$

4 Write down the card that always has the same value as:

   a $a + a$ **e** $xy + yx$
   b $3b + 4b$ **f** $3p - 2p$
   c $a + b + b$ **g** $5pq - 2qp$
   d $a \times a$ **h** $x^2y + yx^2$

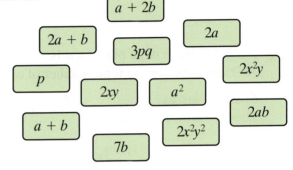

Cards: $a + 2b$, $2a + b$, $2a$, $3pq$, $2x^2y$, p, $2xy$, a^2, $2ab$, $a + b$, $2x^2y^2$, $7b$

5 a Here is an expression.

$$2a + 3 + 2a$$

Which expression below shows it written as simply as possible?
Write down the correct one.

    $7a$ $7 + a$ $2a + 5$

    $4a + 3$ $4(a + 3)$

b Here is a different expression.

$$3b + 4 + 5b - 1$$

Write this expression as simply as possible.

6 The term in each block in these diagrams is found by adding the two blocks below it.
Copy the diagrams and fill in the missing blocks.
Simplify your answers for each block as much as possible by collecting like terms.

a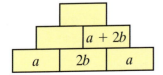

b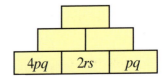

7 **a** Work out the perimeter of each of these shapes.
Simplify your answers as much as possible.

(1) 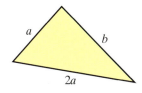 (2) 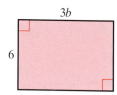 (3)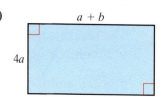

b Draw and label your own shape that has a perimeter of $6a + 12$

8 A teacher has a large pile of cards.
An expression for the **total** number of cards is **$6n + 8$**

a The teacher puts the cards in two piles.
The number of cards in the first pile is **$2n + 3$**

first pile   second pile

Write an expression to show the number of cards in the second pile.

b The teacher puts all the cards together.
Then he uses them to make two equal piles.

Write an expression to show the number of cards in one of the piles.

9 In the grid shown, the value of each square increases by 1 as you move to the right.

The value increases by 10 as you move down a square.

The values of some squares are labelled for you.

a Write down the value of each of the squares labelled *A* to *F*.

b Find the total value of the three squares that you were given.

c Find the total value of the squares labelled *A* to *F*.

F	E			
D	n	$n+1$	A	
	$n+10$	B	C	

1 The language of algebra

Multiplying out an expression in brackets — Level 6

$3(30 + 2)$ means 3 multiplied by $(30 + 2)$

The brackets mean that you add 30 and 2 to get 32 before you multiply the answer by 3.

$3 \times (30 + 2) = 3 \times 32 = 96$

You can **multiply out** the **brackets** instead.

You work out 3×30 and 3×2 and add the answers together.

$3 \times 30 + 3 \times 2 = 90 + 6 = 96$

In algebra $3(x + y)$ means 3 multiplied by $(x + y)$

You can multiply out the brackets in algebraic expressions too.
Multiply each term inside the brackets by the term that is outside.

$3(x + y) = 3 \times x + 3 \times y = 3x + 3y$
$3(x - y) = 3 \times x - 3 \times y = 3x - 3y$
$5(3a + 4) = 5 \times 3a + 5 \times 4 = 15a + 20$
$4(2a - 3b) = 4 \times 2a - 4 \times 3b = 8a - 12b$

You sometimes need to collect like terms when you've multiplied out the brackets.

$3(x + 2y) + 2(2x + 3y)$
$= 3 \times x + 3 \times 2y + 2 \times 2x + 2 \times 3y$
$= 3x + 6y + 4x + 6y$
$= 7x + 12y$

$5(3a + 4b) + 4(2a - 3b)$
$= 5 \times 3a + 5 \times 4b + 4 \times 2a - 4 \times 3b$
$= 15a + 20b + 8a - 12b$
$= 23a + 8b$

Exercise 1:4

1 Multiply out each of these brackets.

- **a** $4(x + y)$
- **b** $2(a + b)$
- **c** $5(p - q)$
- **d** $7(m - n)$
- **e** $8(r + s)$
- **f** $12(l + m)$
- **g** $6(f + 2g)$
- **h** $3(a + 3b)$
- **i** $4(x + 2y)$
- **j** $3(2p - 3q)$
- **k** $4(3v - 2w)$
- **l** $3(g - 2h)$
- **m** $5(2g + 3h)$
- **n** $6(2j - 3k)$
- **o** $5(3c + d)$
- **p** $8(2d - 3e)$
- **q** $5(4m + n)$
- **r** $4(2e - 3f)$

2 Write down the card that always has the same value as

- **a** $3(a + b)$
- **b** $3(a + 2b)$
- **c** $4(a - b)$
- **d** $2(3a + 1)$
- **e** $4(a - 2b)$
- **f** $2(2a + 4b)$

$3a + 6b$	$6a + 2$	$3a + 3b$
$4a - 8b$	$4a - 2b$	$3a + b$
$6a + 1$	$4a + 8b$	$4a - 4b$

3 Jenny wants to multiply out the brackets in the expression $3(2a + 1)$

She writes: $\quad 3(2a + 1) = 6a + 1$

Show why Jenny is **wrong**.

4 $2a \times b$ is the same as $2 \times a \times b$. You write this as $2ab$.
$a \times 2b$ is $a \times 2 \times b$. This is the same as $2 \times a \times b$. You also write this as $2ab$.
Write these products using the correct notation.

- **a** $3a \times c$
- **b** $5c \times d$
- **c** $d \times 4e$
- **d** $g \times 7h$
- **e** $6q \times p$
- **f** $8t \times r$
- **g** $f \times 3e$
- **h** $b \times 9a$

5 This diagram shows you how to multiply out $a(b + c)$.

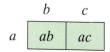

$a(b + c) = ab + ac$

Copy these diagrams and fill them in.

a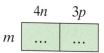

$u(v + w) = \ldots + \ldots$

c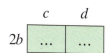

$m(4n + 3p) = \ldots + \ldots$

b

$r(2s + t) = \ldots + \ldots$

d

$2b(c + d) = \ldots + \ldots$

6 Multiply out each of the brackets and collect like terms.

- **a** $3(x + 2y) + 4(2x + 4y)$
- **b** $2(2x + 5y) + 4(3x - 2y)$
- **c** $4(2x + 3y) + 2(x + 3y)$
- **d** $6(x + 2y) + 3(x - 3y)$

7 Multiply out the expression $5(x + 2) + 3(7 + x)$.
Write your answer as simply as possible.

Explore

8 Look at the expressions $2(6x + 3y)$, $3(4x + 2y)$ and $6(2x + y)$.
All of these expressions are equivalent to $12x + 6y$.

$2(6x + 3y) = 12x + 6y \qquad 3(4x + 2y) = 12x + 6y \qquad 6(2x + y) = 12x + 6y$

Write the expression $24x + 8y$ in the form $\ldots(\ldots x + \ldots y)$ in as many different ways as you can.

1 The language of algebra

Watch out... there's a trap about

▶ $n \times n$ is **not** equal to $2n$.
$n \times n$ is equal to n^2.
$n + n$ is equal to $2n$.

▶ $4a + 5b - 2a + 3b = 2a + 8b$

But you cannot simplify $2a + 8b$ any further.

$2a + 8b$ is **not** equal to $10ab$.

You can't just add the numbers and then write the letters down.

▶ $2(3a + 1)$ does not equal $6a + 1$.

You must remember to multiply both terms in the bracket by the term that is outside.
So $2(3a + 1) = 2 \times 3a + 2 \times 1 = 6a + 2$

Test yourself

1 Write an algebraic expression for each of these.

a add 5 to q
b subtract m from 24
c multiply a by 8
d divide 12 by v
e multiply x by itself
f multiply x by 3 then add 6
g divide y by 4 then subtract 5
h add 7 to x then multiply the answer by 2
i add n to 4 then divide the answer by 3
j 7 more than five times m
k 6 more than half n
l the product of x and y

2 Write each of these expressions as simply as you can.

a $n + n + n$
b $p + p + p + p + p$
c $j + j + k + k + k$
d $l + l + l + m + m + m + m$
e $p + p + p + q$
f $r + s + s + s + s$

3 Explain why the two expressions in each part are different.

a $6n$ and $n + 6$
b $7(n + 1)$ and $7n + 1$
c $2x$ and x^2

4 Write down all the terms in the expression $3e^2 - 5f + 7$.

5 A ruler costs *k* pence.
A pen costs *m* pence.
Copy the diagram and match each statement with the correct expression for the amount in pence. The first one is done for you.

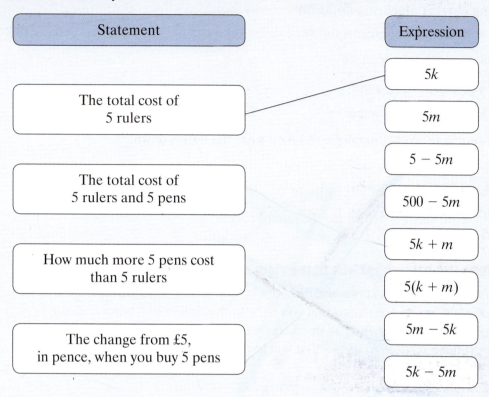

6 Write a sentence to explain the order of the operations in each part.
  a $6n + 7$
  b $2n - 4$
  c $\dfrac{n}{2} + 9$
  d $8(n - 1)$

7 Simplify these expressions by collecting like terms.
  a $7a + 2a$
  b $13bc - 4cb$
  c $3uv + 9 + 8vu - 2$
  d $8p^2q + 2p^2q$
  e $12x^2y + 3yx^2$
  f $7a^2b - 2ba^2$

8 Multiply out each of these brackets.
  a $5(a + b)$
  b $4(2c - d)$
  c $7(2e - 5f)$
  d $3(g - 3h)$
  e $6(4i + j)$
  f $8(5k - 4l)$

9 Multiply out the expression $6(x + 1) + 5(6 + 2x)$.
Write your answer as simply as possible.

10 Write down the card that always has the same value as:
  a $2(3a + 4b)$
  b $3(2a - 3)$
  c $4a \times 3b$
  d $a(2b - 3c)$
  e $5(a + b) + 2(2a + 3b)$
  f $2(2a + 4b) + 3(4a - 2b)$

$16a + 2b$	$6a + 4b$	$2ab - 3ac$
$7ab$	$6a - 9$	$6a + 8b$
$2ab - 3c$	$12ab$	$9a + 11b$

1 The language of algebra

Chapter 1 Summary

Level 5

Using correct algebraic notation

If you start with a number n you need to know how to write expressions that are linked to n.

8 more than the number	$n + 8$
3 less than the number	$n - 3$
Multiplying the number by 5	$5n$
Dividing the number by 3	$\dfrac{n}{3}$
Adding the number to itself	$n + n = 2n$
Multiplying the number by itself	$n \times n = n^2$

Never write $1n$. Just write n for the number itself.

Doing algebraic operations in the right order

You must do multiplications and divisions before you do additions and subtractions.
The expression $3n + 6$ means that you need to **multiply n by 3** before **adding 6**.
But you have to do anything in brackets first.
The expression $3(n + 6)$ means that you have to **add 6 to n** before **multiplying the answer by 3**.

Collecting like terms

You can simplify expressions by collecting like terms.

$$2d + 7d = 9d \qquad 11xy - 3xy = 8xy \qquad 3p^2q + 11p^2q = 14p^2q$$

$$5g + 3k + 2g + k = 7g + 4k \qquad 4y^2z + 8 + 5zy^2 - 2 = 9y^2z + 6$$

Level 6

Multiplying out an expression in brackets

You can multiply out the brackets in algebraic expressions.
Multiply each term inside the brackets by the term that is outside.

$$3(a + b) = 3 \times a + 3 \times b = 3a + 3b$$
$$4(3x - y) = 4 \times 3x - 4 \times y = 12x - 4y$$

Collect like terms when you've multiplied out brackets if you need to.

$$5(2a + 5b) + 4(a - 2b)$$
$$= 5 \times 2a + 5 \times 5b + 4 \times a - 4 \times 2b$$
$$= 10a + 25b + 4a - 8b$$
$$= 14a + 17b$$

2 Multiplying and dividing

Year 6
- Multiplying
- Dividing

1 Multiplication and division methods
2 Measures
3 Order of operations

Chapter 4 Types of numbers
- Factors, multiples and primes
- Number patterns

You should already know:

▶ the multiplication facts up to 10 × 10 = 100 and the related division facts

×	1	2	3	4	5	6	7	8	9	10
1	1	2	3	4	5	6	7	8	9	10
2	2	4	6	8	10	12	14	16	18	20
3	3	6	9	12	15	18	21	24	27	30
4	4	8	12	16	20	24	28	32	36	40
5	5	10	15	20	25	30	35	40	45	50
6	6	12	18	24	30	36	42	48	54	60
7	7	14	21	28	35	42	49	56	63	70
8	8	16	24	32	40	48	56	64	72	80
9	9	18	27	36	45	54	63	72	81	90
10	10	20	30	40	50	60	70	80	90	100

9 × 6 = 54   54 ÷ 9 = 6   54 ÷ 6 = 9

▶ how to double and halve a number by splitting the number up

To double 260:   split 260 into double each part and add the two parts back together.

200 and 60
× 2
400   120
520

▶ how to use written methods for multiplying and dividing

	×	40	3
6		240	18	= 258

6 × 43 = 258

```
  258
- 240
  ---
   18
-  18
  ---
    0
```
6 × 40
6 × 3
43

```
    H T U
      4 3
  ×     6
  -------
    2 5 8
      1
```

258 ÷ 6 = 43

2 Multiplying and dividing

1 Multiplication and division methods

- **Multiplying and dividing integers mentally**
- **Long multiplication**
- **Division**

Key words	
partitioning	product
square	cube
square root	cube root
grid method	column method
estimation	inverse
quotient	dividend
divisor	remainder
fraction	decimal

Multiplying and dividing integers mentally — Level 5

Make some multiplications easier by doubling one number and halving the other.

$150 \times 4 = 300 \times 2 = 600$ double the 150 and halve the 4
$16 \times 5 = 8 \times 10 = 80$ double the 5 and halve the 16

Use **partitioning** by splitting the question into parts like this:

$5 \times 16 = 5 \times 10 + 5 \times 6 = 50 + 30 = 80$ $138 \div 9 = (100 \div 9) + (38 \div 9)$
$\qquad\qquad\qquad\qquad\qquad\qquad\qquad\quad = \ \ 11\ R1\ \ +\ \ 4\ R2$
$\qquad\qquad\qquad\qquad\qquad\qquad\qquad\quad = \ \ 15\ R3$

Use the fact that $9 = 10 - 1$ to multiply by 9 like this: $18 \times 9 = 18 \times 10 - 18 \times 1$
$\qquad\qquad\qquad\qquad\qquad\qquad\qquad\qquad\qquad\qquad\quad = \quad 180 \quad - \quad 18$
$\qquad\qquad\qquad\qquad\qquad\qquad\qquad\qquad\qquad\qquad\quad = \quad 162$

Use factors to split a **product** into two or more steps.

$\quad\ \ 5 \times 16 = 5 \times 8 \times 2 = 40 \times 2 = 80 \qquad\qquad 84 \div 14 = 84 \div 2 \div 7 = 42 \div 7 = 6$
or $5 \times 16 = 5 \times 2 \times 8 = 10 \times 8 = 80 \qquad$ or $\ 84 \div 14 = 84 \div 7 \div 2 = 12 \div 2 = 6$
$18 \times 16 = 18 \times 2 \times 2 \times 2 \times 2 = 36 \times 2 \times 2 \times 2 = 72 \times 2 \times 2 = 144 \times 2 = 288$
$184 \div 8 = 184 \div 2 \div 2 \div 2 = 92 \div 2 \div 2 = 46 \div 2 = 23$

To multiply by 50, you can multiply by 10   or you can multiply by 100 and divide by 2
and then by 5 because $50 = 10 \times 5$ because $50 = 100 \div 2$.

$12 \times 50 = 12 \times 10 \times 5 = 120 \times 5 = 600 \qquad 57 \times 50 = 57 \times 100 \div 2 = 5700 \div 2 = 2850$

You should know these **squares**
$1^2 = 1 \times 1 = 1 \qquad 5^2 = 5 \times 5 = 25 \qquad 9^2 = 9 \times 9 = 81$
$2^2 = 2 \times 2 = 4 \qquad 6^2 = 6 \times 6 = 36 \qquad 10^2 = 10 \times 10 = 100$
$3^2 = 3 \times 3 = 9 \qquad 7^2 = 7 \times 7 = 49 \qquad 11^2 = 11 \times 11 = 121$
$4^2 = 4 \times 4 = 16 \qquad 8^2 = 8 \times 8 = 64 \qquad 12^2 = 12 \times 12 = 144$

these **cubes**
$1^3 = 1 \times 1 \times 1 = 1 \qquad 3^3 = 3 \times 3 \times 3 = 27 \qquad 5^3 = 5 \times 5 \times 5 = 125$
$2^3 = 2 \times 2 \times 2 = 8 \qquad 4^3 = 4 \times 4 \times 4 = 64 \qquad 10^3 = 10 \times 10 \times 10 = 1000$

and be able to work backwards to write down **square roots** and **cube roots** $\sqrt{81} = 9 \quad \sqrt[3]{27} = 3$

Multiplying by 0 always gives 0 as the answer.
You cannot divide by 0.
Multiplying or dividing by 1 always gives the same number as you started with.

Multiplying by 10 makes all the digits move **one column to the left**.

```
  H T U
    3 4
  3 4 0    so 34 × 10 = 340
```

Multiplying by 100 makes all the digits move **two columns to the left**.

```
  Th H T U
        5 9
  5  9 0 0   so 59 × 100 = 5900
```

Multiplying by 1000 makes all the digits move **three columns to the left**.

Dividing by 10 makes all the digits move **one column to the right**.

```
  H T U . t h
    3 4
    3 . 4       so 34 ÷ 10 = 3.4
```

Dividing by 100 makes all the digits move **two columns to the right**.

```
  H T U . t h
    5 9
    0 . 5 9     so 59 ÷ 100 = 0.59
```

Dividing by 1000 makes all the digits move **three columns to the right**.

Exercise 2:1

1 Work these out by doubling one of the numbers and halving the other.
  a 28 × 5   **b** 47 × 4   **c** 50 × 18   **d** 500 × 36

2 a Copy these multiplications and fill in the gaps.
   (1) 7 × 22 = (7 × 20) + (7 × 2) = … + … = …
   (2) 8 × 34 = (8 × 30) + (8 × 4) = … + … = …
   b Use the partitioning method from part **a** to work these out.
   (1) 8 × 17   (3) 6 × 23   (5) 9 × 42   (7) 14 × 21
   (2) 6 × 14   (4) 8 × 31   (6) 13 × 12   (8) 15 × 32

3 24 can be written as 2 × 2 × 2 × 3
   Use this fact to work out these calculations.
   a 14 × 24   **b** 168 ÷ 24   **c** 365 × 24   **d** 528 ÷ 24

2 Multiplying and dividing

4 a Copy these and fill in the gaps.
   (1) $6 \times 14 = 6 \times 7 \times 2 = \ldots \times 2 = \ldots$
   (2) $5 \times 26 = 5 \times 13 \times 2 = 5 \times 2 \times 13 = \ldots \times 13 = \ldots$

   b Work these out.
   (1) 4×35 (2) 5×34 (3) $\frac{1}{2} \times 9 \times 8$ (4) $\frac{1}{2} \times 11 \times 12$

5 Work these out.

   a 18×100 **d** $312 \div 100$ **g** 400×30 **j** $2400 \div 800$
   b 20×1000 **e** $420 \div 1000$ **h** 30×60 **k** $1200 \div 60$
   c $45 \div 10$ **f** 40×20 **i** $900 \div 300$ **l** $6300 \div 30$

6 $99 = 100 - 1$

You can use this fact to help you multiply by 99 like this:
$8 \times 99 = 8 \times 100 - 8 \times 1 = 800 - 8 = 792$

Use this method to do these multiplications.

   a 7×99 **c** 17×99 **e** 7×98 **g** 8×97
   b 9×99 **d** 34×99 **f** 15×98 **h** 14×97

7 a Show that 9×28 is 252.
   b What is 27×28? You can use part **a** to help you.

8 Each amount on a red card is the answer to a question on a blue card.
Match each red card with a blue card.

| 245×1 | 13×99 | 28×98 | 25×99 |

| 2744 | 245 | 2475 | 1287 |

9 Find these squares, cubes, square roots and cube roots.

   a 7^2 **c** 3^3 **e** $\sqrt{16}$ **g** $\sqrt[3]{64}$
   b 9^2 **d** 5^3 **f** $\sqrt{121}$ **h** $\sqrt[3]{1000}$

  10 Copy each of these and fill in the gaps.

   a $320 \div 13 = (300 \div 13) + (20 \div 13)$
               $= \ldots R \ldots + \ldots R \ldots$
               $= \ldots R \ldots$

   b $360 \div 14 = (300 \div 14) + (60 \div 14)$
               $= \ldots R \ldots + \ldots R \ldots$
               $= \ldots R \ldots$

Long multiplication — Level 5

You know about the **grid method** for long multiplication from Year 6.

You can still use this method if you wish.

×	300	70	4
50	15 000	3500	200
6	1800	420	24

$374 \times 56 = 20\,944$

```
  18 700
   3 500
     200
   1 800
     420
+     24
——————
  20 944
```

This is the traditional **column method** for long multiplication.

You work out 413×80 on the first row.

This is the same as $413 \times 8 \times 10$.
Multiplying by **10** will give you a **0** at the end so put that in first.

To work out 413×8 you first do $3 \times 8 = 24$. Put down the **4** and carry the **2**.

Then do $1 \times 8 = 8$ and add the **2** to get **10**. Put down the **0** and carry the **1**.

Then do $4 \times 8 = 32$ and add the **1** to get **33**.

You need to do 413×3 on the second row.
Then you add the two rows up.

You should use **estimation** to check all of your answers.

413×83 is approximately $400 \times 80 = 32\,000$.
$34\,279$ is quite close to $32\,000$ so you can be fairly sure that it's right.

```
        4  1  3
    ×      8  3
   3 ₁3 ₂0  4  0
       1  2  3  9
   3  4  2  7  9
```

Exercise 2:2

1 For each part
 (1) use one multiplication method that you have seen to work out the answer
 (2) use estimation to check your answer.

- **a** 223×76
- **b** 313×58
- **c** 413×87
- **d** 203×47
- **e** 563×39
- **f** 218×72
- **g** 386×84
- **h** 487×48
- **i** 83×69
- **j** 76×43
- **k** 34×69
- **l** 78×31
- **m** 73×671
- **n** 52×368
- **o** 49×825
- **p** 63×327

2 Aidan is buying a laptop that costs £633.50
He decides to spread the cost over 36 months.
This will cost him more. His monthly payments are £25.64
How much extra will Aidan pay for the laptop?

2 Multiplying and dividing

3 Lisa uses a grid to multiply **23** by **15**.

×	20	3
10	200	30
5	100	15

200 + 100 + 30 + 15 = 345

Answer: **345**

Now Lisa multiplies two different numbers.
Copy and complete the grid,
then give the answer.

×	...	40	3
30	...	...	...
...	600	...	18

Facts to figure

4 **Egyptian multiplication**

The ancient Egyptians used a method based on doubling to multiply.

This is how to multiply 13 by 34 using the Egyptian method.

Write 1 in the first column and the larger number, 34,
in the second column.
Double the numbers in both columns.
Keep going until the number in the first column
is bigger than the smaller number, 13.
Find a set of numbers in the first column that add up to 13:
1 + 4 + 8 = 13
Add up the corresponding numbers in the second column.

13 × 34

1	34
2	68
4	136
8	272
16	
	442

13 × 34 = 442

Work these out using Egyptian multiplication.

   a 11 × 47   **b** 17 × 28   **c** 19 × 52

5 **Russian multiplication**

Many cultures use this method of halving and doubling to multiply.

This is how to multiply 13 by 34 using the Russian method.

Write the smaller number, 13, in the first column.
Write the larger number, 34, in the second column.
Halve the first number, ignoring any remainder.
Double the second number.
Stop when you reach 1 in the first column.
Cross out the rows where the first number is even.
Add up the remaining numbers from the second column.

13	34
~~6~~	~~68~~
3	136
1	272
	442

Work these out using Russian multiplication.

   a 23 × 41   **b** 29 × 136   **c** 15 × 218

Division — Level 5

Dividing is the same as repeatedly taking away.

To calculate 30 ÷ 5 you need to work out how many times you can take 5 away from 30.

30 ÷ 5 = 6 because you can take 5 away 6 times before you get to 0.

$$30 \overset{1}{-} 5 \overset{2}{-} 5 \overset{3}{-} 5 \overset{4}{-} 5 \overset{5}{-} 5 \overset{6}{-} 5 = 0$$

Use a written method to divide larger numbers.
To work out 976 ÷ 8 you need to find how many times you can take 8 away from 976.

Subtract blocks of 8 to make it quicker.

Write down the number of 8s that you're taking away at each stage.

So 976 ÷ 8 = 122

```
    976
  − 800      8 × 100
    176
  −  80      8 ×  10
     96
  −  80      8 ×  10
     16
  −  16      8 ×   2
      0   Answer: 122
```

You should use **estimation** to check all of your answers.
Look for estimates that make the division easy.

You can round either or both of the numbers in the question.
976 ÷ 8 is approximately 1000 ÷ 10 = 100.
The estimate is close to the correct answer.

Division is the **inverse** of multiplication.

492 ÷ 12 = 41
so   492 ÷ 41 = 12   41 × 12 = 492   and   12 × 41 = 492
75 × 18 = 1350
so   18 × 75 = 1350   1350 ÷ 75 = 18   and   1350 ÷ 18 = 75

The answer to a division question is called a **quotient**.
The number you're dividing is called the **dividend**.
The number you divide by is called the **divisor**.

Some quotients aren't whole numbers.

When this happens you can write the quotient in different ways, using a **remainder**, a **fraction** or a **decimal**.

If you use a fraction, the fraction is always the remainder over the divisor.

64 ÷ 5 = 12 R4. You can also say 64 ÷ 5 = $12\frac{4}{5}$ and 64 ÷ 5 = 12.8 because $\frac{4}{5} = 0.8$

2 Multiplying and dividing

Exercise 2:3

1 Work out these divisions by copying and completing the working shown.

a 684 ÷ 6 = ...

```
  684
− 600    6 × ...
  ...
−  ...   6 × ...
```

b 424 ÷ 8 = ...

```
  424
− 400    8 × ...
  ...
```

c 1314 ÷ 9 = ...

```
  1314
−  ...   9 × ...
   ...
−  ...   9 × ...
```

2 Work out these divisions.

a 928 ÷ 8
b 959 ÷ 7
c 567 ÷ 9
d 942 ÷ 6
e 1896 ÷ 8
f 1876 ÷ 7
g 1134 ÷ 9
h 1072 ÷ 8

3 Bobby has correctly worked out that 158 × 47 = 7426.
Copy these and fill in the gaps using Bobby's multiplication fact to help you.

a 7426 ÷ 47 = ...
b 7426 ÷ 158 = ...

4 Copy these and fill in the gaps.

a
```
    559
−   ...    13 × 40
    ...
−   ...    13 × ...
     0
```
Answer: ...

559 ÷ 13 = ...

b
```
    348
−   ...    12 × 20
    ...
−   ...    12 × 5
    ...
−   ...    12 × ...
     0
```
Answer: ...

348 ÷ 12 = ...

5 Work out these divisions.

a 444 ÷ 12
b 546 ÷ 13
c 704 ÷ 11
d 592 ÷ 16
e 414 ÷ 18
f 782 ÷ 23
g 3216 ÷ 12
h 3672 ÷ 17
i 4494 ÷ 21
j 3744 ÷ 24
k 3968 ÷ 32
l 9761 ÷ 43

6 Fiona buys a yearly ticket that lets her travel to and from work. It costs £474.

How much is that per month?

7 Work out these divisions.
   Give your answer **(1)** using a remainder   **(2)** as a fraction   **(3)** as a decimal.

   a 25 ÷ 4   c 54 ÷ 4   e 33 ÷ 4   g 54 ÷ 12
   b 52 ÷ 5   d 60 ÷ 8   f 54 ÷ 8   h 52 ÷ 16

8 Farzana works on a farm.
   She collects eggs and puts them into boxes of 6.

   Work out how many boxes she can fill if she collects

   a 45 eggs   b 82 eggs   c 143 eggs.

9 a A club wants to take **3000 people** on a journey to London.
   The club secretary says,

   > 'We can go in coaches.
   > Each coach can carry **52** people.'

   How many coaches do they need for the journey? Show your working.

   b Each coach costs **£420**.
       What is the **total cost** of the coaches?

   c How much is each person's share of the cost?

Facts to figure

10 We use a decimal number system based on the number 10.
   We have digits up to 9 that we use in different positions to show units, tens, hundreds and so on.

   Swedenborg was a Swedish scientist and philosopher.
   In the early seventeenth century he devised a number system based on the number 8.
   In Swedenborg's system, the numbers up to 7 are represented by single letters.
   Bigger numbers combine these letters.

l	1
s	2
n	3
m	4
t	5
f	6
v	7

lo	8
so	16
no	24
mo	32
to	40
fo	48
vo	56

loo	64
soo	128
noo	192
moo	256
too	320
foo	384
voo	448

Work these out using Swedenborg's system.
Use the tables to help you.

a s × *lo*   c s × *loo*   e noo ÷ *lo*
b n × *lo*   d to ÷ *lo*   f moo ÷ *loo*

g In this system *lo* means 8, *loo* means 64 and *looo* means 512. What does *loooo* mean?

2 Multiplying and dividing

2 Measures

▶ **Converting between metric units**

▶ **Making sensible estimates of measures**

> **Key words**
>
> metric units, length, millimetre, centimetre, metre, kilometre
> mass, milligram, gram, kilogram, tonne
> capacity, millilitre, centilitre, litre
> time, second, minute, hour, day, week, month, year, decade, century, millennium
> estimate

▶ **Converting between metric units** Level 5

The **metric units** of **length** are
millimetre (mm), **centimetre** (cm), **metre** (m) and **kilometre** (km).

You need to know these conversion facts:

$$1\,\text{km} = 1000\,\text{m} \qquad 1\,\text{m} = 100\,\text{cm} = 1000\,\text{mm} \qquad 1\,\text{cm} = 10\,\text{mm}$$

1 cm = **10** mm
To change cm into mm multiply by **10**. $18\,\text{cm} = 18 \times \mathbf{10} = 180\,\text{mm}$

1000 m = 1 km
To change m into km divide by **1000**. $3457\,\text{m} = 3457 \div \mathbf{1000} = 3.457\,\text{km}$

1 km = **1000** m and 1 m = **100** cm
To change km into cm multiply by **1000** then by **100**. $4.5\,\text{km} = 4.5 \times \mathbf{1000} \times \mathbf{100} = 450\,000\,\text{cm}$

10 mm = 1 cm and **100** cm = 1 m
To change mm into m divide by **10** then by **100**. $6238\,\text{mm} = 6238 \div \mathbf{10} \div \mathbf{100} = 6.238\,\text{m}$

The metric units of **mass** are **milligram** (mg), **gram** (g), **kilogram** (kg) and **tonne**.
You need to know these conversion facts:

$$1\,\text{tonne} = 1000\,\text{kg} \qquad 1\,\text{kg} = 1000\,\text{g} \qquad 1\,\text{g} = 1000\,\text{mg}$$

1 tonne = **1000** kg
To change tonnes into kg multiply by **1000**. $0.78\,\text{tonnes} = 0.78 \times \mathbf{1000} = 780\,\text{kg}$

1000 mg = 1 g
To change mg into g divide by **1000**. $4520\,\text{mg} = 4520 \div \mathbf{1000} = 4.52\,\text{g}$

The metric units of **capacity** are **millilitre** (mℓ), **centilitre** (cℓ) and **litre** (ℓ).
You need to know these conversion facts:

$$1\,\ell = 100\,\text{c}\ell = 1000\,\text{m}\ell \qquad 1\,\text{c}\ell = 10\,\text{m}\ell$$

The units of **time** are **second**, **minute**, **hour** and **day**. You need to know these facts:

There are 52 **weeks** in a **year**.   12 **months** make a year.   10 years make a **decade**.
A **century** is 100 years.   10 centuries make a **millennium**.

Exercise 2:4

1 Convert each length into metres.
- **a** 2 km
- **b** 5.4 km
- **c** 3.63 km
- **d** 600 cm
- **e** 550 cm
- **f** 472 cm
- **g** 8000 mm
- **h** 6500 mm
- **i** 3245 mm
- **j** 592 cm
- **k** 6.3 km
- **l** 8410 mm

2 Convert each mass into grams.
- **a** 2.5 kg
- **b** 10.3 kg
- **c** 4.3 tonnes
- **d** 9.014 tonnes
- **e** 7500 mg
- **f** 657 mg
- **g** 93 580 mg
- **h** 0.0054 kg

3 Convert each capacity into millilitres.
- **a** 6 ℓ
- **b** 25 cℓ
- **c** 345 cℓ
- **d** 4.75 ℓ

4 Is it possible to calculate 3.4 kg + 6.6 km? Explain your answer.

5 To add or subtract measurements they must be in the same units.

Pick the smallest unit that is used in the question.
Change all of the units into this unit.

So 3 m + 47 cm = 300 cm + 47 cm = 347 cm

Calculate the following, giving the units of each answer.
- **a** 5 m + 53 cm
- **b** 5.6 m − 468 cm
- **c** 85 cm + 785 mm
- **d** 3 kg − 500 g
- **e** 4.8 g + 3400 mg
- **f** 8.05 ℓ + 523 mℓ

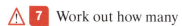

6 A washing machine takes 2 hours to finish 3 loads.
How many minutes does one load take?

7 Work out how many
- **a** minutes there are in 5 hours
- **b** seconds there are in 1 hour
- **c** hours there are in 570 minutes
- **d** days there are in 360 hours
- **e** seconds there are in 2 days 5 hours and 17 minutes
- **f** days there are in 3 normal years and 36 weeks
- **g** days there are in a millennium
- **h** hours there are in a millennium.

8 A farmer ploughs 8 acres of field in 5 hours.
What is the mean time he takes to plough one acre? Give your answer in minutes.

2 Multiplying and dividing

Explore

9 How old are you?
Have you lived for at least
  a 132 months?
  b 4383 days?
  c 114 000 hours?

Making sensible estimates of measures — Level 5

You need to be able to **estimate** length, mass and capacity.

Learn the sizes of these familiar items to help you.

Length

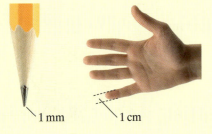

1 mm   1 cm   1 m   100 km

Mass

smartie
1 g

250 g

1 kg

1200 kg

Capacity

5 ml

330 ml

1 l

2 500 000 l

Exercise 2:5

1 Which units would you use to measure these?
Choose your answers from

| mm | minutes | kg | cm^2 | years | ℓ | hours | cm | m | km | seconds | m^2 | mℓ | sg |

    a The length of the classroom
    b The mass of a £1 coin
    c The length of an exercise book
    d The distance from London to Cardiff
    e The time taken to run 100 m
    f The width of a pencil
    g The area of your school hall
    h The capacity of a teapot

2 Choose the most likely measurement for each item.

		A	B	C
a	Width of a front door	85 m	85 cm	85 mm
b	Length of a brick	2 m	20 cm	20 mm
c	Mass of a bar of chocolate	2 kg	200 g	20 g
d	Mass of a fifty pence coin	8 kg	80 g	8 g
e	Capacity of a bucket	5 ℓ	5 cℓ	5 mℓ
f	Capacity of a paddling pool	1000 ℓ	1000 cℓ	1000 mℓ
g	Area of a bathroom floor	6 m^2	60 cm^2	6 cm^2

3 Copy the sentences and fill in the gaps using a number from one of the cards.
You should only use each card once.

    a The amount of cola in a large bottle is … mℓ.
    b The mass of a loaf of bread is … g.
    c The amount of toothpaste in a tube is … mℓ.
    d The distance from New York to London is … km.
    e The time taken to boil an egg is … minutes.
    f The mass of a packet of crisps is … g.

Cards: 3, 800, 30, 2000, 100, 5600

4 Catherine says that the mass of her calculator is between 50 g and 250 g.
She writes this as 50 g < mass of a calculator < 250 g

Copy and complete the following estimates.

    a … < height of a classroom door < …
    b … < mass of a cricket ball < …
    c … < length of a pencil < …
    d … < mass of an apple < …
    e … < width of a classroom chair < …
    f … < capacity of a mug < …

2 Multiplying and dividing

3 Order of operations

▶ **Brackets and BODMAS**

▶ **Using a calculator**

Key words	
operations	order
brackets	BODMAS
power	numerator
denominator	
calculator: key, clear, display	

▶ Brackets and BODMAS   Level 5

$6 \times (5 + 3) - 10$ contains a mixture of **operations**. You must do them in the correct **order**.

The order that you need to use is:

        Brackets
powers **O**f
        Division
        Multiplication
        Addition
        Subtraction

Remember this as **BODMAS**

To work out $6 \times (5 + 3) - 10$ use **BODMAS**.

Work out the **Brackets** first
then do the **Multiplication**
and finally the **Subtraction**.

$6 \times (5 + 3) - 10 = 6 \times 8 - 10$
$6 \times 8 - 10 = 48 - 10$
$48 - 10 = 38$

To calculate $(4 + 6)^2 \times 2 - 150$ use **BODMAS**.

You need to do the **Brackets** first
then the **power Of**
then the **Multiplication**
and finally the **Subtraction**.

$(4 + 6)^2 \times 2 - 150 = 10^2 \times 2 - 150$
$= 100 \times 2 - 150$
$= 200 - 150$
$= 50$

Read 10^2 as 10 **squared** or 10 to the **power of 2**.
Read 10^3 as 10 **cubed** or 10 to the **power of 3**.

$10^2 = 10 \times 10 = 100$
$10^3 = 10 \times 10 \times 10 = 1000$

When more than one multiplication or division appears in a calculation, with no other operations, work **from the left**.

$20 \div 4 \div 2 = 5 \div 2 = 2.5$
$16 \div 2 \times 4 = 8 \times 4 = 32$

When the calculation just contains additions and subtractions, work **from the left**.

$14 - 5 + 9 = 9 + 9 = 18$
$36 - 8 - 5 = 28 - 5 = 23$

When the calculation involves a fraction, work out the **numerator** and the **denominator** before dividing.

$\dfrac{5 + 7}{6 - 2} = \dfrac{12}{4} = 3$

Exercise 2:6

1 Work these out.

a $4 \times 5 + 3$

b $34 - 5 \times 6$

c $3 \times 7 - 100 \div 5$

d $45 \div 9 + 2 \times 4$

e $15 + 6 \div 3 \times 5$

f $\dfrac{9+6}{3+2}$

g $(36 - 16) \div 4$

h $(24 \div 3) \times (12 \div 6)$

i $2 \times (11 - 8)$

j $18 - (4^2 - 9)$

k $(12 + 9 - 18)^2$

l $\sqrt{36 + 13}$

m $(1 + 2)^3 - (8 - 3)^2$

n $\sqrt{(40 - 2^2)}$

o $\dfrac{84 - 9^2}{\sqrt[3]{16 + 11}}$

2 Janet works out that $13 \times 3 - 5 \times 4 = 136$.
Is this correct? Explain your answer.

3 Copy these calculations and add brackets to make them correct.

a $5 \times 5 - 2 - 1 = 14$

b $5 \times 5 - 2 - 1 = 24$

c $5 \times 5 - 2 - 1 = 10$

4 Milo has the following cards.
He arranges the cards to make different calculations.

a What is the largest answer he could make?
Show the calculation.

b What is the smallest whole number answer he could make?
Show the calculation.

5 Find the value of the letter in each of these calculations.

a $(3 + a) \times 5 = 35$

b $64 \div 2 + b \times 3 = 44$

c $(18 - c) \div 2 = 1$

d $2 \times (1 + d)^3 = 16$

Think on!

6 Use the cards to write down

3 calculations with the answer 39

2 calculations with the answer 21

1 calculation with the answer 33

$3 \times (10 + 3) - 2 \times 3 + 6$

$3 \times 10 + (3 - 2) \times 3 + 6$

$3 \times (10 + 3) - 2 \times (3 + 6)$

$3 \times 10 + 3 - 2 \times 3 + 6$

$3 \times 10 + 3 - (2 \times 3 + 6)$

$3 \times 10 + (3 - 2) \times (3 + 6)$

What other answers can you make by moving the brackets?

2 Multiplying and dividing

Using a calculator — Level 5

Scientific calculators use the rules of BODMAS.

When you use a **calculator** make sure that you press the AC key. This will **clear** the **display** before you start.
Enter the calculation as you read it from left to right.

You need to use brackets carefully.

To calculate $(17 - 9)^3$ you need to use brackets and the cube key:

(1 7 − 9) x^3 =

to get the answer 512.

Enter $22 + \sqrt{9 + 7} - 5^2$ using the square root key like this:

2 2 + √ 9 + 7 Replay ▶ − 5 x^2 =

to get the answer 1.

To calculate $\dfrac{9.5 - 2.4}{8.3 + 5.9}$ you should use brackets for both the numerator and denominator like this:

(9 . 5 − 2 . 4) ÷ (8 . 3 + 5 . 9) =

to get the answer $\tfrac{1}{2}$

If you want your answer as a decimal then press the S⇔D key.

Exercise 2:7

1 Use your calculator to work these out.

- **a** $101 \div 10 \div 25$
- **b** $30 \times 17 - 5$
- **c** $120^3 \times 3 + 367^2 + 115$
- **d** $88^2 - 6$
- **e** $17 \times 19 \times 5^2$
- **f** $7774^2 + 958$
- **g** $79 \times 57 + 3$
- **h** $150 \times 40 - 337$
- **i** $139^2 \times 3 - 1913 \times 2 \times 6$
- **j** $15.51 \div 2 \div 11$
- **k** $0.61^2 - 0.00102$
- **l** $42 \times 117 - 15 \times 20$
- **m** $2 \times 50 \times 500 + 337$
- **n** $61^2 + 30$
- **o** $90^2 - 19^2 - 5^2$

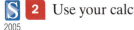

2 Use your calculator to work out

- **a** $(48 + 57) \times (61 - 19)$
- **b** $\dfrac{48 + 57}{61 - 19}$

3 Use your calculator to work these out.
Think carefully about when you need brackets.

a $(11^2 - 18) \times 6$

b $(40^2 + 501) \times 9 \times 2$

c $(8^2 + 2^2)^3 + 23 \times 9 \times 15$

d $(256 + 365)^2 + 343^2 + 88$

e $240^2 + 29 \times 4$

f $\dfrac{4^2 - 1^2}{10^2}$

g $(100 + 0.0079) \times 7 + 10$

h $\sqrt{28.09} + 45 \div 1000$

i $87^2 + \sqrt{22\,201}$

j $50^2 \times 30 - 155^2 + 69 \times 30$

k $\dfrac{304^2 - 303^2}{\sqrt{3^2 - 2^3}}$

l $\dfrac{1432 \times 263^2}{132^2 - 131^2}$

m $\dfrac{4^2 \times 69 \times 761}{5^2 - 1}$

n $\dfrac{17^3 - 523 \times 2}{25^2 \times 8}$

o $\dfrac{(30 + 1) \times 33}{80^2 - 20^2}$

4 Work these out.

a $\dfrac{3^2 + 16}{(3 \times 4 - 7)^2}$

b $\dfrac{5^2 + 5 \times 4}{\sqrt{3^3 \times 75}}$

5 Owen has used his calculator to solve a problem.
This is his calculator display.

Write down Owen's answer

a in £ if the display shows money in £

b in m and cm if the display shows length in m

⚠ **c** in hours and minutes if the display shows time in hours.

> 312.5

6 a Key any number followed by ✕ 4 2 = into your calculator.
What do you need to enter to get back to your starting number?

⚠ **b** Key any number followed by x^2 = into your calculator.
What do you need to enter to get back to your starting number?

Think on!

7 Here are Harjinder's answers to two questions.

a $(30 - 4)^2 = 14$

b $\dfrac{18^2}{9 - 5} = 31$

For each part

(1) explain what Harjinder has done wrong

(2) work out the correct answer.

2 Multiplying and dividing

Watch out ... there's a trap about

▶ You know that **16** is **8 × 2** but **don't** work out 80 ÷ 16 like this:

80 ÷ **16** = 80 ÷ **8 × 2** = 10 × 2 = 20

Although 16 is 8 × 2, you need to divide by 8 and then *divide* by 2.

So 80 ÷ **16** = 80 ÷ **8 ÷ 2** = 10 ÷ 2 = 5

▶ 200 cm is **not** 20 000 m

When you are converting from a **big** unit **to** a **small** unit you **multiply** and when you are converting from a *small* unit *to* a *big* unit you *divide*.

Converting from centimetres to metres is a *small* unit *to* a *big* unit so you *divide*:

200 ÷ 100 = 2 so 200 cm = 2 m

▶ 0.4 of an hour is **not** 40 minutes!

0.4 of an hour = 0.4 × 60 = 24 minutes

Test yourself

1 Work out each of these.

   a 7 × 14   **c** 5 × 32   **e** 40 × 50   **g** 4^3

   b 9 × 15   **d** 12 × 99   **f** 1400 ÷ 70   **h** $\sqrt{81}$

2 Work out each of these.
You need to use a method for long multiplication.

   a 274 × 28   **b** 672 × 25   **c** 638 × 48   **d** 41 × 724

3 On average a person has 1460 dreams a year.
It is Lowenna's 13th birthday.

Work out how many dreams Lowenna has had so far.

4 Work out these divisions.
Give your answer

   (1) using a remainder   **(2)** as a fraction   **(3)** as a decimal.

   a 31 ÷ 4   **b** 34 ÷ 5   **c** 56 ÷ 16   **d** 39 ÷ 12

5 Work these out.

   a 144 ÷ 16
   b 192 ÷ 6
   c 555 ÷ 15
   d 1872 ÷ 9

6 a A teacher needs **220** booklets. The booklets are in **packs** of **16**.
       How many packs must the teacher order? Show your working.

   b Each booklet weighs 48 g.
      How much do the **220** booklets weigh altogether?
      Show your working. Give your answer in **kg**.

7 Copy and complete these.

   a 5 g = … mg
   b 6 kg = … g
   c 5.5 km = … m
   d 85 cm = … mm
   e 2500 mℓ = … ℓ
   f 15 m = … cm

8 Work out each of these. State the units of each answer.

   a 7.6 cm + 3 mm
   b 4 m + 17 cm + 12 mm
   c 2.67 kg − 450 g
   d 7.325 kg − 225 000 mg

9 Which metric units would you use to measure each of these?

   a The height of Blackpool Tower
   b The capacity of a washbasin
   c The time it takes to put on your shoes
   d The mass of a tiger

10 Copy each question and find its answer from the cards.

   a 15 − 7 × 2
   b 3 × (8 − 3)
   c 18 − (13 − 4)
   d 4 × (3 + 9) ÷ 3
   e (15 − 8) × (1 + 2)

   | 16 | 21 |
   | 9 | 1 | 15 |

11 Use a calculator to work out $\dfrac{6^2 - \sqrt{196}}{\sqrt{121}}$

12 Phil has used his calculator to solve a problem.
   This is his calculator display.

   Write down Phil's answer

   a in £ if the display shows money in £
   b in m and cm if the display shows length in m
   c in hours and minutes if the display shows time in hours.

   24.5

2 Multiplying and dividing

Chapter 2 Summary

Level 5

Mental methods for multiplying and dividing

Doubling and halving $150 \times 4 = 300 \times 2 = 600$

Partitioning
$5 \times 16 = 5 \times 10 + 5 \times 6 = 50 + 30 = 80$
$138 \div 9 = (100 \div 9) + (38 \div 9) = 11 \text{ R1} + 4 \text{ R2} = 15 \text{ R3}$

Using multiplication facts $84 \div 14 = 84 \div 7 \div 2 = 84 \div 2 \div 7 = 42 \div 7 = 6$

Square numbers up to 12^2 $11^2 = 11 \times 11 = 121 \quad 12^2 = 12 \times 12 = 144$

Cube numbers $1^3 = 1 \quad 2^3 = 8 \quad 3^3 = 27 \quad 4^3 = 64 \quad 5^3 = 125 \quad 10^3 = 1000$

Square roots and cube roots $\sqrt{81} = 9 \quad \sqrt[3]{27} = 3$

Long multiplication

×	300	70	4
50	15 000	3500	200
6	1800	420	24

$374 \times 56 = 20\,944$

$$\begin{array}{r} 18700 \\ +\ 2244 \\ \hline 20944 \end{array}$$

$$\begin{array}{r} 4\ 1\ 3 \\ \times\ \ \ 8\ 3 \\ \hline 3\ _1 3\ _2 0\ 4\ 0 \\ 1\ 2\ 3\ 9\ \ \\ \hline 3\ 4\ 2\ 7\ 9 \end{array}$$

$413 \times 83 = 34\,279$

Division

$$\begin{array}{r} 976 \\ -\ 800 \\ \hline 176 \\ -\ \ 80 \\ \hline 96 \\ -\ \ 80 \\ \hline 16 \\ -\ \ 16 \\ \hline 0 \end{array}$$

8×100

8×10

8×10

8×2

Answer: $\overline{122}$

Division is the **inverse** of multiplication:

$976 \div 8 = 122$

so $976 \div 122 = 8$, $122 \times 8 = 976$ and $8 \times 122 = 976$

Metric units

Length	1 km = 1000 m	1 m = 100 cm = 1000 mm	1 cm = 10 mm
Mass	1 tonne = 1000 kg	1 kg = 1000 g	1 g = 1000 mg
Capacity	1 ℓ = 100 cℓ = 1000 mℓ	1 cℓ = 10 mℓ	

Order of operations

To work out $6 \times (5 + 3) - 10$ use **BODMAS**.

Work out the **Brackets** first $\quad 6 \times (5 + 3) - 10 = 6 \times 8 - 10$

then do the **Multiplication** $\quad\quad 6 \times 8 \quad - 10 = 48 - 10$

and finally the **Subtraction**. $\quad\quad\quad\ 48 \quad\ - 10 = 38$

3 Coordinates and symmetry

Year 6
- Simple coordinates
- Reflecting shapes in a mirror line

1. Coordinates in all four quadrants
2. Symmetry in 2-D shapes

Chapter 7
2-D and 3-D shapes

Symmetry in 3-D solids

Chapter 17
Algebraic graphs

Drawing graphs

Chapter 18
Transformations

Drawing transformations

You should already know:

▸ **how to write the coordinates of a point in a grid like this**

Point A has coordinates (3, 4)

Point B has coordinates (0, 3)

Point C has coordinates (6, 1)

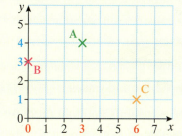

▸ **how to draw the reflection of a shape in a mirror line**

Move each vertex across the mirror line to the point which is the same distance from the mirror line on the other side.

The bottom vertex is on the mirror line so it doesn't move.

Then join up all the points to get the reflected shape.

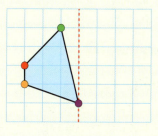

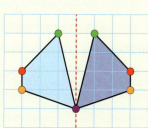

3 Coordinates and symmetry

1 Coordinates in all four quadrants

▶ **Using coordinates in all four quadrants**

▶ Finding the coordinates of the mid-point of a line

Key words

coordinates   x-axis
y-axis   mid-point
x-coordinate   y-coordinate

Using coordinates in all four quadrants   Level 5

You can have negative **coordinates**.

This happens when you have axes like these.

The **x-axis** goes from −5 to 5.

The **y-axis** goes from −5 to 5.

Point A has coordinates (−2, 4)

Point B has coordinates (−4, −3)

Point C has coordinates (5, −1)

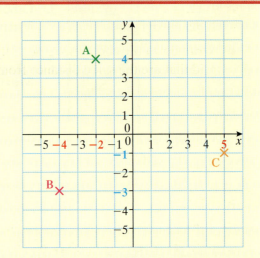

Exercise 3:1

1 a Copy these x and y axes.

b Plot these points and join them up to make a wigwam.

(−4, −5)
(−6, −3)
(−0.5, 2)
(−4, −5)
(−2, −5)
(−0.5, −2)
(1, −5)
(3, −5)
(−0.5, 2)

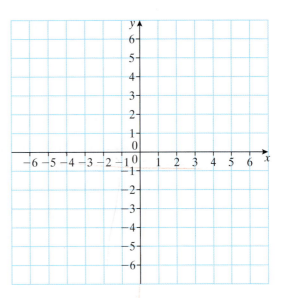

Your wigwam should look like this.

36

2 Imagine the point $(-2, -5)$ on a grid.

Which of the points $(3, 0)$, $(-2, 5)$ or $(3, -5)$ is it closest to?

Explain your answer.

3 The points A and B are an equal distance from point X.
  a Write down the coordinates of the points A and B.
  b Is $(1, -2)$ the same distance from X as points A and B? Explain your answer.
  c Write down the coordinates of all the points on the grid that are the same distance from X as A and B.

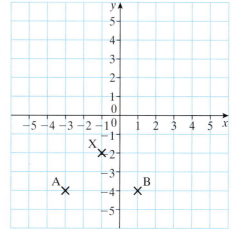

4 a Draw x and y axes from -5 to 5.
  b Plot and label the points $A(-3, 0)$, $B(-1, -2)$ and $C(3, 2)$.
  c ABCD is a rectangle. Mark point D on your diagram.
  d Write down the coordinates of D.

5 a Draw x and y axes from -5 to 5.
  b Plot the points $(2, 3)$, $(-1, 5)$ and $(-4, 3)$.
  c Write down the coordinates of a fourth point that will make an arrowhead.
  d Is it possible to make a rectangle by drawing one more point? Explain your answer.

6 On this square grid, A and B must not move.

When C is at $(6, 2)$, triangle ABC is isosceles.

  a C moves so that triangle ABC is still isosceles. Where could C be now?
     Write the coordinates of its new position.
  b Then C moves so that triangle ABC is isosceles and right-angled. Where could C be now?
     Write the coordinates of its new position.

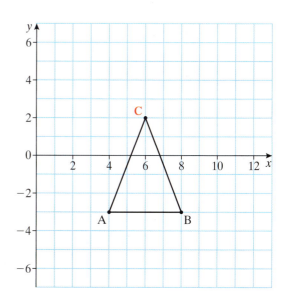

3 Coordinates and symmetry

7 Daniel is plotting points to make a pattern.
  a What are the coordinates of point Q?
  b What are the coordinates of point R?
  c Daniel says, 'The next point in this pattern is (−5, 5).'
    Explain why Daniel is wrong.

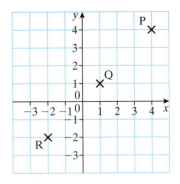

8 a Copy these axes on to squared paper.
  b Plot the points (−2, 1), (−1, 4) and (0, 1).
    Join the points to make a triangle.
  c Plot the points (0, −1), (1, 2) and (2, −1).
    Join the points to make another triangle.
  d Work out the position of the next triangle
    in this pattern. Write down the coordinates
    of the corners of the new triangle.

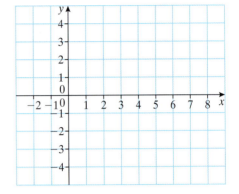

9 a Write down the coordinates of the points
    A, B, C and D.

Dean said, 'I have plotted these points using a rule.'

  b Write down what you think the rule is.
  c Does the point (3, −3) follow the same rule?
    Explain your answer.

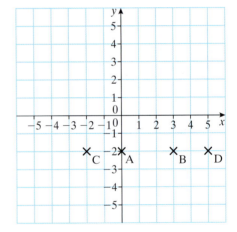

Think on!

10 This grid shows the position of all four quadrants.
From these points
  (2, −4), (−4, −2), (−2, 4), (−2, −2), (5, −3)
  (2, 2), (4, −2), (3, −2), (−1, −2), (−1, 2)
write down
  a 4 points in the fourth quadrant
  b 3 points in the third quadrant
  c 2 points in the second quadrant
  d 1 point in the first quadrant.

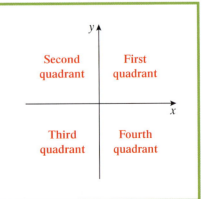

Finding the coordinates of the mid-point of a line — Level 6

The **mid-point** of a line AB is exactly halfway between A and B.

M is the mid-point of the line AB.

The ***x*-coordinate** of A is **1**.

The ***x*-coordinate** of B is **5**.

Moving from A to B changes the *x*-coordinate by **5 − 1 = 4**.

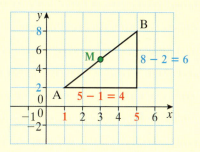

M is halfway along AB.

So moving from A to M changes the *x*-coordinate by half of **4**.

The ***x*-coordinate** of M is $1 + \frac{1}{2} \times 4 = 1 + 2 = 3$

The ***y*-coordinate** of M is $2 + \frac{1}{2} \times 6 = 2 + 3 = 5$

The coordinates of M are (3, 5).

Exercise 3:2

1 Copy this and fill in the gaps.

The *x*-coordinate of **A** is …

The *x*-coordinate of **B** is …

The *x*-coordinate of **M** is … $+ \frac{1}{2} \times$ … = …

The *y*-coordinate of **A** is …

The *y*-coordinate of **B** is …

The *y*-coordinate of **M** is … $+ \frac{1}{2} \times$ … = …

So the coordinates of **M** are (…, …)

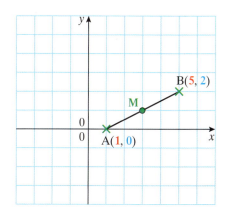

2 Look at the diagram.

  a Shape ABCD is a rectangle.
  What are the coordinates of point D?

  b The point K is halfway between points A and D.
  What are the coordinates of point K?

  c The point L is halfway between points B and D.
  What are the coordinates of point L?

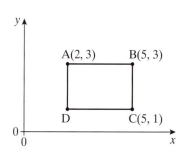

3 Coordinates and symmetry

3 a Copy this diagram onto squared paper.
   b Join the points (−3, 3), (3, 3), (3, −1) and (−3, −1) to make a rectangle.
   c Mark the mid-point of each side.
   d Join the mid-points together to make a quadrilateral. What is the name of the shape that you make?

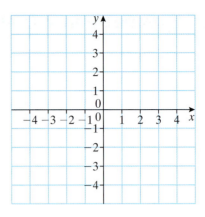

4 a P is the mid-point of line AB.
      Write down the coordinates of point P.

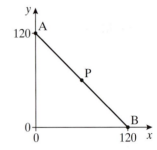

   b Q is the **mid-point** of MN.
      The coordinates of Q are (30, 50).
      Write down the coordinates of points **M** and **N**.

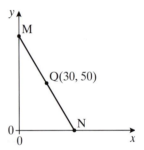

5 Work out the coordinates of the mid-point of the line joining
   a (2, 7) to (8, 11)
   b (−6, −3) to (10, 1).

6 Find the coordinates of the mid-point of the line in each part.
   a AB
   b BC
   c CD
   d BD
   e AC

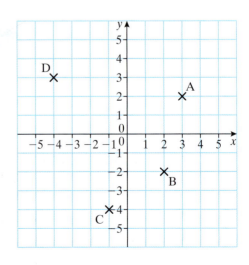

2 Symmetry in 2-D shapes

▶ **Identifying lines of symmetry of a 2-D shape**

▶ **Identifying rotational symmetry of a 2-D shape**

▶ **Classifying triangles**

▶ **Classifying quadrilaterals**

Key words

line of symmetry, rotational symmetry, order of rotational symmetry

triangle: equilateral, isosceles, scalene, right-angled

quadrilateral: square, rectangle, rhombus, parallelogram, trapezium, kite, arrowhead

bisect, concave

▶ **Identifying lines of symmetry of a 2-D shape**   **Level 5**

If you fold a shape along a **line of symmetry** the two parts will fit exactly on top of each other.

You show lines of symmetry using dashed lines.

A square has four lines of symmetry.

A rectangle has two lines of symmetry.

The diagonals of a rectangle are not lines of symmetry.

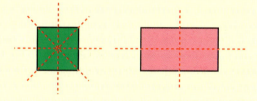

If you fold a rectangle along a diagonal you get an overlap like this:

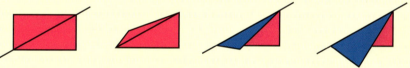

A parallelogram has no lines of symmetry.

This is what happens if you fold it along one of the diagonals.

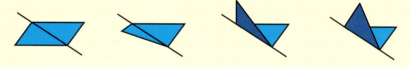

Exercise 3:3

1 Copy each of these shapes.
Draw all the lines of symmetry on each shape.

a   b   c   d

3 Coordinates and symmetry

2 Zalia makes different paper shapes.
To do this she folds a piece of square paper along the diagonal, draws a shape, cuts it out and then unfolds it.

Here is Zalia's drawing.
Sketch the shape that she makes.

3 In each diagram the red line is a line of symmetry.

Copy and complete each diagram.

a
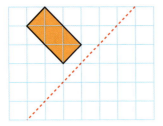

c
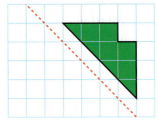

b
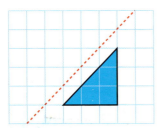

d
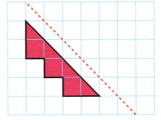

Explore

4 A Rangoli pattern is a colourful design used by Hindu and Sikh families, to decorate their homes during festivals.
It is usually drawn on the floor near the entrance of a house.
Most Rangoli patterns have line symmetry.

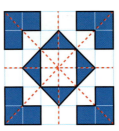

To draw a Rangoli pattern:
- draw a **design** on a square grid
- reflect the **design** in all the **red lines of symmetry**
- colour in the whole pattern.

Draw a few of your own Rangoli patterns.

3

Identifying rotational symmetry of a 2-D shape   Level 5

A shape has **rotational symmetry** if it looks the same more than once as you rotate it.

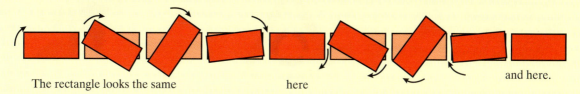

The rectangle looks the same   here   and here.

A rectangle has rotational symmetry and line symmetry.

A parallelogram has rotational symmetry but no line symmetry.

The **order of rotational symmetry** is the number of times the shape looks the same as you rotate it through one full turn.

An equilateral triangle has rotational symmetry of order 3

A square has rotational symmetry of order 4

This shape has rotational symmetry of order 1.

It only looks the same as itself when you rotate it through a full turn of 360°.

You wouldn't say that the shape is symmetrical though!

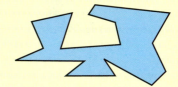

Exercise 3:4

1 Write down the order of rotational symmetry of each of these shapes.

a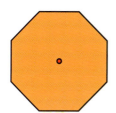

c

e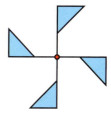

b

d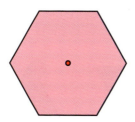

f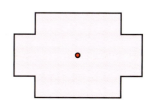

3 Coordinates and symmetry

2 Write down the order of rotational symmetry of each of these.

a    b    c

3 Fleur is drawing a shape with rotational symmetry of order 4.
This is her drawing. But she has not finished!
Copy and complete her drawing.

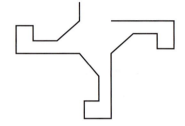

4 An equilateral triangle has **3 lines of symmetry**

It has **rotational symmetry** of **order 3**

a Copy this table.

Number of lines of symmetry

		0	1	2	3
Order of rotational symmetry	1				
	2	B			
	3				A

b Write the letter of each shape in the correct space in the table.
You may use a mirror or tracing paper to help you.
The letters for the first two shapes have been written for you.

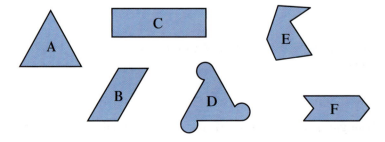

Classifying triangles

Level 5

An **equilateral triangle** has three equal sides.

It also has three equal angles. Each of its angles is 60°.

It has three lines of symmetry and rotational symmetry of order 3.

An **isosceles triangle** has two equal sides.

It also has two equal angles.

It has one line of symmetry and rotational symmetry of order 1.

A **scalene triangle** has no equal sides.

It has no equal angles.

It has no lines of symmetry and has rotational symmetry of order 1.

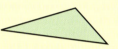

A **right-angled triangle** may be scalene or isosceles.

A right-angled isosceles triangle has two equal angles of 45°.

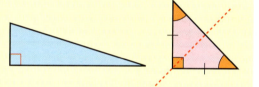

Exercise 3:5

1 a Measure the sides of this triangle.
Copy and complete

$a = $ …… cm

$b = $ …… cm

$c = $ …… cm

The triangle has …… equal sides.

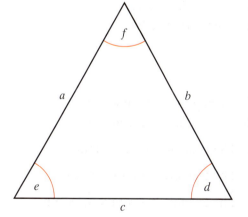

b Measure the angles of this triangle.
Copy and complete

$d = $ ……°

$e = $ ……°

$f = $ ……°

The triangle has …… equal angles.

c Jamie says, 'This triangle has one line of symmetry.'
Is Jamie correct?

d Copy and complete this sentence.

An ……… triangle has …… equal sides, …… equal angles and …… lines of symmetry.

3 Coordinates and symmetry

2 Ali drew this triangle.

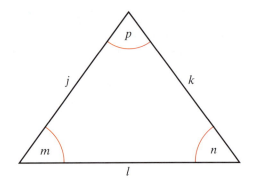

a Measure and write down the sizes of the angles and sides of Ali's triangle.

b Ali said, 'I have drawn a scalene triangle.' Give two reasons why he is wrong.

3 Measure the sides of this scalene triangle.

Measure the angles.

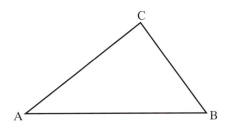

Copy and complete:

AB = ……,   BC = ……,   AC = ……

∠BAC = ……,   ∠ABC = ……,   ∠ACB = …….

A scalene triangle has …… equal sides and …… equal angles.
A scalene triangle has rotational symmetry of order ……

4 For each part, write down the type of triangle being described. But be careful! There may be more than one answer.

a The triangle has line symmetry.

b The triangle has a right angle.

c The triangle has rotational symmetry of order more than 1.

5 A right-angled triangle has a 90° angle.

a Can a right-angled triangle also be an equilateral triangle? Explain your answer.

b Can a right-angled triangle also be an isosceles triangle? Explain your answer.

Classifying quadrilaterals

Level 6

A **quadrilateral** has four sides. Some quadrilaterals have special names.

A **square** has four equal sides.
It also has four equal angles. Each of its angles is 90°.
It has four lines of symmetry and rotational symmetry of order 4.
The diagonals are equal and they **bisect** each other at right angles.

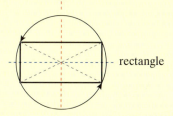
square

A **rectangle** has two pairs of equal sides.
It has four equal angles. Each of its angles is 90°.
It has two lines of symmetry and rotational symmetry of order 2.
The diagonals are equal and they bisect each other
but not at right angles.

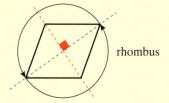
rectangle

A **rhombus** has four equal sides.
Opposite sides are parallel. Opposite angles are equal.
It has two lines of symmetry and rotational symmetry of order 2.
The diagonals bisect each other at right angles
but they are not equal.

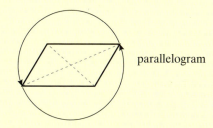
rhombus

A **parallelogram** has two pairs of equal sides.
Opposite sides are parallel. Opposite angles are equal.
It has no lines of symmetry and
rotational symmetry of order 2.
The diagonals bisect each other but not at right angles.
The diagonals are not equal.

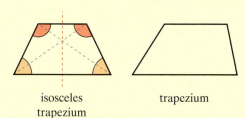
parallelogram

A **trapezium** has one pair of parallel sides.
It may have one line of symmetry.
It has rotational symmetry of order 1.
If it has a line of symmetry then it has
two pairs of equal angles and the
diagonals are the same length.

isosceles trapezium   trapezium

A **kite** has two pairs of equal sides.
It has one pair of equal angles.
It is like two isosceles triangles back-to-back.
It has one line of symmetry and rotational symmetry of order 1.
The diagonals intersect each other at right angles but they are not equal.

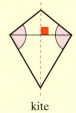
kite

An **arrowhead** has two pairs of equal sides.
It has one reflex angle. It is a **concave** shape.
It has one pair of equal angles.
It has one line of symmetry and rotational symmetry of order 1.
The diagonals intersect at right angles outside the shape.

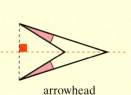
arrowhead

3 Coordinates and symmetry

Exercise 3:6

1 Jenny put these three shapes together to make a rectangle.
  a Make a drawing to show how she did this.
  b Describe all the properties of a rectangle.

2 Use the clues to sketch the shape in each part.
Label each sketch with the name of the shape.

  a It is a quadrilateral with no lines of symmetry.
Opposite angles are equal.
It has two pairs of equal sides.
It has rotational symmetry of order 2.

  b It has one line of symmetry.
It has two pairs of equal angles.
It has one pair of equal sides.
It has rotational symmetry of order 1.

3 a Plot each group of points on a new copy of the grid.
Join each set of points and label the name of the shape you produce in each part.

  (1) (1, 1) (1, 3) (3, 3) (4, 1) (1, 1)
  (2) (0, 2) (3, 3) (4, 2) (3, 1) (0, 2)
  (3) (2, 0) (4, 2) (2, 4) (0, 2) (2, 0)
  (4) (0, 1) (1, 3) (3, 3) (4, 1) (0, 1)
  (5) (1, 4) (2, 4) (4, 0) (3, 0) (1, 4)
  (6) (2, 0) (3, 2) (2, 4) (1, 2) (2, 0)
  (7) (1, 1) (1, 4) (2, 4) (2, 1) (1, 1)
  (8) (4, 4) (2, 2) (4, 0) (0, 2) (4, 4)

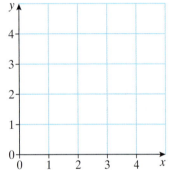

  b Draw the diagonals on each of the shapes you have drawn.
  c Which shapes have diagonals that cross at right angles?

4 Put each quadrilateral through this classification diagram.
Where does each shape come out?

  a Arrowhead

  b Isosceles trapezium

  c Kite

  d Parallelogram

  e Rhombus

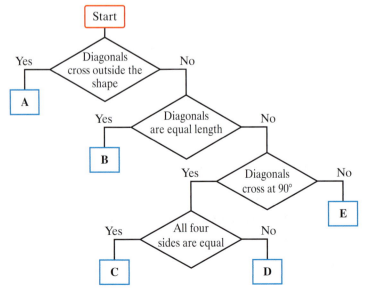

48

5 Write down the name of the quadrilateral that has
  a two different pairs of equal sides and four equal angles
  b two pairs of equal sides with no lines of symmetry and rotational symmetry of order 2
  c two pairs of equal sides with one pair of equal angles and one line of symmetry.

6 On this square grid, the points **A**, **B** and **C** must **not** move.
D is another point on the grid.
The coordinates of D are whole numbers.
When **D** is at (2, 8), quadrilateral ABCD is a kite.

  a Point **D** moves so that quadrilateral ABCD is still a kite.
  Where could **D** be now?
  Write down the coordinates of both possible new positions.

  b Point **D** moves so that quadrilateral ABCD is an arrowhead.
  Where could **D** be now?
  Write down the coordinates of all the possible new positions.

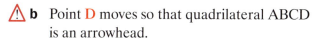

7 Put each quadrilateral through this classification diagram.
Where does each shape come out?

  a Rhombus

  b Isosceles trapezium

  c Kite

  d Parallelogram

  e Arrowhead

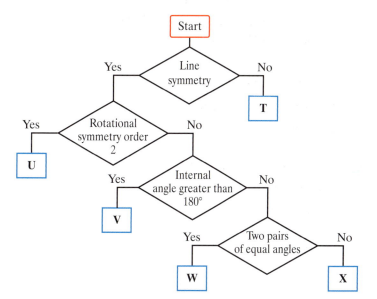

8 Explain the similarities between the shapes in each part.
  a Rectangle and parallelogram
  b Isosceles trapezium and rhombus
  c Rhombus and square

3 Coordinates and symmetry

Watch out ... there's a trap about

▶ Remember that a rectangle only has two lines of symmetry.

The red and blue lines are lines of symmetry.
The grey diagonal lines are **not** lines of symmetry.

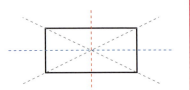

▶ Some people think that the order of rotational symmetry of this shape must be 0 because it isn't symmetrical. But the order of rotational symmetry of this shape is 1. There is no shape that has rotational symmetry of order 0.

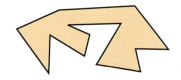

Test yourself

1 Copy these x and y axes.

  a Plot the points $(2, 3)$, $(-1, 4)$ and $(-3, -2)$.

  b Write down the coordinates of the point that will make a rectangle.

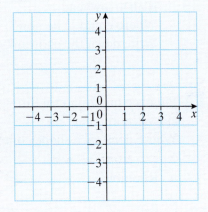

2 P is the mid-point of line AB.
Write down the coordinates of point P.

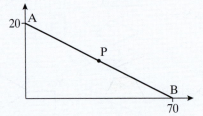

3 In each diagram the red line is a line of symmetry.
Copy and complete each diagram.

  a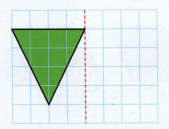

  b

4 Ben makes paper shapes.
To do this he folds a piece of paper in half, draws a shape, cuts it out and then unfolds it.

Ben cuts out the blue shape.

   a Sketch the shape that he makes.

   b Write down the order of rotational symmetry for Ben's shape.

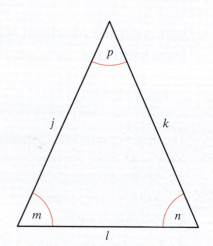

5 Rani drew this triangle.

   a Measure the angles and sides of her triangle.

   b Construct an accurate drawing of her triangle.

   c Draw any lines of symmetry on your drawing.

   d Rani said, 'I have drawn an equilateral triangle'.
       Give **four** reasons why she is wrong.

6 Write down the name of the shape that has

   a three sides of different lengths

   b four equal sides and four equal angles

   c two different pairs of equal sides and two different pairs of equal angles.

7 Put each quadrilateral through this classification diagram.
Where does each shape come out?

   a Arrowhead

   b Isosceles trapezium

   c Kite

   d Parallelogram

   e Rhombus

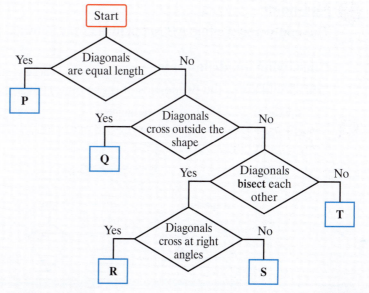

3 Coordinates and symmetry

Chapter 3 Summary

Level 5

Coordinates in all four quadrants

Point A has coordinates (−1, 2)
Point B has coordinates (−3, −2)
Point C has coordinates (2, −3)
Point D has coordinates (3, 1)

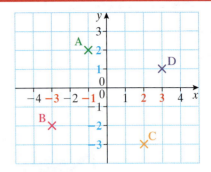

Reflection and rotational symmetry

If you fold a shape along a **line of symmetry** the two parts will fit exactly on top of each other.
A square has four lines of symmetry.

The **order of rotational symmetry** is the number of times the shape looks the same as you rotate it.
An equilateral triangle has rotational symmetry of order 3.

Classifying triangles

You should know the properties of these triangles.

    equilateral triangle   **isosceles triangle**   **scalene triangle**

  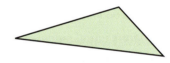

Level 6

Mid-point

The **mid-point** of a line AB is exactly halfway between A and B.

Classifying quadrilaterals

You should know the properties of these quadrilaterals.

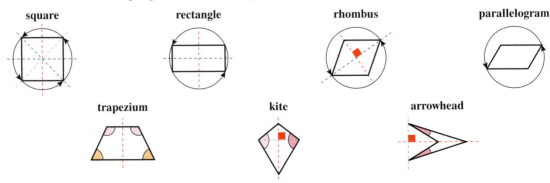

4 Types of numbers

Year 6
- Finding multiples
- Finding factors
- Working out square numbers
- Adding and subtracting whole numbers
- Using negative numbers to describe temperature

1. Multiples and factors
2. Prime numbers and divisibility
3. Directed numbers

Chapter 6 Formulae and algebraic operations
Using positive and negative numbers in formulae

Chapter 12 More fractions and percentages
- Cancelling down fractions
- Adding and subtracting fractions

You should already know:

▶ **your multiplication tables up to 10 × 10 and associated division facts**

$7 \times 5 = 35$ so $35 \div 5 = 7$ and $35 \div 7 = 5$

▶ **how to find multiples**

You can find a multiple of a number by multiplying it by any **whole number**.

$7 \times 2 = 14 \quad 7 \times 5 = 35 \quad 7 \times 8 = 56$

So 14, 35 and 56 are **multiples** of 7.

▶ **how to find factors**

The best way to find factors is in pairs.

$1 \times 10 = 10 \quad 2 \times 5 = 10$

so the factors of 10 are 1, 2, 5 and 10.

▶ **how to find the square numbers**

Squaring a number means multiplying it by itself. The first five **square numbers** are

$1^2 = 1 \quad 2^2 = 4 \quad 3^2 = 9 \quad 4^2 = 16 \quad 5^2 = 25$

▶ **how to describe temperature using negative numbers**

Temperatures below freezing are below 0°C.
−4°C means 4 degrees **below** freezing.

4 Types of numbers

1 Multiples and factors

▶ Finding the Lowest Common Multiple (LCM)

▶ Finding the Highest Common Factor (HCF)

Key words
multiple   common multiple
Lowest Common Multiple (LCM)
factor   common factor
Highest Common Factor (HCF)

▶ Finding the Lowest Common Multiple (LCM)   Level 5

The **multiples** of 10 are   10, 20, 30, 40, 50, 60, 70, 80, 90, 100, …

The multiples of 15 are   15, 30, 45, 60, 75, 90, 105, …

30, 60, 90, appear in both lists. They are **common multiples** of 10 and 15.

30 is the **Lowest Common Multiple (LCM)** of 10 and 15.

To find the lowest common multiple of two numbers, write out the lists of the multiples of the numbers until you find the first number that appears in both lists.

Exercise 4:1

1 **a** Write down the first 10 multiples of 4.
  b Write down the first 10 multiples of 6.
  c What is the LCM of 4 and 6?

2 Work out the LCM of the numbers in each part.

  a 3 and 6   **d** 8 and 10   **g** 6 and 12   **j** 3, 4 and 5
  b 3 and 4   **e** 10 and 15   **h** 5 and 12   **k** 4, 5 and 6
  c 6 and 7   **f** 12 and 18   **i** 2, 3 and 4   **l** $\frac{1}{2}, \frac{1}{3}$ and $\frac{1}{4}$

3 Two shift workers, Becky and Chris, share a flat.
Becky gets every fourth day off.
Chris gets every fifth day off.

Becky and Chris both had a day off on April 1st.
What is the date of the next day off that they share?

4 A ship is sailing in the Irish Sea.
The captain can see three lighthouses flashing.
Hilbre Island lighthouse flashes its light once every 3 seconds.
Trwyn Du lighthouse flashes its light once every 5 seconds.
Point Lynas lighthouse flashes its light once every 10 seconds.

Sometimes the captain sees all three lights flash at the same time. How often does this happen?

Trwyn Du lighthouse

Finding the Highest Common Factor (HCF) Level 5

The **factors** of 20 are   1, 2, 4, 5, 10 and 20

The factors of 24 are   1, 2, 3, 4, 6, 8, 12 and 24

1, 2 and 4 are **common factors** of 20 and 24.
They are all factors of both numbers.

4 is the **Highest Common Factor (HCF)** of 20 and 24.

To find the highest common factor of two numbers, write out the lists of all the factors of the numbers and look for the biggest number that appears in both lists.

Exercise 4:2

1 a Write down all the factors of 24.

b Write down all the factors of 42.

c What is the HCF of 24 and 42?

2 Work out the HCF of the numbers in each part.

a	8 and 12	**d**	8 and 16	**g**	16 and 20	**j**	6, 15 and 21
b	3 and 6	**e**	16 and 24	**h**	7 and 13	**k**	8, 16 and 20
c	15 and 20	**f**	12 and 18	**i**	8, 24 and 32	**l**	7, 11 and 23

3 This is a factor loop.
Each pair of circles is joined with a line.
There is a number on each line.

This number is the HCF of the numbers in the two circles.

a Copy this factor loop.
Fill in the missing numbers.

b Make up your own factor loop.

c Make up a factor loop with the numbers 2, 6, 8 and 10 between the circles.

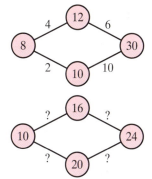

Explore

4 The HCF of two numbers is 24.
The LCM of the numbers is 144.
Neither number is 24.

What are the two numbers?

4 Types of numbers

2 Prime numbers and divisibility

- Using tests for divisibility
- Understanding prime numbers
- Using prime factor decomposition

Key words
tests for divisibility, divisible, prime number, prime factor, prime factor decomposition, factor tree

Using tests for divisibility — Level 5

Here are some **tests for divisibility**.

Divisible by	Test	Example
2	The number is **even**. It **ends in 0, 2, 4, 6** or **8**	2**8**, 4**6** and 100**2** are all **divisible** by 2
3	The sum of the digits of the number is divisible by 3	174 is divisible by 3 because 1 + 7 + 4 = 12 and 12 is divisible by 3
4	The number formed by the **last two digits** of the number is **divisible by 4**	3**24** is divisible by 4 because 24 is divisible by 4
5	The number **ends in 0** or **5**	2**5**, 23**5** and 635**0** are all divisible by 5
6	The number is divisible by 2 **and** 3	34**2** is divisible by 6 because it ends in 2 **and** 3 + 4 + 2 = 9 which is divisible by 3
8	Half of the number is divisible by 4	504 is divisible by 8 because 504 ÷ 2 = 252 and 2**52** is divisible by 4
9	The sum of the digits of the number is divisible by 9	783 is divisible by 9 because 7 + 8 + 3 = 18 and 18 is divisible by 9
10	The number **ends in 0**	2**0**, 30**0** and 4000**0** are all divisible by 10

Exercise 4:3

1 Look at this list of numbers.

   12   87   258   432   546   625   877   898   900   8700   8743

Write down all the numbers in the list that are divisible by

- **a** 2
- **b** 3
- **c** 4
- **d** 5
- **e** 6
- **f** 8
- **g** 9
- **h** 10

2 Mohinder says that any number that is divisible by 2 **and** 3 is also divisible by 6.
Claire says that any number that is divisible by 2 **and** 4 is also divisible by 8.
Which one of them is wrong? Explain why.

Think on!

3 Greta thinks of a 3-digit even number.
It is divisible by 5 and by 9.
It is less than 200.
What is Greta's number?

4 Copy and complete each sentence with a number from this box.
Use each number only once.

| 429 | 452 | 456 | 540 | 622 | 642 | 645 | 660 |

a … is divisible by 2
b … is divisible by 3
c … is divisible by 4
d … is divisible by 5
e … is divisible by 6
f … is divisible by 8
g … is divisible by 9
h … is divisible by 10

Understanding prime numbers   Level 5

A **prime number** has exactly two factors.
These numbers are 1 and the number itself.

So 13 is a prime number. Its only factors are 1 and 13.
There are no other integers that multiply together to give 13.

The prime numbers less than 30 are
   2, 3, 5, 7, 11, 13, 17, 19, 23 and 29.

1 is **not** a prime number because it doesn't have two factors.
Its only factor is 1.

Exercise 4:4

1 a Explain why 2 is the only even prime number.
  b Write down all the prime numbers between 30 and 40.

2 Jacob is thinking of two prime numbers.
The sum of his numbers is 24.
The difference between his numbers is 10.
Find the pair of prime numbers that Jacob is thinking of.

3 Some prime numbers make a different prime number
when you reverse their digits.
They are called emirp numbers. Really!
Find all the 2-digit emirp numbers.

4 Types of numbers

Facts to figure

4 Around 200 BC Eratosthenes worked out a method to find prime numbers. It is called the sieve of Eratosthenes.

1	2	3	4	5	6	7	8	9	10
2	4	6	8	10	12	14	16	18	20
3	6	9	12	15	18	21	24	27	30
4	8	12	16	20	24	28	32	36	40
5	10	15	20	25	30	35	40	45	50
6	12	18	24	30	36	42	48	54	60
7	14	21	28	35	42	49	56	63	70
8	16	24	32	40	48	56	64	72	80
9	18	27	36	45	54	63	72	81	90
10	20	30	40	50	60	70	80	90	100

a Make a copy of this number square.

b Cross out the 1.

c Put a circle around the 2.
Cross out all the numbers that are divisible by 2.

d Put a circle around the 3.
Cross out all the numbers that are divisible by 3.

e Do the same with 5 and 7.

f List all the numbers you have not crossed out.
They should all be prime numbers.

5 A Russian mathematician called Pafnuty Chebyshev had a theory.
He said:

> 'Between every whole number bigger than 1 and its double there is at least one prime number.'

For example, between 3 and its double, 6, there is the prime number 5.

Check Chebyshev's theory for the numbers from 2 to 20.

6 Twin primes are pairs of prime numbers that have a **difference** of 2.

3 and 5 is a pair of twin primes because 5 − 3 = 2.

Paul Stäckel, a German mathematician, was the first person to call them twin primes.

a Find all the pairs of twin primes that are less than 100.

b Add each pair together. What do you notice?

7 A famous mathematician called Christian Goldbach wrote down a conjecture in 1742.
A conjecture is a statement which you are not sure is true.
He said:

> 'All even numbers bigger than four can be written as the sum of two odd prime numbers.
> All odd numbers bigger than seven can be written as the sum of three odd prime numbers.'

Test Goldbach's conjecture for the numbers up to 40.

Using prime factor decomposition   Level 6

You already know that 1, 2, 4, 5, 10 and 20 are the factors of 20.
You also know that 2 and 5 are prime numbers.
So 2 and 5 are the **prime factors** of 20.

You can write every integer as the product of prime factors.
This means you can find prime numbers that multiply together to give the number.

For example $2 \times 2 \times 5$ is the **prime factor decomposition** of 20.

You can find the prime factor decomposition of a number using a **factor tree**.

First, split the number into any two factors.

If either of the two numbers is prime, put a circle around it.

If a factor is not prime, split it into two factors.

Carry on until all the branches have a circle at the end.

So $36 = 2 \times 2 \times 3 \times 3$

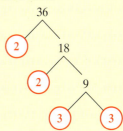

Exercise 4:5

1 a Write down all the factors of 60.
  b List the prime factors of 60. Start with the smallest.

2 Copy and complete these factor trees.
Use them to write out the prime factor decomposition of each number.

a 24

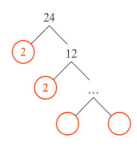

b 64

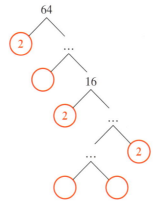

c 180

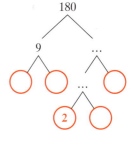

$24 = 2 \times 2 \times \_\_ \times \_\_$ $64 = 2 \times \_\_ \times \_\_ \times \_\_ \times \_\_ \times \_\_$ $180 = 2 \times \_\_ \times \_\_ \times \_\_ \times \_\_$

3 Use a factor tree to find the prime factor decomposition of each of these numbers.
  a 22   **c** 32   **e** 100   **g** 160
  b 30   **d** 81   **f** 108   **h** 250

3 Directed numbers

- Writing directed numbers in order
- Adding and subtracting directed numbers
- Multiplying and dividing directed numbers

Key words
negative   minus
positive   plus

Writing directed numbers in order — Level 5

You can put numbers in order of size using a number line.
Numbers get bigger as you move to the right.
⁻4 is bigger than ⁻5. Write this as ⁻4 > ⁻5.

numbers getting bigger

This number line shows the numbers 5, ⁻4, ⁻2, 0 and ⁻6.

Starting with the smallest, the numbers in order of size are ⁻6, ⁻4, ⁻2, 0 and 5.
You should read ⁻4 as '**negative** 4'. '**Minus** 4' means subtract 4.
You don't usually write ⁺4. Just write 4 for '**positive** 4'. '**Plus** 4' means add 4.
Zero is neither positive nor negative.

Exercise 4:6

1 Look at this weather map of Europe.

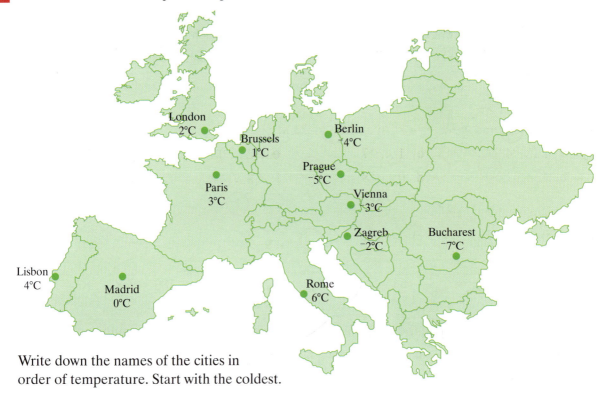

Write down the names of the cities in order of temperature. Start with the coldest.

2 Look at these temperatures.

−5°C, −7°C, 0°C, 4°C, −1°C, 6°C

Write the temperatures in order. Start with the coldest.

3 This table shows the scores of some golfers in Round 2 of the Shanghai Championship in 2007.

Paul Casey had a score of −5.
This means he used five strokes fewer than expected.

In a game of golf the player with the lowest score wins.

a Which of these players is in the lead?

b List the players in order.
   Start with the current leader.

Name	Score
Paul Casey	−5
Nick Dougherty	−3
Bradley Dredge	+2
Ross Fisher	−8
Padraig Harrington	−4
Ian Poulter	+4
Steve Webster	−5
Lee Westwood	0

4 At the end of January, Sharon's bank account is overdrawn.
She owes the bank £55. This is like having −£55 in her account.

This table shows the amount of money in Sharon's bank account from January to June.
It shows the amount at the end of each month.

Month	Jan	Feb	Mar	Apr	May	Jun
Amount in bank	−£55	−£125	£83	−£133	£87	−£228

a At the end of which month did she have the most money?

b At the end of which month did she **owe** the most money?

c Write the amounts of money in order.
   Start with the biggest amount that she **owed**.

5 Copy these and write > or < in each to make a correct statement.

a 2 ... −4   c 1 ... −7   e −2 ... 0   g −23 ... −22
b −3 ... 1   d 0 ... −8   f −8 ... −2   h −40 ... −41

6 Write the numbers in order of size.
Start with the smallest.

7, −1, −2, 3, −6, 0, −4

7 Write the numbers in order of size.
Start with the smallest.

3.2, −0.1, 6.2, −1.9, −3.4, −2, 3.5, −6.1, 0, −3.6

4 Types of numbers

Adding and subtracting directed numbers — Level 5

You can think about temperatures when you have to add and subtract directed numbers. Think about positive numbers as amounts of heat and negative numbers as amounts of cold.

Adding a positive number is just adding!
Adding heat makes the temperature go up.

$6 + {}^+7 = 6 + 7 = 13$
$^-4 + 6 = 2$

$+\ ^+ = +$

Adding a negative number is the same as subtracting.
Adding cold makes the temperature go down.

$12 + {}^-4 = 12 - 4 = 8$
$^-5 + {}^-2 = {}^-5 - 2 = {}^-7$

$+\ ^- = -$

Subtracting a positive number is subtracting.
Taking away heat makes the temperature go down.

$15 - {}^+6 = 15 - 6 = 9$
$^-4 - 7 = {}^-11$

$-\ ^+ = -$

Subtracting a negative number is the same as adding.
Taking away cold makes the temperature go up.

$11 - {}^-3 = 11 + 3 = 14$
$^-8 - {}^-8 = {}^-8 + 8 = 0$

$-\ ^- = +$

Exercise 4:7

1 On University Challenge, you lose 5 points if you interrupt and answer the question incorrectly.

   a Jim interrupts the first question of the show and gets the answer wrong.
   How many points does his team have?

   b Jim answers the second question correctly and earns 10 points.
   How many points does his team have now?

2 The temperatures in four cities were recorded during the day and at night.
How much warmer is the day temperature than the night temperature for each city?

Paris Day 12°C Night $^-2$°C   **Kabul**   Day 22°C Night $^-1$°C
Oslo   Day 7°C   Night $^-8$°C   **Moscow** Day 16°C Night $^-5$°C

3 At the end of February, Sadie's bank statement shows that her account is overdrawn by £228.20

   a She pays in £955.
   How much does she have in her account now?

   b Sadie keeps a list of the money she spends during March.
   What amount will her bank statement show at the end of March?

March
Rent — £240
Food — £185.27
Clothes — £127.95
Going out — £104.33
Holiday deposit — £200

4 Copy these magic squares and fill in the missing numbers. Remember that all vertical, horizontal and diagonal lines in a magic square add to the same total.

a
⁻2		⁻7
	⁻5	
⁻3		

b
⁻6		
⁻2	⁻9	⁻4

c
⁻1	⁻8	0
	2	

5 Work these out.

a ⁻8 + ⁺3   e ⁻2 − ⁺4   i 5 − ⁻3   m ⁻3 + 11
b ⁻7 + 5   f ⁻5 − 2   j 2 − ⁻5   n ⁻2 + ⁻5
c 7 + ⁻3   g ⁻1 + ⁻6   k ⁻7 − ⁻3   o ⁻4 − ⁻5
d 8 + ⁻3   h ⁻1 + 6   l 2 + ⁻3   p ⁻1 − 7

6 Copy these and fill in the missing numbers.

a ⁻1 + ⁺3 = …   c 7 − … = ⁻3   e ⁻15 − … = ⁻17   g 12 − ⁻3 = …
b ⁻14 + … = ⁻8   d ⁻12 − 5 = …   f ⁻7 + … = ⁻2   h ⁻12 − … = ⁻9

7 Extend the patterns shown in these calculations by writing down the next five rows.

a 6 + 1 = 7
   6 + 0 = 6
   6 + ⁻1 = 5
   6 + ⁻2 = 4

b ⁻4 − 2 = ⁻6
   ⁻4 − 1 = ⁻5
   ⁻4 − 0 = ⁻4
   ⁻4 − ⁻1 = ⁻3

8 Matt thinks of two integers.
He takes one away from the other and gets an answer of ⁻4.

a Write down three pairs of numbers that Matt could have used.

b If Matt took his integers away in the opposite order, write down the answer that he would get.

Explore

9 a Write down five different pairs of integers that have
    (1) a sum of ⁻7   (2) a difference of ⁻7.

b Write down a pair of integers that has a sum of ⁻7 **and** a difference of ⁻7.

4 Types of numbers

Multiplying and dividing directed numbers — Level 6

Multiplication is repeated addition. $3 \times {}^-4 = {}^-4 + {}^-4 + {}^-4 = {}^-4 - 4 - 4 = -12$

When you **multiply** a **positive** number by a **negative** number you get a **negative** answer.

So $5 \times {}^-3 = -15$ because ${}^+ \times {}^- = {}^-$ and $5 \times 3 = 15$.

Division is the reverse of multiplication. So ${}^-15 \div {}^-3 = 5$. There are 5 lots of -3 in -15.

When you **divide** a **negative** number by a **negative** number you get a **positive** answer.

Also ${}^-15 \div 5 = -3$ so when you **divide** a **negative** number by a **positive** number you get a **negative** answer.

Because $\dfrac{15}{-5} = \dfrac{-15}{5} = -\dfrac{15}{5} = -3$ this also means that when you **divide** a **positive** number by a **negative** number you get a **negative** answer.

$15 \div {}^-5 = -3$. Reversing this to give a multiplication tells you that ${}^-5 \times {}^-3 = 15$ so when you **multiply** a **negative** number by a **negative** number you get a **positive** answer.

You should remember all of these rules.

${}^+ \times {}^+ = {}^+$	${}^+ \times {}^- = {}^-$	${}^+ \div {}^+ = {}^+$	${}^+ \div {}^- = {}^-$
${}^- \times {}^- = {}^+$	${}^- \times {}^+ = {}^-$	${}^- \div {}^- = {}^+$	${}^- \div {}^+ = {}^-$

Exercise 4:8

1 Extend the patterns shown in these calculations by writing down the next five rows.

   a $2 \times 6 = 12$
      $1 \times 6 = 6$
      $0 \times 6 = 0$
      ${}^-1 \times 6 = {}^-6$

   b $2 \times {}^-4 = {}^-8$
      $1 \times {}^-4 = {}^-4$
      $0 \times {}^-4 = 0$
      ${}^-1 \times {}^-4 = 4$

2 **a** Copy this multiplication table and fill it in.

Colour in the positive numbers, the negative numbers and the zeros using different colours.

b Look at the patterns in the table. Describe one pattern that you have found.

×	${}^-3$	${}^-2$	${}^-1$	0	1	2	3
3							
2							
1							
0							
${}^-1$							
${}^-2$							
${}^-3$							

3 Copy these and fill in the missing numbers.

a ⁻2 × 7 = ...   c ⁻12 ÷ 6 = ...   e ⁻9 × ⁻3 = ...   g 16 ÷ ... = ⁻4

b ⁻14 × ... = ⁻28   d ⁻15 ÷ ... = 3   f ⁻12 ÷ ... = ⁻6   h ... × ⁻1 = ⁻9

4 a Two numbers **multiply** together to make ⁻15.
They **add** together to make **2**.
What are the two numbers?

b Two numbers **multiply** together to make ⁻15,
but **add** together to make ⁻**2**.
What are the two numbers?

c Two numbers **multiply** together to make **8**,
but **add** together to make ⁻**6**.
What are the two numbers?

d The square of 5 is 25.
The square of **another** number is also 25.
What is that other number?

5 a Copy this multiplication grid three times.

b Fill in your grid in three different ways.

c How many different ways are there
to fill in this grid using integers?

×		3	⁻2
			⁻6
⁻4			
	8		
			⁻7

6 a How many ⁻3s are there in ⁻15?

b How many ⁻5s are there in ⁻20?

c How many 8s are there in ⁻24?

d How many ⁻5s are there in 20?

Think on!

7 Sort these cards into pairs that give the same answer.

| ⁻12 − ⁻2 | | ⁻3 − 3 + ⁻3 | | ⁻2 × 0 | | 6 − ⁻8 |

| 4 − ⁻2 + ⁻6 | | ⁻7 × ⁻2 | | ⁻2 × 5 |

| 28 ÷ ⁻2 | | 4 − 18 | | ⁻36 ÷ 4 |

4 Types of numbers

Watch out ... there's a trap about

▶ The first factor tree is wrong.
12 = 1 × 2 × 2 × 3 is **not** the prime factor decomposition.
1 is not a prime number.

The second factor tree is correct.
12 = 2 × 2 × 3 is the correct prime factor decomposition.

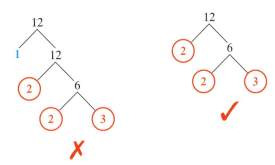

▶ ⁻7 − 2 does **not** equal 9.

Some people think that a negative and a negative always makes a positive so the answer is 9.

But ⁻7 − 2 = ⁻9

This is because you start at ⁻7 on the number line and go **down 2** places.

Test yourself

1 **a** Write down the first 6 multiples of 8.
b Write down the first 6 multiples of 12.
c Write down the common multiples in your two lists.
d What is the LCM of 8 and 12?

2 Work out the LCM of 6 and 8.

3 **a** Write down all the factors of 16.
b Write down all the factors of 36.
c Write down all the common factors of 16 and 36.
d What is the HCF of 16 and 36?

4 Use the tests of divisibility to decide which of the numbers 2, 3, 4, 5, 6, 8, 9 and 10 are factors of 360.

5 **a** Write down the first 10 prime numbers.
b Find a pair of prime numbers with a sum of 84 and a difference of 2.

6 a Write down all the factors of 42.

  b Write down the prime factors of 42.

7 Copy and complete this prime factor decomposition of 350.

$350 = 2 \times 5 \times \underline{} \times \underline{}$

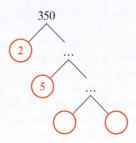

8 Find the prime factor decomposition of 112.

9 Look at these temperatures.

  ⁻7°C, 0°C, 2°C, 1°C, ⁻6°C, ⁻1°C

Write the temperatures in order. Start with the coldest.

10 Copy these and put > or < in each to make a correct statement.

  a 2 … ⁻1   **b** ⁻2 … ⁻4   **c** ⁻2 … 4   **d** ⁻2 … 1

11 Work these out.

  a ⁻7 + ⁺4   **c** ⁻3 − ⁺5   **e** 8 − ⁻6   **g** ⁻5 + 15
  b ⁻5 + 2   **d** ⁻7 − 3   **f** ⁻4 − ⁻10   **h** ⁻14 + ⁻6

12 Copy this multiplication table and fill it in.

×	⁻1	4	⁻2
		⁻8	
⁻5			
	6		
3			⁻9

13 Copy these and fill in the missing numbers.

  a ⁻4 × 7 = …   **c** ⁻15 ÷ 3 = …   **e** 6 × … = ⁻30   **g** ⁻16 ÷ … = 4
  b ⁻2 × ⁻6 = …   **d** 16 ÷ … = ⁻2   **f** 0 × ⁻3 = …   **h** 12 ÷ ⁻6 = …

4 Types of numbers

Chapter 4 Summary

Level 5

Lowest common multiple (LCM)

The multiples of 10 are 10, 20, **30**, 40, 50, **60**, …
The multiples of 15 are 15, **30**, 45, **60**, 75, **90**, …

The LCM of 10 and 15 is the first number in both lists. **30** is the LCM of 10 and 15.

Highest common factor (HCF)

The factors of 20 are **1**, 2, 4, **5**, 10 and 20.
The factors of 25 are **1**, **5** and 25.

The HCF of 20 and 25 is the biggest number in both lists. **5** is the HCF of 20 and 25.

Prime numbers

A prime number has exactly two factors. These numbers are 1 and the number itself.
The first 10 prime numbers are 2, 3, 5, 7, 11, 13, 17, 19, 23 and 29.

Writing positive and negative numbers in order

You can put numbers in order of size by thinking about where the numbers are on a number line.

This number line shows the numbers 3, ⁻4, 1, 0 and ⁻2

```
 ⁻4  ⁻3  ⁻2  ⁻1   0   1   2   3
```

So, starting with the smallest, the numbers in order of size are ⁻4, ⁻2, 0, 1 and 3.

Adding and subtracting positive and negative numbers

You should remember all of these **rules**.

⁻5 + ⁻2 = ⁻5 − 2 = ⁻7   11 − ⁻3 = 11 + 3 = 14

| + ⁺ = + | − ⁺ = − |
| + ⁻ = − | − ⁻ = + |

Level 6

Prime factor decomposition

You can find the **prime factor decomposition** of a number using a factor tree.

28 = **2** × **2** × **7**

```
      28
     /  \
    2   14
       /  \
      2    7
```

Multiplying and dividing positive and negative numbers

You should remember all of these **rules**.

⁺5 × ⁺3 = ⁺15
⁻4 × ⁻6 = ⁺24

| + × ⁺ = + | + × ⁻ = − |
| − × ⁻ = + | − × ⁺ = − |

| + ÷ ⁺ = + | + ÷ ⁻ = − |
| − ÷ ⁻ = + | − ÷ ⁺ = − |

⁺18 ÷ ⁻3 = ⁻6
⁻50 ÷ ⁺10 = ⁻5

5 Data and diagrams

You should already know:

▶ **how to group data**

These test marks have been grouped.

All the groups are the same size and they don't overlap.

Mark	Tally	Frequency
0 – 9	||||		6
10 – 19	|||| |||| ||||	15
20 – 29	|||| ||||	9

▶ **how to find the mode and the range**

The **mode** of a set of data is the most common or most popular value.
It is sometimes called the **modal value**.

These are the weights of 10 crisp packets, measured to the nearest gram.

20 g, 19 g, 21 g, 20 g, 20 g,
19 g, 22 g, 20 g, 18 g, 20 g

The modal weight is 20 g.

The **range** measures how spread out the data is.
The range is
the largest value take away the smallest value.

These are the heights of 6 people.

148 cm   152 cm   163 cm
167 cm   175 cm   189 cm

The range is 189 cm − 148 cm = 41 cm.

▶ **how to draw bar charts**

These are the rules you should remember.
- Bars are all the same width.
- There are equal gaps between the bars.
- The bar chart must have labels and a title.
- Each bar must be labelled in the centre.

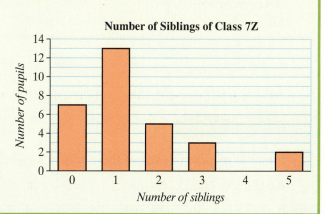

5 Data and diagrams

1 Averages and the range

- Finding the median
- Finding the mean
- Finding the mean from a frequency table
- Understanding and using averages and the range

Key words

mode, modal value, median, mean, frequency table, biased

Finding the median — Level 5

There are three types of average.

You already know about the **mode**.

The mode of a set of data is the most common or most popular value. It is sometimes called the **modal value**.

The second type of average is the **median**.

To find the median of a set of data:
- write the data in order from smallest to largest
- the median is the middle number in your list.

To find the median of the numbers: 3, 6, 10, 2, 6, 4, 1, 7, 2

Write them in order: 1, 2, 2, 3, 4, 6, 6, 7, 10

The median is the middle number, which is 4.

If there is an even number of data values, there will be two middle numbers.
If this happens, the median is halfway between these two numbers.

These are the heights of six people.

148 cm   152 cm   **163 cm**   **167 cm**   175 cm   189 cm

Their median height is $\dfrac{163 + 167}{2} = 165$ cm.

Exercise 5:1

1 Find the median of each of these sets of numbers.

   a 12, 15, 16, 23, 25   **c** 56, 32, 24, 58, 89, 67, 9, 12, 7

   b 132, 145, 167, 189, 190, 201   **d** 23, 145, 56, 23, 67, 89, 35, 23, 67, 89, 102, 38

2 These are the times, in seconds, taken by 10 pupils to run 100 m.

13.5   16.2   14.8   15.1   16.3   18.9   17.6   16.8   15.3   16.1

Find the median time.

3 These are the times of eight advert breaks on TV in seconds.

120   150   120   180   150   180   120   240

Find the median time.

4 The table shows the shoe sizes of the pupils in Class 7F.

Shoe size	4	5	6	7	8	9
Number of pupils	3	4	7	5	3	2

Find the median shoe size.

Finding the mean   Level 5

The third type of average is the **mean**. It is the most commonly used of the three.

To find the mean of a set of data:
- add up all the data values
- divide this total by the number of data values.

These are the amounts earned per hour by 8 people:

£7.40   £8.40   £5.90   £6.50   £7.90   £8.20   £9.30   £6.40

The total is £7.40 + £8.40 + £5.90 + £6.50 + £7.90 + £8.20 + £9.30 + £6.40 = £60

The mean is £60 ÷ 8 = £7.50

Exercise 5:2

1 Find the mean of each of these sets of numbers.

   a 16, 18, 24, 28, 34
   b 13, 265, 37, 48, 433, 38
   c 21.3, 34.6, 24.7, 45.7, 23.6, 34.8, 23.7, 55.6
   d 0.34, 0.56, 0.45, 0.8, 0.38, 0.56, 0.7, 0.76, 0.35, 0.7

2 The amounts of time Daniel spends on his homework in a week are:

45 min   35 min   25 min   65 min   40 min

Find the mean amount of time Daniel spends on his homework.

5 Data and diagrams

3 Eight of the judges in a diving competition awarded a diver these points:

5.8   5.6   5.9   5.7   5.5   5.7   5.7   5.5

a What is the mean score?

b What is the modal score?

c The ninth judge gave the diver a score of 5.9
   If this score is included, will the mean go up or down?
   Explain your answer.

4 The mean of five numbers is 65. What is the total of the numbers?

5 Mike has a mean score of 78% for the first five tests of the year.
After his sixth test, his mean score goes down to 76%.
What score did Mike get in his sixth test?

6 Gina has a mean score of 85% for the first five tests of the year.
She gets 61% on her last test of the year.
What is her mean score for the year?

Finding the mean from a frequency table — Level 5

You can also find the mean when data is in a **frequency table**.
This is a frequency table showing the number of goals scored in 28 football matches.

Number of goals	Number of matches	Total number of goals
0	4	0 × 4 = 0
1	7	1 × 7 = 7
2	8	2 × 8 = 16
3	3	3 × 3 = 9
4	6	4 × 6 = 24
Total	28	56

The entries in the third column show the total number of goals on each row.
There were **8** matches with **2** goals scored. This is a total of 2 × 8 = 16 goals.
Do this for every row and add up the last column to get the total number of goals.

To find the mean you divide the total number of goals by the total number of matches.

The mean number of goals is 56 ÷ 28 = 2.

Exercise 5:3

1 A sample of 50 boxes of matches is taken from a production line in a factory.
The number of matches in each box is counted and recorded.
The boxes should have an average contents of 40 if the packing machine is working properly.

This frequency table shows the results of the sample.

Number of matches in a box	Number of boxes
38	6
39	8
40	15
41	11
42	10

a Calculate the mean number of matches in the boxes.
b Do you think the machine is working properly?
Explain your answer.

2 Nathaniel counts the number of chocolate buttons in 50 packets. These are his results.

Number of buttons in a packet	Number of packets
26	3
27	5
28	8
29	11
30	19
31	4

Calculate the mean number of buttons in a packet.

3 Two seaside towns record the number of hours of sunshine they have on each day in August.
The amounts of sunshine are given to the nearest hour.
The results are shown in the table.

Hours of sunshine	Town A	Town B	Hours of sunshine	Town A	Town B
0	3	2	5	2	5
1	5	4	6	4	2
2	4	6	7	1	1
3	6	5	8	2	1
4	2	3	9	2	2

Compare the two towns and decide which town is the sunnier!

5 Data and diagrams

Understanding and using averages and the range — Level 5

You need to understand when to use the different averages and the range.

The **median** is the middle value. This allows you to make statements like:
'The median test score is 45%. So half of the class scored at least 45%.'
The median is not **biased** if one or two values are much bigger or smaller than the others.

The **mode** is the most common value. It is useful when reporting the results of surveys.
'The modal answer was red. Most people preferred red cars.'
Unlike other averages, the mode does not have to be a number.

The **mean** takes all the values into account. It is the average that most people usually use.
'The mean pocket money for a class is £7' means that each pupil would get £7 if you shared all the pocket money for the class equally between all the pupils.
It can be biased by a value that is very different from the others.

The **range** is used to show how spread out the data is. The bigger the range, the bigger the gap between the smallest and the biggest values.

Martin and Andy both have a batting average of 46 in cricket.
The range of Andy's scores is 15 runs.
The range of Martin's scores is 37 runs.
This means that Andy's scores are more consistent.
They are less spread out.
Andy is the more reliable player.
Martin might get a very high score but he might get a very low score.
You can choose which one you would rather have on your team!

Exercise 5:4

1 Look at this data for the monthly hours of sunshine in two different countries.

Month	Jan	Feb	Mar	Apr	May	Jun	Jul	Aug	Sep	Oct	Nov	Dec
Country 1	154	161	165	170	173	185	190	198	187	164	153	140
Country 2	50	80	120	165	190	236	260	301	276	197	101	64

a Work out the mean number of hours of sunshine for each country.

b Draw a bar chart for each country.
Draw a horizontal line on each of your bar charts to show the mean number of hours of sunshine for each country.

c Work out the range for each country.

d Explain the main differences between the two countries using your answers to parts **a** to **c**.

2 Write down which average might be best to use in each of these cases.
Explain your answers.

   a Pocket money received by each pupil in your class.

   b Which football team each of your class supports.

   c The time taken by each of your class to run 100 m.

   d The shoe sizes of all the pupils in your class.

3 Calculate, where possible, the mean, median and mode for each of these sets of data.
Explain which average you think is best in each part.

   a The number of CDs owned by 18 people.

   12, 14, 43, 54, 24, 36, 0, 32, 7, 5, 21, 31, 40, 28, 17, 4, 12, 16

   b The average temperature to the nearest °C in July over a 15-year period.

   23, 22, 21, 23, 26, 22, 23, 25, 21, 20, 23, 21, 22, 23, 24

   c The maths test scores of 12 people.

   55% 44% 49% 44% 55% 65% 75% 79% 44% 55% 40% 55%

   d The hourly wage rate of 10 people.

   £4.50 £4.70 £4.50 £3.30 £23.00 £4.50 £6.50 £35.00 £4.90 £5.60

4 Katy and Corrine both play cricket.
This table shows their scores in their last six games.

| Katy | 44 | 73 | 39 | 60 | 68 | 40 |
| Corrine | 120 | 7 | 84 | 26 | 9 | 90 |

   a Work out the mean score for both girls.

   b Work out the range for both girls.

   c Copy and complete these sentences.

   Katy and Corrine's mean scores are very _____.

   The range of Katy's scores is _____ but Corrine's range is _____.

   Of the two girls, _____ is more consistent but _____ might get you a very high score if you needed one.

5 These are the number of goals scored by each member of a football team in one season.

   0   0   1   2   3   3   4   5   9   11   17

   a Work out the mean, the median and the mode of these scores.

   b Write down one reason for and one reason against using the mean as the average.

5 Data and diagrams

6 Hannah went on a cycling holiday.

The table shows how far she cycled each day.

Monday	Tuesday	Wednesday	Thursday
32.3 km	38.7 km	43.5 km	45.1 km

Hannah says, 'On average I cycled **over 40 km** a day.'

Show that Hannah is wrong.

7 The number of shots taken by 50 golfers at the 18th hole is shown in this bar chart.

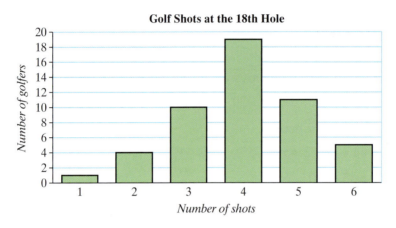

a Show the data in a frequency table.

b Work out the mean number of shots taken for this hole.

The hole is a par 4. This means that, on average, it should take 4 shots.

c Are these golfers doing better or worse than average? Explain your answer.

8 George is a car salesman.

This table shows the number of cars he has sold in the last six weeks.

Week	1	2	3	4	5	6
Cars	3	4	12	3	3	2

George is discussing his sales with his manager.

George says his average sales are good. His manager disagrees.

Say which average you think each of them is using. Show your working.

Explore

9 a Write down five sets of five numbers that have a mean of 12.

b Write down five numbers whose mean is 12 and whose range is 5.

c Write down four numbers whose mean is 12 and whose range is 5.

2 Diagrams and continuous data

- **Reading information from diagrams**
- Drawing time-series graphs
- Continuous data
- Drawing frequency diagrams

Key words

pie chart	line graph
sector	time-series graph
trend	discrete
continuous	frequency diagram

Reading information from diagrams   Level 5

You need to be able to read information from many different diagrams.
As well as reading bar charts, you also need to be able to read **pie charts** and **line graphs**.

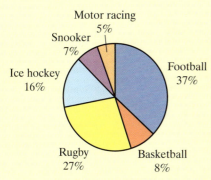

This pie chart shows Year 7's favourite type of sport to watch on TV.

Football is the most popular.
It has the biggest **sector**.

Motor racing is the least popular.
It has the smallest sector.

The percentage of pupils preferring each sport is labelled. It is difficult to read exact values from a pie chart if it is not labelled like this.

This line graph shows the percentage of cat food that was sold in tins between 1998 and 2004.

The line shows the trend of the sales.
It is a downward trend.

In 1998, 80% of cat food sold was in tins.
By 2004, this had reduced to 35%.

Exercise 5:5

1 This line graph shows the percentage of people in the UK who own a DVD player. Write down

  a the percentage owning a DVD player in 2000

  b the increase between 2000 and 2002

  c the two years between which there was the biggest rise in ownership

  d why you think the graph rises very slowly at first.

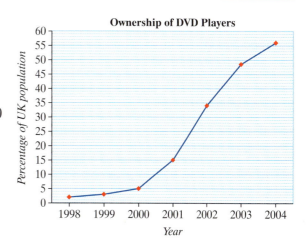

5 Data and diagrams

2 This graph shows the average temperature in Solihull for 2007.

Describe what happened to the temperature during the year.

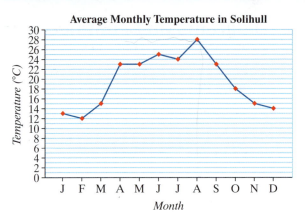

3 This pie chart shows the proportions of tabloid newspapers sold on Sunday.

   a Write down which newspaper is the most popular.
   b How many times higher are sales of the Sunday Express than sales of the Star?
   c Explain why you cannot use this pie chart to work out how many Sunday Mirrors were sold.

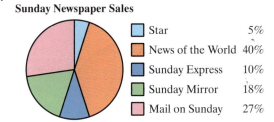

4 A school records how many pupils are late each day. The bar chart shows the results for one week.

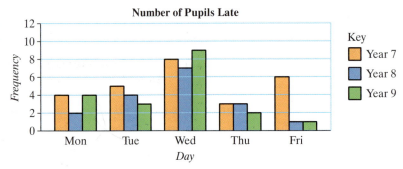

   a How many pupils were late on Monday?
   b How many Year 9 pupils were late during the week?

The bus broke down on one day during the week.

   c Which day do you think this was? Explain your answer.

5 This bar chart shows how pupils at Keighley High School choose to eat their lunch.

   a What is the most popular option in Year 7?
   b What is the most popular option in Year 9?
   c How many pupils are there in Year 8?
   d How many pupils eat at home altogether?

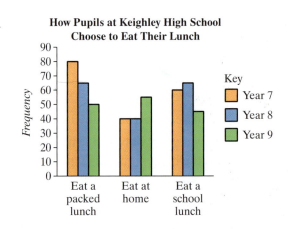

6 This pie chart shows the percentage of people who are members of each religion in the UK.

a Estimate the percentage of people who said they were Christians.

b Estimate the percentage who answered 'None'.

c Estimate the percentage of the population who gave no reply.

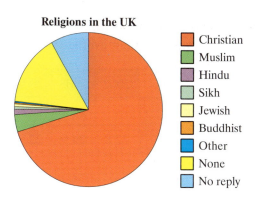

Religions in the UK
- Christian
- Muslim
- Hindu
- Sikh
- Jewish
- Buddhist
- Other
- None
- No reply

Think on!

7 Which **red sector** represents the smallest number of pupils?

(A) This pie chart represents 200 pupils

(B) This pie chart represents 100 pupils

(C) This pie chart represents 90 pupils

(D) This pie chart represents 100 pupils

Drawing time-series graphs — Level 6

A **time-series graph** is very similar to a line graph.

It always shows time on the horizontal scale.

Points are joined with straight lines. These lines show the **trend** over a period of time.

This time-series graph shows that the results in all the subjects shown are now improving.

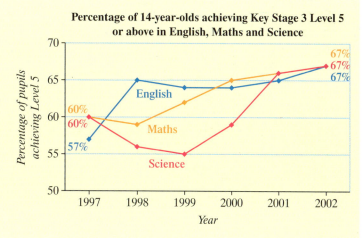

Exercise 5:6

1 This table shows the profits of Terry's Taxis over a seven-year period.

Year	2001	2002	2003	2004	2005	2006	2007
Profit (£ thousands)	12	10	11	13	15	18	21

Draw a time-series graph to show the profits.

5 Data and diagrams

2 Two seaside towns are in competition with each other.
They record their average summer temperatures in °C over a period of six years.

	2002	2003	2004	2005	2006	2007
Seatown	23.1	25.4	22.9	22.3	21.1	22.6
Beachside	22.8	24.9	22.3	22.7	22.1	23.9

a Draw one time-series graph showing both sets of data. Use different colours for the two towns.

b Which parts of the graph do you think each town would choose to use in their advertisements? Explain your answer.

3 This table shows the populations of Ireland and England during the nineteenth century. The populations are in millions.

	1840	1850	1860	1870	1880	1890	1900
Ireland	8.0	6.5	5.8	5.3	5.1	4.8	4.5
England	16.0	17.6	20.2	22.5	25.9	28.7	32.2

a Draw a single time-series graph to show this data.
Draw the lines for the two countries in different colours.

b Describe what happened to the population of each country.

Continuous data   Level 6

There are two types of data. They are known as **discrete** and **continuous**.

Data is **discrete** when it can only take certain individual values.

Examples of discrete data are:
   the number of people in a family
   the number of computer games you own
   the shoe sizes stocked in a shop.

Notice that the last example is still discrete even though the data is not whole numbers.

Discrete data can take values like 3, $3\frac{1}{2}$, 4, $4\frac{1}{2}$, 5 etc.

There are no other shoe sizes between 3 and 4 such as $3\frac{1}{4}$ or 3.7

Data is **continuous** when it can take any value in a certain range.

Examples of continuous data are:
   the height of a person (you don't grow a whole centimetre at a time!)
   the length of an earthworm
   the time when the first goal is scored in a football match.

Exercise 5:7

1 Read these descriptions of sets of data.
For each one, write down whether the data is **discrete** or **continuous**.
   a The number of pupils in each Year 7 class in your school
   b The weights of 30 cats
   c The number of complete laps run by each person in a sponsored run
   d The distance run by each person in a sponsored run
   e The area of each county in the UK
   f The time taken by athletes to run 100

2 Mr Raphson sets his maths class a test. It is marked out of 25.
   a Mr Raphson only gives whole marks. Is this data discrete or continuous?
   b Mr Raphson then changes the marks into percentages. Is this data discrete or continuous?

3 Your age is one of the few numbers that is never rounded up.
You are still 11 years old when you are 11 years, 364 days, 23 hours and 59 minutes old!
You do not say that you are 12 when you pass $11\frac{1}{2}$.
Is your age continuous or discrete? Explain your answer.

Explore

4 There are four basketball teams in a competition.
The heights of the team members are given in this table correct to the nearest cm.

Team	Heights (cm)							
Green Valley	149	152	160	158	160	162	158	156
Red Ferns	155	156	154	158	152	157	160	157
St Peters	143	147	150	152	155	149	150	153
Albion	150	146	159	152	144	158	157	158

   a Find the modal height, range, mean and median for each team.

This table gives the scores for the last eight games of each team.

Team	Scores							
Green Valley	35	17	33	35	36	16	27	41
Red Ferns	16	24	22	31	29	15	31	32
St Peters	18	21	31	22	12	39	20	19
Albion	14	16	18	31	31	32	30	22

   b Find the modal score, range, mean and median for each team.
   c Does there seem to be any relationship between the heights of the players and the scores?

5 Data and diagrams

Drawing frequency diagrams Level 6

You should draw a **frequency diagram** to display **continuous** data.
A frequency diagram should always have:
- bars of equal width with no gaps between them
- a title and labels on the axes
- a continuous scale on the horizontal axis – not labels under each of the bars.

This frequency table shows the distance some Year 7 pupils live from school.

Distance from school, d (miles)	$0 \leqslant d < 1$	$1 \leqslant d < 2$	$2 \leqslant d < 3$	$3 \leqslant d < 4$	$4 \leqslant d < 5$	$5 \leqslant d < 6$
Number of pupils	18	12	25	14	9	3

$1 \leqslant d < 2$ means that pupils in this group live between 1 and 2 miles away.
The $\leqslant$ symbol means that 1 mile is included in this group.
The $<$ symbol means that 2 miles is **not** included.
Pupils living 2 miles away go into the $2 \leqslant d < 3$ group.

Here is a frequency diagram to show this data.

Notice that a frequency diagram looks quite similar to a **bar chart**.

But remember that a bar chart is only used for discrete data and it has gaps between the bars.

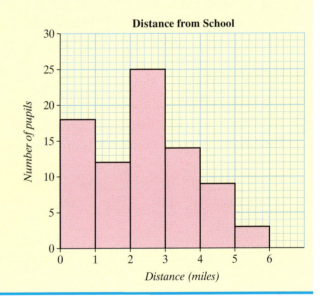

Exercise 5:8

1 This table shows the heights of 30 Year 7 pupils.

Height (m)	1 up to 1.2	1.2 up to 1.4	1.4 up to 1.6	1.6 up to 1.8
Number of pupils	12	13	4	2

Draw a frequency diagram to display this data.
Your horizontal scale should look like this:

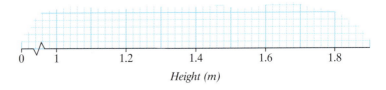

2 This table shows the ages of young people involved in road accidents.

Age, A (years)	0 ≤ A < 5	5 ≤ A < 10	10 ≤ A < 15	15 ≤ A < 20
Frequency	560	580	1020	980

Draw a frequency diagram to display the data.

3 These are the weights of some hamsters.

Weight (g)	24 ≤ Weight < 26	26 ≤ Weight < 28	28 ≤ Weight < 30	30 ≤ Weight < 32
Frequency	13	17	18	21

Draw a frequency diagram to display the data.

4 This data shows the time in seconds for 30 pupils to complete a race.

```
42.1   45.6   54.3   39.7   46.2   48.5
38.9   48.7   54.1   46.9   43.3   59.9
48.6   39.9   40.4   43.9   46.8   48.1
51.1   48.8   52.2   51.0   46.6   48.9
45.9   42.7   43.8   42.9   39.9   45.6
```

a Design a suitable frequency table for this data.
b Tally the data into your frequency table.
c Draw a frequency diagram to display the data.

5 The weights of 30 stick insects were measured as part of a scientific study. The weights are in grams.

```
12.350   12.506   13.106   12.640   13.503   12.541
12.450   13.467   12.986   13.034   12.453   13.756
12.783   12.842   13.304   13.036   12.548   12.354
13.473   12.520   12.012   13.753   13.864   12.750
12.650   12.205   12.640   12.642   12.963   12.853
```

a Design a frequency table with suitable groups for this data.
b Tally the data into your frequency table.
c Draw a frequency diagram to display the data.

5 Data and diagrams

Watch out ... there's a trap about

▶ This is Paul's working for a question about finding a mean from a frequency table.

He has been asked to calculate the mean number of goals scored in 30 hockey matches.

Although the answer 3 seems reasonable, it is **wrong**.

Paul has not worked out the total number of goals.

You mustn't just divide the totals of the two columns. The correct working is

$1 \times 8 = 8$
$2 \times 12 = 24$
$3 \times 7 = 21$
$4 \times 3 = 12$

Mean $= (8 + 24 + 21 + 12) \div 30$
$= 2.17$ (to 2 d.p.) ✓

Number of goals	Frequency
1	8
2	12
3	7
4	3
10	30

Mean $= 30 \div 10$
$= 3$

Test yourself

1 These are the times, in seconds, taken by nine pupils to run 200 m.

28.5   32.1   29.5   36.5   27.4   30.4   29.9   37.4   34.4

Find the median time.

2 These are the amounts of time, in minutes, that Mohammed spends watching the TV each day in one week.

50   70   0   120   30   150   35

a Find the mean of these times.
b Explain why you can't find the mode of these times.
c Find the range of these times.

3 These are the shoe sizes of 10 members of Class 7A.

7   5   6   8   4   7   2   6   7   10

a Calculate the mean, median and mode of these shoe sizes.
b Say which average you think is best and why.

4 Dennis recorded the number of eggs laid by his chickens for the 31 days of July.
Here are his results.

Number of eggs	Number of days
15	15
16	7
17	4
18	4
19	1

Work out the mean number of eggs laid by the chickens in July.

5 Bill's mean score in his three maths tests so far this year is 67%.
Bill's Dad says he will buy him a computer game if his mean gets up to 70%.
What does Bill need to score in his next test to get his computer game?

6 This frequency table shows the temperatures of 50 holiday resorts in Europe.

Temperature, T (°F)	$65 \leq T < 70$	$70 \leq T < 75$	$75 \leq T < 80$	$80 \leq T < 85$	$85 \leq T < 90$
Number of resorts	2	17	23	6	2

Draw a frequency diagram to display the data.

7 Explain why
  a the weight of a bag of sweets is an example of continuous data
  b the number of sweets in a bag is an example of discrete data.

8 Look at this time-series graph.

Copy and complete this table using data that you read from the graph.

Year	Births (millions)	Deaths (millions)
1921		
1931		
1941		
2001		
2021		
2041		

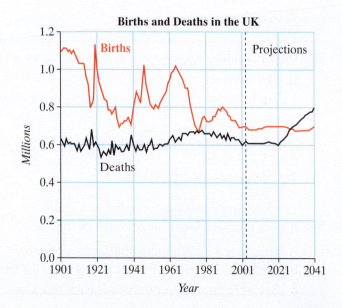

Births and Deaths in the UK

5 Data and diagrams

Chapter 5 Summary

Level 5

Median and mean

To find the **median** of a set of data:
- write the data in order from smallest to largest
- the median is the middle number in your list.

1 4 5 4 6 3 4 18 2 4 4
1 2 3 4 4 **4** 4 4 5 6 18
median = **4**

To find the **mean** of a set of data:
- add up all the data values
- divide this total by the number of data values.

$1 + 2 + 3 + 4 + 4 + 4 + 4 + 4 + 5 + 6 + 18 = 55$

mean = $55 \div 11 = 5$

You can also find the mean when data is in a frequency table.
This is a table showing the number of goals scored in 60 football matches.

Number of goals	Number of matches	Total number of goals
0	8	0 × 8 = 0
1	12	1 × 12 = 12
2	19	2 × 19 = 38
3	18	3 × 18 = 54
4	3	4 × 3 = 12
Total	60	116

To find the mean you divide the total number of goals by the total number of matches.
The mean number of goals is $116 \div 60 = 1.93$ (to 2 d.p.)

Level 6

Data is continuous when it can take any value in a certain range.

Examples are the weight of a person or the length of a mouse.

You use **frequency diagrams** to display continuous data.

There are no gaps between the bars.

The horizontal axis has a continuous scale.
It does not have labels under each of the bars.

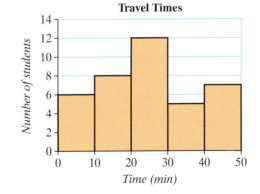

A frequency diagram looks similar to a bar chart.
But remember that a bar chart is only used for discrete data and it has gaps between the bars.

6 Formulae and algebraic operations

**Chapter 1
The language of algebra**

- Using letters to stand for unknown numbers
- Using correct algebraic notation
- Doing algebraic operations in the correct order

1 Formulae

2 Order of operations

**Chapter 9
Equations**

- Using function machines
- Solving equations

You should already know:

▶ how to use letters for unknowns

An **equation** contains an equals sign.
$n + 2 = 16$ is an equation.
$n = 14$ is the **solution** of the equation.
$n = 14$ is the only value of n that makes the equation true.

An **expression** does not contain an equals sign.
$n + 8$ is an expression.
n can be any number. n is called a **variable**.

▶ how to write algebra correctly

If n is a number then these are expressions linked to n.

8 more than the number $n + 8$
3 less than the number $n - 3$
Multiplying the number by 5 $5n$
Dividing the number by 3 $\dfrac{n}{3}$
Adding the number to itself $n + n = 2n$
Multiplying the number by itself $n \times n = n^2$
Never write $1n$. Just write n.

▶ that the order of algebraic operations is important

Do multiplications and divisions before additions and subtractions.
$3n + 6$ means **multiply n by 3** then **add 6**.
Do anything in brackets first.
$3(n + 6)$ means **add 6 to n** then **multiply the answer by 3**.

6 Formulae and algebraic operations

1 Formulae

- **Substituting into expressions**
- **Substituting into formulae**
- **Deriving formulae**

Key words
expression	variable
value	evaluate
substitute	formula
formulae	derive

Substituting into expressions
Level 5

You already know that an **expression** is a collection of letters and numbers.

$n + 7$ is an expression. The letter n is a **variable**.

This means that n can take any **value**.

If $n = 4$ you can **evaluate** the expression.

You **substitute** 4 into the expression.

This means that you replace the n with the value 4.

So $n + 7$ becomes $4 + 7 = 11$.

To evaluate the expression $3(x + 1)$ when $x = 7$ substitute 7 into the expression instead of the x.

$$3(x + 1) = 3(7 + 1)$$
$$= 3 \times 8$$
$$= 24$$

To evaluate the expression $2a - b + 3c$ when $a = 5$, $b = 4$ and $c = 6$ substitute for each letter in the expression.

$$2a - b + 3c = 2 \times 5 - 4 + 3 \times 6$$
$$= 10 - 4 + 18$$
$$= 24$$

Exercise 6:1

1 Work out the value of these expressions.

- **a** $10 + n$ when $n = 6$
- **b** $16 - x$ when $x = 5$
- **c** $p + q$ when $p = 9$ and $q = 5$
- **d** $r - s + t$ when $r = 12$, $s = 5$ and $t = 4$
- **e** $4t$ when $t = 8$
- **f** $9a$ when $a = {}^-4$
- **g** y^2 when $y = {}^-3$
- **h** $\frac{b}{2}$ when $b = 16$
- **i** $\frac{24}{c}$ when $c = 3$
- **j** $\frac{m}{n}$ when $m = 28$ and $n = 4$
- **k** $2d + 3e - 4f$ when $d = 2$, $e = 0$ and $f = 1$
- **l** $28 - 3g$ when $g = 9$
- **m** $4j - 2k$ when $j = 8$ and $k = {}^-3$
- **n** $4x^2 + 3$ when $x = {}^-1$

2 When $k = 10$, write down the value of each expression.

- **a** $8 + k$
- **b** $3k$
- **c** k^2

3 a When $x = 8$, what is the value of **$5x$**?
   Choose the correct answer from these boxes.

   | 5 | 13 | 40 | 58 | None of these |

b When $x = 8$, what is the value of $3x - x$?
   Choose the correct answer from these boxes.

   | 0 | 3 | 16 | 30 | None of these |

c When $x = 8$, what is the value of x^2?
   Choose the correct answer from these boxes.

   | 8 | 10 | 16 | 64 | None of these |

4 Evaluate these expressions.

   a $3(x + 2)$ when $x = 5$
   b $4(x + y)$ when $x = 3$ and $y = 2$
   c $2(x - 4)$ when $x = 10$
   d $2(1 + 3x)$ when $x = 2$
   e $7(x - 2y)$ when $x = 2$ and $y = 3$
   f $5(3x + 2y)$ when $x = {}^-2$ and $y = 3$
   g $x(x + 1)$ when $x = 4$
   h $x(x + 2y)$ when $x = 3$ and $y = 1$

5 a When $w = 5$, find the value of the following.
   (1) $4(w + 3)$ **(2)** $4w + 3$ **(3)** $4w + 43$ **(4)** $4w + 12$
   b Copy and complete. $4(w + 3) = 4w + \ldots$

6 a If $b = {}^-1$, evaluate each of the following.
   (1) $b + b + b + b$ **(2)** $b + 2b + b$ **(3)** $2b + 2b$ **(4)** $4b$
   b What is the simplest way of writing the **expressions** in part **a**?

Explore

7 If n is an integer, $2n$ has to be an even number.
   So the expressions $2n$, $2n + 2$ and $2n + 4$ represent three consecutive even numbers.
   a What value of n would produce the three even numbers 4, 6 and 8?
   b What value of n would produce the three even numbers 16, 18 and 20?
   c Explain how to find the value of n for any three consecutive even numbers.
   d Write down the expression for one more than $2n$.
   e You know that $2n$ has to be an even number. What sort of number is $2n + 1$?
   f Write down three expressions that produce consecutive odd numbers for any integer, n.

6 Formulae and algebraic operations

Substituting into formulae   Level 5

A **formula** is a rule.
Formulae can be written in words or using letters.

The formula for the area of a rectangle is   Area = *l*ength × *w*idth
You can write this as $A = l \times w$ or $A = lw$

The formula tells you how to work out the area, A, for any values of the length, l, and width, w.

To find the area of this rectangle you substitute
$l = 12$ and $w = 9$ into the formula like this

$A = lw$
$A = 12 \times 9$
$ = 108$

9 cm

12 cm

The rectangle has an area of $108 \, cm^2$.

The formula for the perimeter of a rectangle is $P = 2(l + w)$

To find the perimeter of the rectangle you substitute
$l = 12$ and $w = 9$ into the formula like this

$ = 2(12 + 9)$
$ = 2 \times 21$
$ = 42$

The perimeter is 42 cm.

Exercise 6:2

1 A full bottle of medicine holds 125 mℓ. A spoonful of medicine is 5 mℓ.
The formula to work out the amount of medicine left in a bottle, a, when s spoonfuls have been used is $a = 125 - 5s$.

Work out the amount left in the bottle after taking

a 3 spoonfuls

b 5 spoonfuls

c 9 spoonfuls.

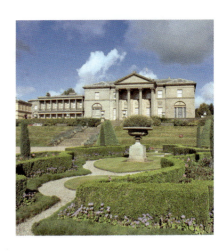

2 This is a picture of Tatton Park in Cheshire.

If you visit Tatton Park by car, it costs £4.20 to park.

It also costs £5 per adult and £3 per child to get in.

The formula to work out the total cost, £t, for the number of people in a car with a adults and c children is
$$t = 5a + 3c + 4.2$$
Use the formula to find the total cost for a car with

a 2 adults and 2 children

b 2 adults and 4 children

c 4 adults and 3 children.

3 Rhiannon is using $A = 3 \times r \times r$ to calculate the approximate area of a circle.

Find the approximate area when

a $r = 5$ **b** $r = 7$ **c** $r = 9.4$ **d** $r = 12.1$

4 Chika uses the formula $v = u + at$ during a physics lesson.

Find v when

a $u = 5, a = 10$ and $t = 3$

b $u = 16, a = 9.8$ and $t = 10$

c $u = 25, a = {}^-2$ and $t = 12$.

5 a Substitute $h = 7, a = 11$ and $b = 13$ into each of these formulae.

(1) $A = \dfrac{h(a + b)}{2}$ (2) $A = \tfrac{1}{2}ah + \tfrac{1}{2}bh$ (3) $A = \dfrac{ah + bh}{2}$ (4) $A = \left(\dfrac{a + b}{2}\right)h$

b Explain what your answers tell you about these formulae.

6 $A = 6s^2$ is the formula for finding the surface area of a cube with side s.

a Find A when

(1) $s = 3$ (2) $s = 5$.

b For what value of s does $A = 600$?

Facts to figure

7 Mathematicians have been using formulae for thousands of years.

Aryabhata was an Indian mathematician born in 476 AD.

In one of his books he wrote

'Tribhujasya phalashariram samadalakoti bhujardhasamvargah.'

This roughly translates to give the formula for the area of a triangle:

$$A = \tfrac{1}{2}bh$$

where A is the area in cm², b is the length of the base in cm and h is the height in cm.

Use Aryabhata's formula to find the area of each of these triangles

a base = 70 cm, height = 6 cm

b base = 15 cm, height = 11 cm

c base = 10.5 cm, height = 20 cm.

Statue of Aryabhata in India

6 Formulae and algebraic operations

Deriving formulae — Level 5

You need to be able to **derive** a formula.

This just means that you need to work out the formula for yourself.

Look at the number of lines that you can draw on this diagram that join a red dot to a blue dot.

There are 8 lines.

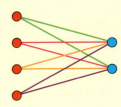

Now look at this diagram.
Here there are 9 lines.

Can you see the formula for the number of lines for any number of red and blue dots?
In the first diagram there are 4 red dots and 2 blue dots and there are 8 lines.
In the second diagram there are 3 red dots and 3 blue dots and there are 9 lines.

If you have r red dots and b blue dots the formula for the number of lines, L, is $L = r \times b$
This is the formula written properly following the rules of algebra $\quad L = rb$
L, r and b are **variables**.

Now you can use the formula to work out the number of lines on any diagram.
To find the number of lines on a diagram with 12 red dots and 7 blue dots,
substitute $r = 12$ and $b = 7$ into the formula. $\qquad L = rb$
$\qquad L = 12 \times 7 = 84$

So there would be 84 lines on a diagram with 12 red dots and 7 blue dots.

Exercise 6:3

1 Damien sketched this trapezium on isometric dotty paper.
He looked at the length of each side.

$a = 3$, $b = 2$, $c = 3$ and $d = 5$.

This is a 3, 2, 3, 5 trapezium.

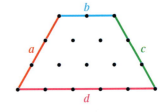

a	b	c	d
3	2	3	5

a Draw five different trapezia on isometric paper.
All the sides must follow the lines of dots.

b Copy and fill in this table to show the lengths of the sides of your trapezia.

c Write down a formula to show the relationship between a and c.

d Write down a formula to show the relationship between a, b and d.

e If $a = 4$ and $d = 9$ use your formulae to work out b and c.

2 Here is a sequence made from octagons *n* and squares *s*.

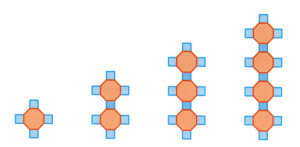

Number of octagons (*n*)	Number of squares (*s*)
1	4
2	7
3	10
4	13

   a Draw the next pattern in this sequence.

   b Write down the number of squares needed to make it.

   c How many squares will there be in the pattern with 20 octagons? Explain your answer.

   d Copy and fill in the following sentence.

      To work out the number of squares, *s*, you … the number of octagons, *n*, by … and add …

   e Write down a formula that connects *n* and *s*.

3 Here is a sequence of shapes made using counters.

   a Copy and fill in the table.

   b Explain how the number of blue counters changes for each shape.

   c What do you notice about the number of red counters in each shape?

   d Write down a formula that connects *s* and *t*.

shape 1   shape 2   shape 3

Shape number (*s*)	1	2	3	4
Number of blue counters	8	…	…	…
Number of red counters	4	…	…	…
Total number of counters (*t*)	12	…	…	…

Explore

4 a Brooke lays paths around garden ponds. All the ponds are 1 metre wide and have a length that's a whole number of metres, *l*.

     She makes a path out of 1 metre square paving stones.

     Find a formula for the number of stones, *s*, that Brooke uses for a path around a pond that measures *l* metres by 1 metre.

 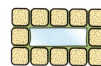

1 m by 1 m pond   3 m by 1 m pond

  b Brooke decides to experiment with ponds of different widths. Find a formula for the number of stones, *s*, that Brooke uses for a path around a pond that measures *l* metres by *w* metres.

2 m by 2 m pond

6 Formulae and algebraic operations

2 Order of operations

▶ **Using BODMAS in algebra**

▶ **Understanding inverse operations**

Key words	
order	brackets
BODMAS	order of operations
inverse	square
square root	

Using BODMAS in algebra   Level 5

You have already seen that there is a correct **order** to do calculations.

You have to do multiplications and divisions **before** you do additions and subtractions.

The expression $5n + 2$ means that you need to **multiply n by 5** and then **add 2**.

The expression $2 + 5n$ is the same as $5n + 2$.

So $2 + 5n$ also means that you need to **multiply n by 5** and then **add 2**.

Anything in **brackets** must be done first.

So $5(n + 2)$ means that you have to **add 2 to n** and then **multiply the answer by 5**.

You have also seen that **BODMAS** tells you the order to do calculations involving numbers.

The rules of BODMAS also apply to the **order of operations** in algebra.

Brackets
p**o**wers **O**f
Division
Multiplication
Addition
Subtraction

Using the rules of **BODMAS**, the expression $4n^2 - 6$ means that you work out **n squared** before you **multiply by 4** and then **subtract 6**.

Using the rules of **BODMAS**, the expression $7(n - 6) + 3$ means that you **take 6 away from n** before you **multiply the answer by 7** and then **add 3**.

Some expressions can look quite similar but mean different things.

$7n - 6$ means multiply by 7 first and then take away 6 from the answer.

$7(n - 6)$ means that you take away 6 first and then multiply your answer by 7.

Make sure that you understand why these expressions are different!

Exercise 6:4

1 The expression $7 - 3n$ means multiply n by 3 and then subtract the answer from 7.
Write a sentence to explain the order of the operations in each part.

a $3 + 6n$ **c** $\dfrac{n}{7} + 1$ **e** $4(2 - n)$ **g** $3n^2 + 5$

b $4(n - 3)$ **d** $\dfrac{n - 9}{5}$ **f** $10 - \dfrac{n}{2}$ **h** $20 - 4n^3$

2 Each part contains two expressions that are different.
Explain the difference between the two expressions in each part.

a $4n - 3$ and $4(n - 3)$ **d** $\dfrac{n - 5}{7}$ and $\dfrac{7}{n - 5}$

b $\dfrac{n}{3} + 6$ and $\dfrac{n + 6}{3}$ **e** $3(n^2 + 5)$ and $3(n + 5)^2$

c $3n$ and n^3 **f** $3n^2 + 5$ and $(3n)^2 + 5$

3 Ali, Barry and Cindy each have a bag of counters.
They do not know how many counters are in each bag.
They know that:

> Barry has **two more** counters than Ali.
> Cindy has **four times as many** counters as Ali.

a Ali calls the number of counters in her bag **a**.
Write **expressions using a** to show the number of counters in Barry's bag and in Cindy's bag.

b Barry calls the number of counters in his bag **b**.
Write **expressions using b** to show the number of counters in Ali's bag and in Cindy's bag.

c Cindy calls the number of counters in her bag **c**.
Which one of these **expressions** shows the number of counters in Barry's bag?

$4c + 2$ $4c - 2$ $\dfrac{c}{4} + 2$ $\dfrac{c}{4} - 2$ $\dfrac{c + 2}{4}$ $\dfrac{c - 2}{4}$

4 A magazine costs m pounds.
A newspaper costs n pounds.

a Write down a correct expression from these cards for each statement.
  (1) The total cost of 4 magazines and 1 newspaper.
  (2) How much more 4 magazines cost than 4 newspapers.

b You should have two expressions left.
Explain what each of these expressions represents.

$4(m + n)$ $4(m - n)$ $4m + n$ $4m - n$

6 Formulae and algebraic operations

Think on!

5 Look at the pupil's statement in each part and say whether it is **always true**, **sometimes true** or **never true**.

Explain each of your answers.

If you decide that a statement is sometimes true,
give one example showing when it's true
and one example showing when it's false.

a Lucy: 'The expression $\frac{n-3}{2}$ has the same value as the expression $\frac{n}{2} - 3$.'

b Amber: 'The expression ab^2 has the same value as the expression b^2a and they both have the same value as $a \times b \times b$.'

c Callum: 'The expression $4n - 1$ has the same value as the expression $4(n - 1)$.'

d Mika: 'The expression ab^2 has the same value as the expression $(ab)^2$.'

e Dawn: 'The expression $\frac{n}{3}$ has the same value as the expression $\frac{3}{n}$.'

Understanding inverse operations — Level 5

$a + b = 8$ is the same as $8 = a + b$.
If the sum of two numbers is 8, then when you subtract one of the numbers from 8 you will get the other number.

So if $a + b = 8$, then you know that $a = 8 - b$ and $b = 8 - a$.
This is because adding and subtracting are **inverse** operations.

So **add 6** and **subtract 6** are inverse operations.

$a \times b = 12$ is the same as $12 = a \times b$.
If the product of two numbers is 12, then when you divide 12 by one of the numbers you will get the other number.

So if $a \times b = 12$, then you know that $a = \frac{12}{b}$ and $b = \frac{12}{a}$.

This is because multiplying and dividing are **inverse** operations.

So **multiply by 4** and **divide by 4** are inverse operations.

If you know that $a^2 = 25$ then you know that $a = \sqrt{25} = 5$.

This is because **squaring** and **square rooting** are **inverse** operations.

In the expression $5n + 2$ you have to **multiply** n by 5 and then **add 2**.

To undo these operations to get back to where you started,
you need to do the inverse operations in the opposite order.

So to get back to where you started you have to **subtract 2** and then **divide your answer by 5**.

Exercise 6:5

1 Write down the inverse of each of these operations.
- **a** add 8
- **b** subtract 3
- **c** × 8
- **d** ÷ 3
- **e** double
- **f** square root
- **g** square
- **h** halve

2 Copy these and fill them in.
- **a** If $a + b = 12$ then $a = 12 - \ldots$ and $b = \ldots - \ldots$
- **b** If $c \times d = 10$ then $c = \frac{10}{\ldots}$ and $d = \frac{\ldots}{\ldots}$
- **c** If $e = 16 - f$ then $f = 16 - \ldots$ and $e + f = \ldots$
- **d** If $g = \frac{12}{h}$ then $g \times h = \ldots$ and $h = \frac{12}{\ldots}$
- **e** If $p = q^2$ then $q = \sqrt{\ldots}$
- **f** If $h = k^2$ then $\ldots = \sqrt{h}$

3 Erin thinks of some numbers.
Find the number that she thinks of in each part.
- **a** She multiplies it by 2 and adds 4. She gets 18.
- **b** She subtracts 3 and multiplies by 6. She gets 30.
- **c** She adds 6 and divides by 3. She gets 12.
- **d** She divides it by 4 and subtracts 2. She gets 0.
- **e** She squares it and adds 6. She gets 10.
- **f** She subtracts 4 and square roots. She gets 9.

4 Reece thinks of a number. He multiplies it by 4, adds 8 and gets 36.
- **a** What was Reece's starting number?
- **b** Reece wants to explain to Erin how to get back to the number he started with.
  He says that he divides the number by 4 and then takes 8 away.
  - **(1)** Work out what number Reece would get if he used his method.
  - **(2)** Write down what Reece should say to Erin.

5 Marita thinks of a number. She squares it and then she adds 6.
Then she divides her answer by 7. She gets 10.
- **a** Write down the operations that she needs to use to get back to her starting number.
- **b** What was Marita's starting number?

6 The expression $6n - 4$ means you multiply n by 6 and subtract 4.
- **a** Write down the operations that you need to do to give the inverse of the expression.
- **b** Write down the algebraic expression that is the inverse of $6n - 4$.

6 Formulae and algebraic operations

Watch out ... there's a trap about

▶ You have seen that the formula for the number of lines, L, connecting r red dots to b blue dots is $L = rb$.

If there are 2 red dots and 3 blue dots then you substitute $r = 2$ and $b = 3$ into the formula to find L.

Don't substitute like this: $L = rb$ so $L = 23$. ✗   There aren't 23 lines!
In algebra, rb means $r \times b$
so $L = 2 \times 3 = 6$. ✓   There are 6 lines.

▶ $3(n - 5)$ is **not** the same as $3n - 5$.
$3(n - 5)$ means **subtract 5 from** n and then **multiply by 3**.
$3n - 5$ means **multiply** n **by 3** and then **subtract 5**.

If $n = 9$, $3(n - 5) = 3(9 - 5)$ If $n = 9$, $3n - 5 = 3 \times 9 - 5$
$ = 3 \times 4$ $= 27 - 5$
$ = 12$ $= 22$

These answers are different so the two expressions can't be the same.

Test yourself

1 Work out the value of these expressions.

a $a + 6$ when $a = 7$ g $2i - 5j - 2k$ when $i = 5, j = 0$ and $k = 1$

b $21 - b$ when $b = 3$ h $3l - 4m$ when $l = 12$ and $m = 5$

c $6c$ when $c = 7$ i $2(n + 4)$ when $n = 3$

d $\dfrac{12}{d}$ when $d = 3$ j $4(10 - 4p)$ when $p = 2$

e $4e + 2$ when $e = 6$ k $5(q + 2r)$ when $q = 4$ and $r = 1$

f $f - g + h$ when $f = 15, g = 9$ and $h = 4$ l $3(2s - 3t)$ when $s = 3$ and $t = 2$

2 Zachary is a member of a judo club.
He pays a £5 joining fee and £3.50 per lesson.
The formula to work out the total cost, £t, to be a member of the club is

$$t = 3.5d + 5$$

where d is the number of lessons.
Work out the total cost if Zachary attends

a   2 lessons   b   10 lessons   c   5 lessons.

3 Tickets for entry to Knowsley Safari Park cost £11 for adults and £8 for children. The formula to work out the total cost of entry, £t, for a adults and c children is

$t = 11a + 8c$

Work out the total cost of entry for

a 2 adults and 2 children

b 3 adults and 4 children.

4 Here is a sequence of shapes made using counters.

shape 1   shape 2   shape 3

a Copy and complete the table.

Shape number (s)	1	2	3	4
Number of blue counters	3	6	…	…
Number of red counters	1	1	…	…
Total number of counters (t)	4	7	…	…

b Explain how the number of blue counters changes for each new shape.

c What do you notice about the number of red counters in each shape?

d Copy and complete this formula: $s \times … + … = t$

5 Each part contains two expressions that are different.
Explain the difference between the two expressions in each part.

a $6n - 3$ and $6(n - 3)$

b $\frac{n}{5} + 3$ and $\frac{n + 3}{5}$

c $\frac{n}{4}$ and $\frac{4}{n}$

d $n - 8$ and $8 - n$

6 Write down the inverse of each of these operations.

a add 8
b subtract 5
c multiply by 4
d $- 12$
e $\times 6$
f $\div 8$
g halve
h square root

7 Kesia thinks of some numbers.
Find the number that she thinks of in each part.

a She multiplies it by 4 and adds 2. She gets 22.

b She adds 10 and multiplies by 5. She gets 60.

c She multiplies it by 3 and subtracts 9. She gets 12.

d She subtracts 5 and divides it by 2. She gets 10.

e She divides it by 3 and subtracts 4. She gets 5.

6 Formulae and algebraic operations

Chapter 6 Summary

Level 5

Substituting values into expressions and formulae

To evaluate the expression $2a - b + 3c$ when $a = 5$, $b = 4$ and $c = 6$ substitute into the expression like this:

$$2a - b + 3c = 2 \times 5 - 4 + 3 \times 6$$
$$= 10 - 4 + 18$$
$$= 24$$

To work out the value of p in the formula $p = 3t + 2$ when $t = 4$ substitute into the formula like this:

$$p = 3t + 2$$
$$= 3 \times 4 + 2$$
$$= 12 + 2$$
$$= 14$$

Using BODMAS in algebra

Brackets
Powers **O**f
Division
Multiplication
Addition
Subtraction

To work out $6 \times (5 + 3) - 10$ use **BODMAS**.

$$6 \times (5 + 3) - 10 = 6 \times 8 - 10$$
$$= 48 - 10$$
$$= 38$$

Understanding inverse operations

$7 + 3 = 10$ and $10 - 3 = 7$
So **add 3** and **subtract 3** are inverse operations.

$7 \times 4 = 28$ and $28 \div 4 = 7$
So **multiply by 4** and **divide by 4** are inverse operations.

$5^2 = 25$ and $\sqrt{25} = 5$
So **square** and **square root** are inverse operations.

The expression $5n + 2$ means you have to **multiply n by 5** and then **add 2**.

To get back to where you started you have to **subtract 2** and then **divide your answer by 5**.

7 2-D and 3-D shapes

Year 6
- Making 3-D models
- Drawing 2-D shapes

Chapter 3 Coordinates and symmetry
Symmetry in 2-D shapes

1. 3-D shapes
2. 2-D representations of 3-D shapes

Chapter 14 Area, volume and measures
- Drawing nets

Year 8
- Drawing plans and elevations
- The locus of a moving object

You should already know:

▶ the names of these 3-D shapes

cube cuboid 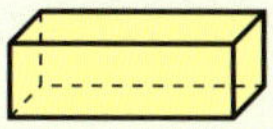 square-based pyramid

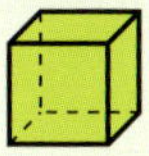

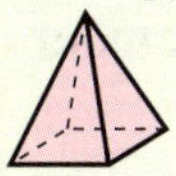

sphere 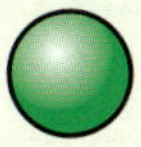 hemisphere  cylinder

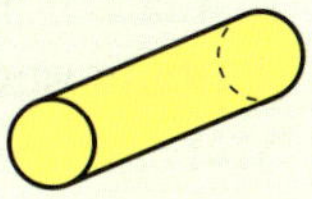

cone 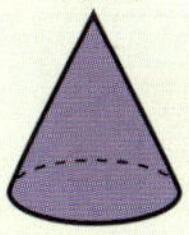 triangular prism 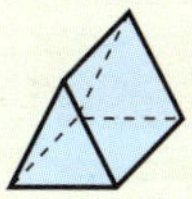 tetrahedron

▶ the names of these polygons

triangle quadrilateral 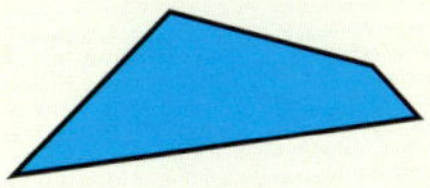 pentagon

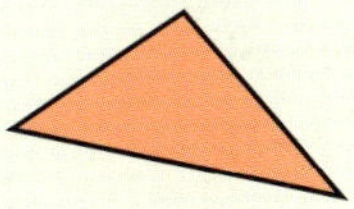

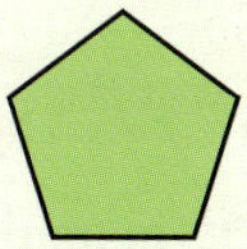

hexagon 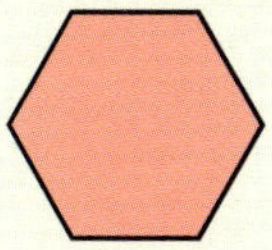 octagon 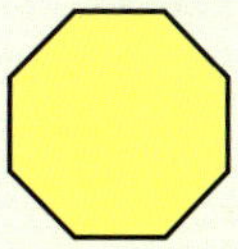 decagon

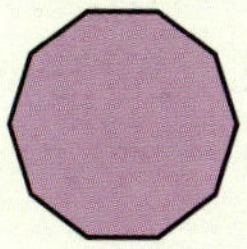

101

7 2-D and 3-D shapes

1 3-D shapes

Describing 3-D shapes

Key words	
face	edge
vertex	vertices
plane	plane of symmetry

Describing 3-D shapes   Level 5

A **face** is a surface of a 3-D shape.
The top face of this cube is red.
The front face is blue.
The side face that you can see is green.
There are three other faces that you can't see.

An **edge** is where two faces meet.
The pink edge is where the top face and the front face meet.

A **vertex** is where three or more edges meet.
The three pink edges meet at the orange vertex.
Think of a vertex as a corner of the shape.

When you describe a 3-D shape you should give the number of faces, edges and vertices.

A cuboid has 6 faces, 12 edges and 8 vertices.

You can also talk about whether the shape is symmetrical.
Instead of a line of symmetry, 3-D shapes have **planes of symmetry**.
A **plane** is a 2-D surface.
You can think of a plane of symmetry as the surface of a mirror.
A cuboid has three planes of symmetry.

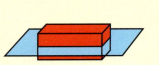  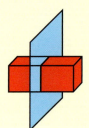

Exercise 7:1

1 Gavin made this model of a tetrahedron using modelling clay and straws.

  a How many balls of modelling clay did he use?
  b How many straws did he use?

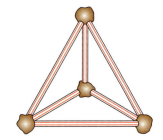

2 Omar says, 'A pyramid has an even number of edges.'
Write down the number of edges of each pyramid and decide if Omar is correct.

 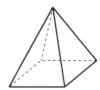 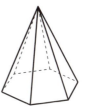

3 For the shape in each part, write down the number of

(**1**) faces   (**2**) edges   (**3**) vertices.

a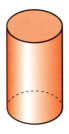

b

4 Derek has a wooden cube.
He cuts off one corner of the cube like this.

  a What shape is the new face?

  b Describe Derek's new solid.
    Give the number of faces, edges
    and vertices in your description.

Derek cuts off another corner like this.

  c Describe Derek's solid now.

Derek carries on cutting the corners off the original cube.

⚠ **d** Describe the solid he has left when he has cut all the original corners off.

5 Write down the number of planes of symmetry for each shape.

a   b   c 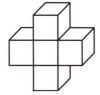   d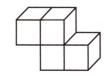

7 2-D and 3-D shapes

6 Jafar was asked to draw a plane of symmetry on this shape. This is what he drew.

Explain what he has done wrong.

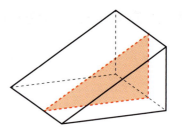

7 These models show the chemical structure of different greenhouse gases. How many planes of symmetry does each model have?

a

Dichlorodifluoromethane

b

Trichlorofluoromethane

⚠ c

Sulfur hexafluoride

Explore

8 You are going to discover the relationship between the number of faces, edges and vertices for all solids that have plane faces. This is called Euler's rule, named after the mathematician who first discovered it.

a Copy this table and fill it in.

	Faces	Vertices	Edges
Cube			
Cuboid			
Square-based pyramid			
Tetrahedron			
Triangular prism			

b Look at the numbers in each row. Write down what you notice about the value of faces + vertices and the number of edges for each of the shapes.

c Write down a rule that starts edges = …

2 2-D representations of 3-D shapes

▸ **Recognising 2-D representations of 3-D shapes**

▸ **Drawing nets**

▸ **Recognising plans and elevations**

Key words

isometric paper net
plan elevation
front elevation side elevation

Recognising 2-D representations of 3-D shapes Level 6

This diagram is drawn on 1 cm dotty **isometric paper**. Every dot is 1 cm away from the dots around it.

Isometric paper has a right way up.
The vertical space between the dots must be 1 cm.

This diagram shows two 1 cm cubes next to each other. So this diagram shows a cuboid with dimensions 2 cm by 1 cm by 1 cm.

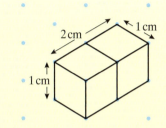

You can also have isometric paper which has a grid of lines instead of dots. This paper is the right way up when you can see vertical lines like this.

You use it the same way as dotty isometric paper.

This diagram shows a cuboid that is 3 cm by 3 cm by 2 cm.

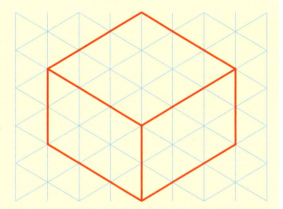

To **sketch a cube** without using isometric paper:

Start by drawing a square.

Then draw three equal parallel lines sloping backwards like this.

Then join the ends of these lines.

Any edges you cannot see need to be shown with dashed lines.

So add dashed edges to complete a square at the back and the fourth sloping line like this and you have sketched a cube.

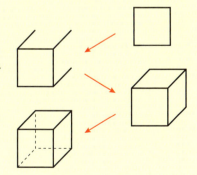

Exercise 7:2

1 You will need dotty isometric paper for this question.
This cuboid is made from four small cubes.

Draw a cuboid which is
twice as **high**, **twice** as **long** and **twice** as **wide**.

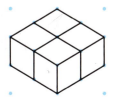

105

7 2-D and 3-D shapes

2 On dotty isometric paper, draw **all** the different ways that there are of joining four cubes together.

You could use multilink cubes to make them first.

This diagram shows you one way.

You have seen another way in **Question 1**.

3 a Draw a 3 cm by 2 cm by 1 cm cuboid on 1 cm isometric paper like this.

b Draw five more cuboids of your own on your isometric paper. Write the dimensions of each cuboid underneath its drawing.

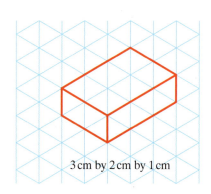

3 cm by 2 cm by 1 cm

4 The diagram shows a solid made from two cuboids. One of the cuboids is placed on top of the other.

a Copy the diagram onto isometric paper.

b How many faces does the solid have?

c How many edges does the solid have?

d How many vertices does the solid have?

e Clodagh wants to make the solid using cubes. How many cubes does she need?

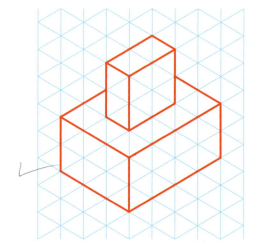

5 Follow these instructions and draw a sketch of a square-based pyramid.

a Draw a parallelogram like this. This is the base of the pyramid. You need two dashed edges and two solid edges.

b Draw the diagonals to find the middle of the parallelogram.

c Draw a vertical line from the middle of the base to the **top point**.
Rub out the diagonals and the vertical line.

d Join the top point to each of the vertices on the base. Use a dashed line for the edge at the back like this.

e Repeat these steps to draw a sketch of a hexagonal-based pyramid.
Remember to start with a hexagon!

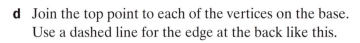

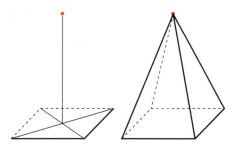

106

Drawing nets

Level 6

This is a **net** of a solid cube.

This is how it folds up to give the cube.

If you actually want to make a 3-D shape from a net, you have to add flaps to the net so that you can stick it together like this.

But you mustn't draw flaps if you're asked to draw a net.

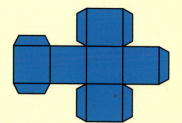

This is a net for a cuboid that is 2 cm by 1 cm by 1 cm.

When you draw a net, you have to draw the lengths accurately. You may have to use a scale for your drawing. Choose a scale so that the net fits on your page and it's not too small.

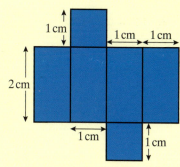

This is how the net folds up to give a cuboid.

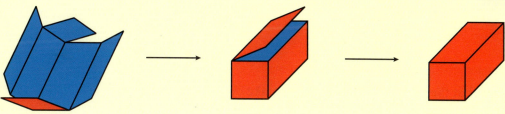

Exercise 7:3

1 Copy the diagrams. Colour in one square to make the net of an open cube. The black square shows the base of each cube.

a   b   c

107

7 2-D and 3-D shapes

2 These pictures are all mixed up. Match each net to its 3-D shape.

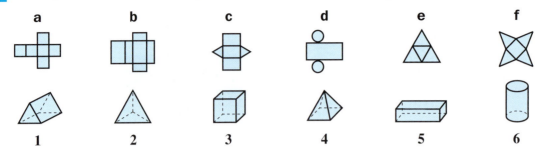

3 This net folds to make a 3-D shape.
What is the name of the 3-D shape?

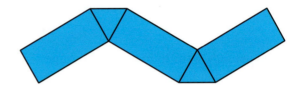

4 Copy and complete this diagram to show a net of a cuboid that is 3 cm by 2 cm by 1 cm.

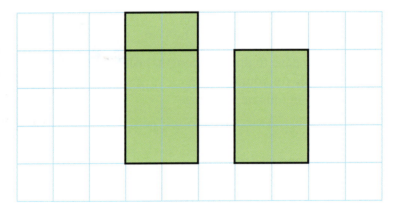

5 Alex says that these shapes will **not** fold to make cuboids.
Explain why he is right in each part.

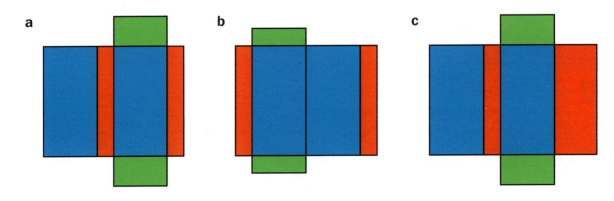

6 Look at these diagrams. They show a cuboid and its net.

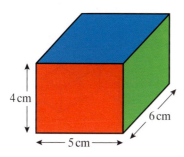 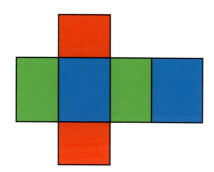

Write down the size of each rectangle.

a 　　b 　　c

7 Draw the net of each cuboid on squared paper.

a 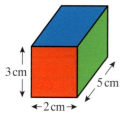　　b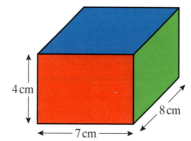

Explore

8 This is an octahedron.
It has 8 faces and 5 planes of symmetry.

A 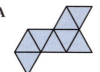　　C

B 　　D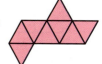

Which of the shapes on the right does **not** fold to make an octahedron?

7 2-D and 3-D shapes

Recognising plans and elevations   Level 6

Look at this 3-D shape.

It is made from 11 cubes.

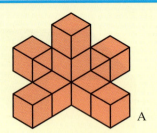

If you looked down on it from directly above this is what you'd see.

This is called the **plan** view.

A **plan** is the view you would see from directly above.

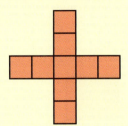

If you look at the object from point A, this is what you'd see. This is called an **elevation**.

If A is at the front of the shape, this is called the **front elevation**.

If A is at the side of the shape, then this is called the **side elevation**.

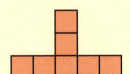

Exercise 7:4

1 Andy made this shape using multilink cubes.

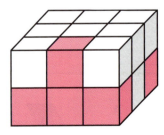

  a Which of the diagrams is a plan of the shape?

  b Which of the diagrams is not a view of the shape?

A 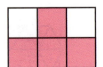   B   C 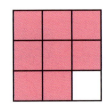   D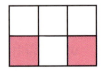

2 Match each shape to the correct plan view.

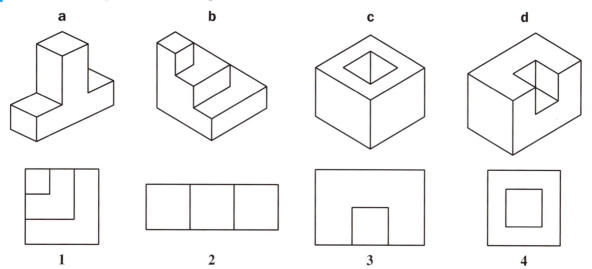

3 Jessie made different cuboids using three black and three white multilink cubes.
Draw the side elevation of the shape from the point X in each part.

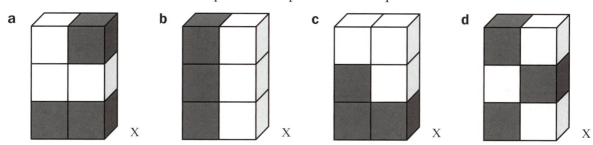

4 Max made a 3-D shape using seven cubes.
Here are the plan, front elevation and side elevation for his shape.

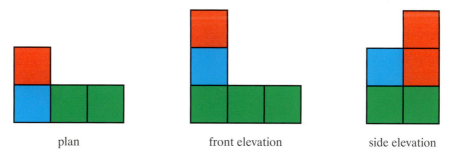

plan　　　　front elevation　　　　side elevation

Which diagram shows the shape Max made?

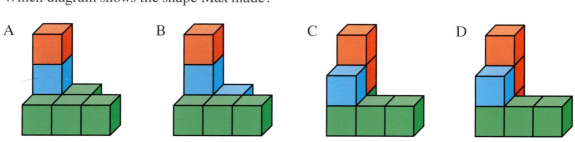

111

7 2-D and 3-D shapes

Watch out ... there's a trap about

▶ Make sure that you count all the hidden faces, edges and vertices when you're looking at a diagram of a 3-D object.

You can only see **2 faces**, **5 edges** and **4 vertices** on this square-based pyramid.

But there are actually **5 faces**, **8 edges** and **5 vertices**.

▶ Isometric paper **must not** be used the wrong way round.

This is wrong! The vertical dots are not 1 cm apart.

This diagram looks like a sketch that you would draw without isometric paper.

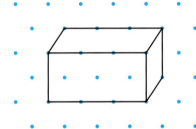

Test yourself

1 Callum made this model of a triangular prism using modelling clay and straws.

  a How many balls of modelling clay did he use?
  b How many straws did he use?

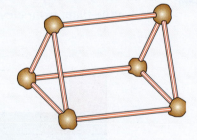

2 Orlando draws these planes of symmetry for a cuboid.

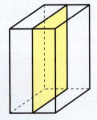 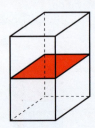 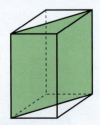 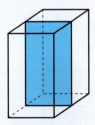

He has made a mistake.
Explain what he has done wrong.

3 I join six cubes face to face to make each 3-D shape below.

Then I join the 3-D shapes to make a cuboid.
Draw this cuboid on dotty isometric paper.

4 Copy each diagram and colour in two extra squares to give you the net of a cube.

a 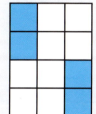   b 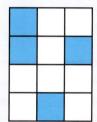   c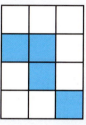

 5 The sketch shows the net of a triangular prism.
The net is folded up and glued to make the prism.

  a Which edge is **tab 1** glued to?
  b Which edge is **tab 2** glued to?
  c Which two vertices meet the corner marked • ?

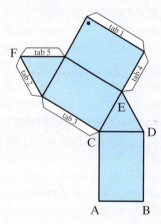

6 Tyler made this shape using multilink cubes.
Three cubes are red. The other seven are white.

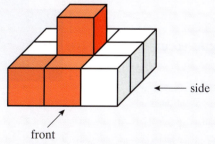

Copy and complete each view of the shape by colouring in the squares that are red.

a 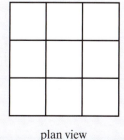   b    c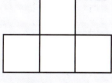

  plan view   front elevation   side elevation

7 2-D and 3-D shapes

Chapter 7 Summary

Level 5

Describing 3-D shapes

Say how many faces, edges and vertices there are.
You can also talk about whether the shape has a **plane of symmetry**.
A **plane** is a 2-D surface.
You can think of a plane of symmetry as the surface of an actual mirror.
A cuboid has three **planes of symmetry**.

 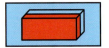 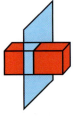

Nets

A **net** of a 3-D shape is a 2-D shape that you can fold up to make the shape.

Level 6

2-D representations of 3-D objects

You can draw 3-D objects accurately on isometric paper   or   as a sketch

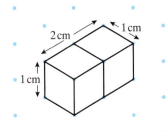 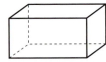

Nets

This is a net for a cuboid that is 2 cm by 1 cm by 1 cm.
When you draw a net, you have to draw the lengths accurately.
You may have to use a scale for your drawing.

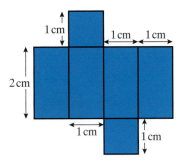

Plans and elevations

A **plan** is a view from directly above a 3-D shape.
An **elevation** is a view from one side of a 3-D shape.

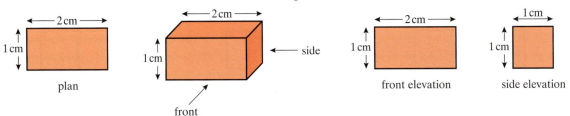

8 Decimals, fractions and percentages

Year 6

Rounding

Chapter 2 Multiplying and dividing

Multiplying and dividing integers using mental and written methods

→

1. Rounding and estimating
2. Multiplying and dividing with decimals
3. Fractions and percentages

→

Chapter 12 More fractions and percentages

- Simplifying, adding and subtracting fractions
- Writing one number as a fraction or percentage of another
- Equivalent fractions, decimals and percentages

You should already know:

▶ **how to round numbers**

28 is closer to 30 than 20.
28 rounds to 30 to the nearest 10.

450 is halfway between 400 and 500.
450 rounds to 500 to the nearest 100.

6295 is closer to 6000 than 7000.
6295 rounds to 6000 to the nearest 1000.

▶ **how to multiply and divide using mental methods**

Doubling and halving $150 \times 4 = 300 \times 2 = 600$

Partitioning $5 \times 16 = 5 \times 10 + 5 \times 6 = 50 + 30 = 80$

Using multiplication facts to help with divisions
$84 \div 14 = 84 \div 7 \div 2 = 84 \div 2 \div 7 = 42 \div 7 = 6$

▶ **how to multiply and divide whole numbers using written methods**

```
  H T U
      4 3
    ×   6
    ─────
    2 5 8
        1
```
$43 \times 6 = 258$

```
  258
− 240    6 × 40
  ───
   18
−  18    6 × 3
  ───
    0
   ───
    43
```
$258 \div 6 = 43$

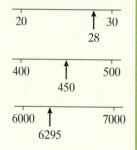

$413 \times 83 = 34\,279$

115

8 Decimals, fractions and percentages

1 Rounding and estimating

- **Rounding decimals**
- **Checking answers**

Key words
round
to one decimal place (to 1 d.p.)
to two decimal places (to 2 d.p.)
estimate   approximate
inverse operation

Rounding decimals   Level 5

Decimal numbers can be **rounded** to the nearest whole number.

6.8 is between 6 and 7. It is closer to 7.

6.8 **rounds** to 7 to the nearest whole number.

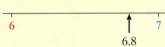

You can also round to a given number of decimal places.
This tells you how many digits there must be after the decimal point.

14.34 is between 14.3 and 14.4
14.34 is closer to 14.3 than to 14.4
14.34 rounds to 14.3 **to one decimal place (to 1 d.p.)**.

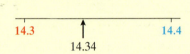

1.473 metres is between 1.47 metres and 1.48 metres.
It is closer to 1.47 metres.

1.473 m rounds to 1.47 m **to two decimal places (to 2 d.p.)**.

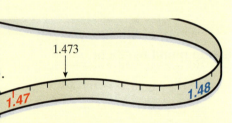

To round to 2 d.p. you can also look at the digit
in the thousandths column.

If it is **5 or more**, add one to the digit in the
hundredths column.
If it is **less than 5**, leave the hundredths column unchanged.

U	.	t	h	th		
1	.	4	7	2	=	1.47 to 2 d.p.
0	.	7	3	5	=	0.74 to 2 d.p.
6	.	8	9	7	=	6.90 to 2 d.p.

6.897 is 6.90 when rounded to 2 d.p.
The 0 is needed to show that the decimal has been rounded to 2 d.p.

Exercise 8:1

1 a π (pi, which you say as 'pie') is a number used in maths.
It is a never-ending decimal that starts 3.1415…
Round π to one decimal place.

b *e* is another number used in maths.
It is also a never-ending decimal.
It starts 2.71828…
Round *e* to two decimal places.

2 Here are the current World Records from some athletics events.

Round each measurement to

a the nearest whole number

b one decimal place.

Men's events	
100 m	9.74 s
400 m hurdles	46.78 s
Triple jump	18.29 m
High jump	2.45 m
Shot put	23.12 m
Javelin	104.80 m

3 You need to think about the meaning of a rounded answer.

In some questions it doesn't make sense to follow the usual rules of rounding.

Here are Warren's answers to these questions.

a A pen costs 21p.
How many pens can Sammi buy with £5?

b 32 people go by horse-drawn carriage to a wedding reception.
The carriage holds up to 10 people.
How many carriage trips are needed?

Explain what Warren has done wrong in his calculations.

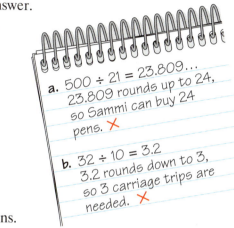

a. 500 ÷ 21 = 23.809…
23.809 rounds up to 24, so Sammi can buy 24 pens. ✗

b. 32 ÷ 10 = 3.2
3.2 rounds down to 3, so 3 carriage trips are needed. ✗

4 This table shows the world record weights of some fruit and vegetables.

Round each measurement to

a the nearest whole number

b one decimal place

c two decimal places.

Apple	1.849 kg
Lemon	5.265 kg
Pumpkin	666.322 kg
Carrot	10.314 kg

5 Kerry says,

'If I round 8.45 to the nearest whole number, the answer is 9. This is because 8.45 rounds to 8.5, then 8.5 rounds to 9.'

Is Kerry correct? Explain your answer.

Think on!

6 Each number on a red card can be rounded to a number on a blue card.

Put the cards in pairs so that each red card is paired with a blue card.

But be careful! Some red cards have more than one possible partner.

Red cards: 109.275, 109.37, 109.47, 109.57, 109.67, 109.77, 109.87, 109.975

Blue cards: 110, 109.8, 110.0, 109, 109.9, 109.5, 109.3, 109.6

8 Decimals, fractions and percentages

Checking answers — Level 5

You can use an **estimate** to check if a calculation is correct.
Round the original values and use these rounded values to work out an **approximate** answer.
Compare your two answers to see if they are about the same size.

Tim works out that 88.63 + 32.8 = 121.43

To check if Tim is correct
you can round 88.63 to 89 and 32.8 to 33.

Then an approximation is 89 + 33 = 122.
121.43 is quite close to 122
so you can be fairly sure that Tim is correct.

Alex works out that 88.63 − 32.8 = 85.35

To check if Alex is correct
you can round 88.63 to 89 and 32.8 to 33.

Then an approximation is 89 − 33 = 56.
85.35 is not very close to 56 so Alex is probably wrong.
In fact, 88.63 − 32.8 = 55.83 so Alex is wrong!

You can also use **inverse operations** to check if a calculation is correct.

Addition and Subtraction are inverse operations.

You can check that   123.5 + 12.6 = 136.1
by working out   136.1 − 123.5   or   136.1 − 12.6

Multiplication and Division are inverse operations.

Squaring and Square rooting are inverse operations.

Exercise 8:2

1 In each part
  (1) work out the exact answer using the column method
  (2) estimate an answer by rounding each number to the nearest whole number.

  a 52.5 + 31.4   **c** 29.64 + 41.95   **e** 22.6 + 4.65 + 3.45
  b 46.9 + 46.3   **d** 237.2 + 37.65   **f** 47.45 + 7.9 + 23.07

2 In each part
  (1) work out the exact answer using the column method
  (2) estimate an answer by rounding each number to the nearest whole number.

  a 38.5 − 21.4   **c** 64.2 − 30.7   **e** 87.24 − 34.15
  b 61.8 − 32.3   **d** 68.67 − 21.85   **f** 64.21 − 31.5

3 The table shows the times for four runners from Class 7S and four runners from Class 7T.

Class 7S		Class 7T	
Name	Time in seconds	Name	Time in seconds
Paddy	13.92	Lucia	14.12
Tosin	13.88	James	14.08
Joshua	13.79	Cynthia	13.49
Danielle	13.85	Bilal	13.63

a Only the three fastest times for each team count towards the total time for the team. Write down the three fastest times for
  (1) Class 7S **(2)** Class 7T.

b Add up the three fastest times for
  (1) Class 7S **(2)** Class 7T.

c Estimate each of the totals to check your answers to part **b**. Show your working.

4 Ben says that $16.3 - 9.7 = 6.6$
Explain how Ben could do an addition to check if he is right.

5 Jenny has worked out that $14.8 + 5.6 = 20.4$
Write down two subtractions that Jenny could do to check her answer.

6 Write down an inverse calculation you could do to check each of Pavel's calculations.
  a $58.1 + 36.2 = 94.3$
  b $50.1 - 28.6 = 21.5$
  c $52.8 \times 2.6 = 137.28$
  d $37.5 \div 1.5 = 35$
  e $\sqrt{20.25} = 4.5$
  f $2.19 + 39.52 = 42.71$
  g $21.92 - 10.98 = 10.94$
  h $219.28 \times 8 = 1754.24$
  i $586.8 \div 18 = 32.6$
  j $8.2^2 = 67.24$
  k $40.96 + 10.25 = 51.22$
  l $53.87 - 19.08 = 44.79$
  m $37.64 \times 1.2 = 451.68$
  n $123.21 \div 111 = 1.11$
  o $12.5^2 = 165.25$

7 In **Question 6**, six of the calculations are incorrect.
  a Use the checks you have written down to find the six incorrect calculations.
  b Write down the correct answers for the six calculations.

8 Ella calculates that $46.89 + 23.12 = 70.01$
Ella combines an estimate **and** an inverse operation to check her calculation.
She works out $70 - 23 = 47$, so her answer is about right.

Write down a calculation that you could use to check each of these.
Use estimation **and** an inverse operation like Ella.
  a $5.8 + 9.1 = 14.9$ **b** $31.9 - 11.2 = 20.7$ **c** $93.12 \times 5.1 = 474.912$

8 Decimals, fractions and percentages

2 Multiplying and dividing with decimals

- Multiplying and dividing decimal numbers by 10, 100 and 1000
- Multiplying and dividing using mental methods
- Multiplying with decimal numbers
- Dividing with decimal numbers

Key words

increases, multiply, decreases, divide, partitioning, doubling, halving, column method, estimate, approximately, equivalent

Multiplying and dividing decimal numbers by 10, 100 and 1000 — Level 5

The value of a positive number **increases** when it is multiplied by 10, 100 or 1000.

Multiplying by 10 makes all the digits move one column to the left.

$0.03 \times 10 = 0.3$

```
H  T  U . t  h
         0 . 0  3
         0 . 3
```

Multiplying by 100 makes all the digits move two columns to the left.

$4.95 \times 100 = 495$

```
H  T  U . t  h
         4 . 9  5
   4  9  5 .
```

Multiplying by 1000 makes all the digits move three columns to the left.

The value of a positive number **decreases** when it is divided by 10 or 100.

Dividing by 10 makes all the digits move one column to the right.

$0.5 \div 10 = 0.05$

```
H  T  U . t  h
         0 . 5
         0 . 0  5
```

Dividing by 100 makes all the digits move two columns to the right.

$41 \div 100 = 0.41$

```
H  T  U . t  h
   4  1 .
         0 . 4  1
```

Dividing by 1000 makes all the digits move three columns to the right.

Exercise 8:3

1 Work out each of these.

- **a** 3.5×10
- **b** 9.8×100
- **c** 0.07×1000
- **d** $23 \div 10$
- **e** $450 \div 100$
- **f** $8600 \div 1000$
- **g** $420 \div 1000$
- **h** $39 \div 100$
- **i** $6.8 \div 10$
- **j** 0.02×100
- **k** 2.53×1000
- **l** 0.9×10

2 Copy the table and fill in the gaps.

	× 10	÷ 100	× 1000	
a	0.05			50
b	2.4			
c		7.3		
d			0.009	
e				6250

3 Copy these statements and fill in the gaps.

a … × 10 = 3   e … ÷ 10 = 0.3   i … × 10 = 0.2   m … ÷ 1000 = 3.16
b … × 100 = 3   f … ÷ 10 = 0.06   j … × 1000 = 57   n … ÷ 10 = 0.1
c 0.2 … 10 = 0.02   g 0.2 × … = 200   k 4.1 ÷ … = 0.041   o … ÷ 10 = 0.77
d 18 ÷ … = 0.18   h 4.38 × … = 438   l 0.9 … 10 = 9   p 0.44 … … = 4.4

4 Dust mite droppings are a big problem for people with asthma.
They are too small to see with the naked eye.
In fact they are 100 times smaller than the width of a pinhead.
A pinhead is 0.2 cm wide.

How big are dust mite droppings?

Dust mite

Facts to figure

5 Decimal numbers haven't always been written with a decimal point.

John Napier, a Scottish mathematician, popularised the decimal point when he used it in a book, called *Descriptio*, in 1616.

Before that, people used to use a **bar over the units digit** to show decimals.

So, instead of writing 24.9, they would write 2$\bar{4}$9

Even today, not everyone uses a decimal point.
In most European countries people use a **comma** to show a decimal.
So, instead of writing 24.9, they write 24,9

In Arab countries a *momayyez* is used. It looks like a **forward slash**.
So, instead of writing 24.9, they write 24/9

Copy and complete these using the symbol for a decimal point shown in each part.

a 2$\bar{4}$9 ÷ 100 =   c 15$\bar{3}$8 ÷ 1000 =   e 45,23 × 10 =
b 6,7 ÷ 10 =   d 0/422 × 100 =   f 93/25 × 1000 =

8 Decimals, fractions and percentages

Multiplying and dividing using mental methods — Level 5

You need to be able to multiply and divide with decimals without a calculator.

Here are some tricks to use:

Multiplying by 0.2 is the same as **multiplying by 2** and then **dividing by 10**

$8 \times 0.2 = 8 \times 2 \div 10$
$= 16 \div 10$
$= 1.6$

Multiplying by 0.03 is the same as **multiplying by 3** and then **dividing by 100**

$7 \times 0.03 = 7 \times 3 \div 100$
$= 21 \div 100$
$= 0.21$

Multiplying by 30 is the same as **multiplying by 10** and then **multiplying by 3**

$2.3 \times 30 = 2.3 \times 10 \times 3$
$= 23 \times 3$
$= 69$

Dividing by 6 is the same as **dividing by 3** and then **dividing by 2**

$15.6 \div 6 = 15.6 \div 3 \div 2$
$= 5.2 \div 2$
$= 2.6$

Multiplying by 50 is the same as **multiplying by 100** and then **dividing by 2**

$1.36 \times 50 = 1.36 \times 100 \div 2$
$= 136 \div 2$
$= 68$

Dividing by 5 is the same as **dividing by 10** and then **multiplying by 2**

$4.7 \div 5 = 4.7 \div 10 \times 2$
$= 0.47 \times 2$
$= 0.94$

Use **partitioning** like this:

$5.6 \times 11 = (5.6 \times 10) + (5.6 \times 1)$
$= 56 + 5.6$
$= 61.6$

Use **doubling** and **halving**:

$12.5 \times 6 = 25 \times 3 = 75$ double the 12.5 and halve the 6
$8 \times 3.5 = 4 \times 7 = 28$ double the 3.5 and halve the 8

Remember all the alternatives that are true given one multiplication fact.
$3.6 \times 4 = 14.4$ so you also know that

$4 \times 3.6 = 14.4$ $14.4 \div 3.6 = 4$ and $14.4 \div 4 = 3.6$

Look at these alternatives you can make from one multiplication fact:

Because you know that $8 \times 7 = 56$
you also know that $0.8 \times 7 = 5.6$
and $0.08 \times 7 = 0.56$

So you can use the fact that $8 \times 7 = 56$ to write down that 0.08×7 is 0.56

Exercise 8:4

1 Copy these and work them out.
- **a** 3×0.4
- **b** 9×0.5
- **c** 6×0.7
- **d** 9×0.9
- **e** 6×0.04
- **f** 7×0.03
- **g** 0.02×6
- **h** 0.07×5

2 Copy each statement and fill in the missing number.
- **a** $\ldots \times 0.3 = 1.5$
- **b** $\ldots \times 0.07 = 0.56$
- **c** $\ldots \times 0.4 = 16$
- **d** $\ldots \times 0.2 = 0.06$
- **e** $\ldots \times 0.02 = 70$
- **f** $\ldots \times 0.06 = 1.8$
- **g** $6 \times \ldots = 0.24$
- **h** $35 \times \ldots = 7$
- **i** $12 \times \ldots = 7.2$

3 Tyra parked her car for 8 hours.
Calculate how much she should pay.

4 A bag of chips costs £0.97
Jenny buys 9 bags.
How much will she have to pay?

5 Look at these cards.

     [0.2] [2] [0.3] [6] [10]

Which two cards would you multiply together to get the smallest answer?

6 Copy each of these and fill in the gaps.

- **a** $4.1 \times 30 = 4.1 \times 10 \times 3$
  $= \ldots \times 3$
  $= \ldots$
- **b** $6.7 \times 40 = \ldots \times 10 \times \ldots$
  $= \ldots \times \ldots$
  $= \ldots$
- **c** $3.7 \times 60 = \ldots \times 10 \times \ldots$
  $= \ldots \times \ldots$
  $= \ldots$
- **d** $3.4 \times 50 = \ldots \times 100 \div \ldots$
  $= \ldots \div \ldots$
  $= \ldots$
- **e** $8.2 \times 50 = \ldots \times \ldots \div \ldots$
  $= \ldots \div \ldots$
  $= \ldots$
- **f** $2.4 \div 5 = \ldots \div \ldots \times \ldots$
  $= \ldots \times \ldots$
  $= \ldots$

7 Copy each of these and fill in the gaps.

- **a** $18.6 \div 6 = 18.6 \div 3 \div 2$
  $= \ldots \div 2$
  $= \ldots$
- **b** $42.4 \div 8 = 42.4 \div 4 \div 2$
  $= \ldots \div 2$
  $= \ldots$
- **c** $80.1 \div 9 = 80.1 \div 3 \div 3$
  $= \ldots \div 3$
  $= \ldots$
- **d** $66.4 \div 8 = 66.4 \div 2 \div 2 \div 2$
  $= \ldots \div 2 \div 2$
  $= \ldots \div 2$
  $= \ldots$

8 Decimals, fractions and percentages

8 Copy each of these and fill in the gaps.

a 3.7 × 11 = (3.7 × 10) + (3.7 × 1)
          = … + …
          = …

b 4.8 × 12 = (4.8 × 10) + (4.8 × 2)
          = … + …
          = …

c 2.7 × 13 = (2.7 × …) + (2.7 × …)
          = … + …
          = …

d 4.2 × 12 = (4.2 × …) + (4.2 × …)
          = … + …
          = …

e 3.3 × 9 = (3.3 × 10) − (3.3 × 1)
         = … − …
         = …

f 2.6 × 8 = (2.6 × 10) − (2.6 × …)
         = … − …
         = …

9 Work these out by doubling one of the numbers and halving the other.

a 2.5 × 6
b 6.5 × 8
c 12.5 × 12
d 6 × 4.5
e 14 × 2.5
f 32.5 × 4

10 Matt has worked out that 7.6 × 8 = 60.8
Write down three multiplication and division statements that he also knows are true.

11 Copy these calculations. Fill in the gaps.

a 9 × 5 = …
   0.9 × 5 = …
   0.09 × 5 = …

b 8 × 6 = …
   0.8 × 6 = …
   0.08 × 6 = …

c 4 × 7 = …
   0.4 × 7 = …
   0.04 × 7 = …

12 a Work out the value of 15 × 6.
  b Use your answer to part **a** to write down the value of each of these.
   (1) 1.5 × 6   (2) 0.15 × 6   (3) 0.015 × 6

13 Lee is paid £4.60 an hour.
He works 8 hours a day for 5 days each week.
How much does Lee get paid in a week?

14 Frank and Linda are gardeners.
Frank works for 4 hours and
Linda works for 2 hours on the same job.
They get paid £64.80 for the job.
How much should Frank be paid for his share of the work?

Multiplying with decimal numbers — Level 5

You have already seen the traditional **column method** for long multiplication.

You work out 216×30 on the first row.

This is the same as $216 \times 3 \times 10$.
Multiplying by **10** will give you a **0** at the end so put that in first.

To work out 216×3, you do $6 \times 3 = 18$. Put down the **8** and carry the **1**.

Work out $1 \times 3 = 3$ and add the **1** to get **4**.

Then do $2 \times 3 = 6$.

Then you work out 216×7 on the second row and add the two rows up.

```
        2   1   6
    ×       3   7
    6  ₁4   8   0
    1  ₁5  ₄1   2
    7   9   9   2
```

You can use this to help you to multiply decimal numbers.

To work out 2.16×3.7 you need to spot that $2.16 = 216 \div 100$ and $3.7 = 37 \div 10$.

So you work out 216×37 as above and then divide the answer by **1000**.
So $2.16 \times 3.7 = 7.992$.

You should still use an **estimate** to check your answer.

Round 2.16 to 2 and 3.7 to 4.
So 2.16×3.7 is **approximately** $2 \times 4 = 8$.

7.992 is close to 8 so you can see that it's the right size of answer for the calculation.

Exercise 8:5

1 a Work out the value of 218×7.
   b Use an estimate for 218×7 to check your answer to part **a**.
   c Use your answer to part **a** to write down the value of each of these.
       (1) 21.8×7 **(2)** 2.18×7

2 a Work out the value of 354×42.
   b Use an estimate for 354×42 to check your answer to part **a**.
   c Use your answer to part **a** to write down the value of each of these.
       (1) 35.4×4.2 **(2)** 3.54×0.42

3 a Estimate and work out the exact value of 2.75×5.3.
   b Estimate and work out the exact value of 14.26×8.7.

8 Decimals, fractions and percentages

4 In each part
   (1) work out the exact value
   (2) use an estimate to check your answer.

   a 23.7 × 5
   b 46.5 × 8
   c 67.2 × 61
   d 72.8 × 26
   e 60.7 × 4.7
   f 5.02 × 9.1
   g 6.1 × 5.2
   h 2.46 × 7
   i 7.13 × 0.6
   j 4.28 × 3.7
   k 1.07 × 0.67
   l 3.15 × 0.08

5 A market stall sells hardware.
   For each part
   (1) estimate the answer
   (2) work out the actual cost.

   a 24 hinges at £3.56 each.
   b 18 packs of screws at £1.79 each.
   c 6 plug sockets at £14.68 each.

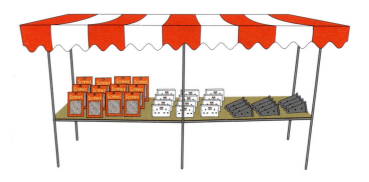

6 a Phoebe is buying bulbs for her garden.
   Work out the cost of
   (1) 28 lilies at £2.49 each
   (2) 36 day lilies at £2.24 each
   (3) 27 phlox at £1.94 each
   (4) 39 incarvillea at £1.29 each.

   b Phoebe also buys 15 bags of topsoil at £3.38 per bag.
   How much does she spend altogether?

7 I pay £16.20 to travel to work each week.
   I work for 45 weeks each year.
   How much do I pay to travel to work each year?

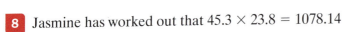

8 Jasmine has worked out that 45.3 × 23.8 = 1078.14

   a Write down an inverse calculation that you could use to check Jasmine's multiplication.
   b What answer should you get if Jasmine is correct?

9 Zafar collects money for charity.

   He has £45 in £1 coins, £21 in 50p coins
   and £5.20 in 10p coins.

   A £1 coin is 3.15 mm thick, a 50p coin is 1.78 mm thick,
   and a 10p coin is 1.85 mm thick.

   Zafar makes a pile of £1 coins, a pile of 50p coins
   and a pile of 10p coins.
   How high is each stack of coins?

Dividing with decimal numbers — Level 5

You have already seen how to do divisions with whole numbers.

The same method works for decimal numbers.

This is how to work out $109.76 \div 8$

```
   109.76
 -  80       8 × 10
   ─────
    29.76
 -  24       8 × 3
   ─────
     5.76
 -   5.6     8 × 0.7
   ─────
     0.16
 -   0.16    8 × 0.02
   ─────
     0.00
   Answer: 13.72
```

So $109.76 \div 8 = 13.72$

Again you should use an **estimate** to check your answer to the calculation.
You should choose numbers that make calculating the estimate easy.
You can round the number that is being divided like this:

$109.76 \div 8$ is **approximately**
- $112 \div 8 = 14$
- $104 \div 8 = 13$
- $108 \div 8 = 13.5$

Or you can round both the numbers in the calculation.
$109.76 \div 8$ is approximately $110 \div 10 = 11$. This is much easier to do in this example.
13.72 is close to any of these estimates so you can be fairly sure that it's right.

You can also do decimal divisions by doing an **equivalent** whole number division.

To work out $493 \div 3.4$ you need to realise that this is equivalent to $4930 \div 34$.

Then work this out using whole number division.

$4930 \div 34 = 145$ so $493 \div 3.4 = 145$

```
   4930
 - 3400      34 × 100
   ────
   1530
 - 1360      34 × 40
   ────
    170
 -  170      34 × 5
   ────
      0
   Answer: 145
```

$493 \div 3.4$ is approximately $480 \div 3 = 160$ and 145 is close enough to this to believe it is correct.

Exercise 8:6

1 Copy and complete these divisions.

a
```
    158.4
 -  120       6 × 20
    ───
    ...
 -  ...       6 × ...
    ───
    ...
 -  ...       6 × ...
    ───
    0.0
    Answer: ___
```

b
```
    257.12
 -  240       8 × ...
    ──────
    ... ...
 -  ...       8 × 2
    ──────
    ... ...
 -  ... ...   8 × ...
    ──────
    ... ...
 -  ... ...   8 × ...
    ──────
    0.00
    Answer: ___
```

8 Decimals, fractions and percentages

2 a Write down an inverse calculation that you could use to check each of your answers in **Question 1**.
  b Work out each of your inverse calculations.

3 The total of six numbers is 453.6
Work out the mean of the numbers.

4 Phoebe buys some bags of bulbs.
Work out the cost of one bulb if a bag of
  a 8 lilies costs £1.92
  b 14 nabranthus costs £2.24

5 Evie is buying curtain material.
She buys 7 m of material and pays £125.23
How much does the material cost per metre?

6 Copy this division and complete it to work out the value of 914.4 ÷ 7.2

```
    9144
  − 7200      72 × ...
    ...
  − 1400      72 × ...
    ...
  −  504      72 × ...
       0
         Answer:  ...
```

7 In each part
  (1) work out the exact value
  (2) use an estimate to check your answer.
  a 154.2 ÷ 6   **d** 592 ÷ 3.2   **g** 843.2 ÷ 3.4   **j** 1162.8 ÷ 1.7
  b 11.92 ÷ 8   **e** 893 ÷ 3.8   **h** 969.3 ÷ 2.7   **k** 1005.2 ÷ 2.8
  c 192.22 ÷ 7   **f** 868 ÷ 5.6   **i** 676.2 ÷ 4.6   **l** 2073.6 ÷ 3.6

⚠ 8 Josh is buying guttering.
Each length of guttering is 2.5 m long.
He needs enough guttering to fit around the roof of his house which is a total length of 23.5 m.
  a Work out 23.5 ÷ 2.5
  b How many pieces of guttering does Josh need to buy?

Explore

9 a When a number is divided by 8.5, the answer is 4.12 What is the number?
  b When a number is multiplied by 4.6, the answer is 103.5 What is the number?

3 Fractions and percentages

▶ **Finding a fraction of an amount**

▶ **Finding a percentage of an amount**

Key words
fraction	denominator
numerator	integer
percentage	decimal
increase	decrease

▶ Finding a fraction of an amount **Level 5**

You can find a **fraction** of an amount like this:

To find $\frac{3}{5}$ of 500 g

Find $\frac{1}{5}$ of 500 $500 \div 5 = 100$
Then multiply by 3 $100 \times 3 = 300$

So $\frac{3}{5}$ of 500 g = 300 g

To find a fraction of a quantity you   divide by the **denominator**
and   multiply by the **numerator**.

So $\frac{2}{3}$ of 36 cm = $36 \div 3 \times 2 = 12 \times 2 = 24$ cm

When you divide by the denominator you may not get an **integer** answer.
If this happens, change the integer to a fraction using a denominator of **1**.

To find $\frac{3}{7}$ of 50 seconds, write 50 as the fraction $\frac{50}{1}$

Then $\frac{3}{7}$ of 50 seconds = $\frac{3}{7} \times \frac{50}{1} = \frac{3 \times 50}{7 \times 1} = \frac{150}{7} = 21\frac{3}{7}$ seconds

Exercise 8:7

1 a Work these out.

 (1) $\frac{7}{8}$ of 24   (2) $24 \times 7 \div 8$ (3) $24 \div 8 \times 7$ (4) $\frac{7}{8} \times 24$

   b Write down what you notice about your answers to part **a**.

2 Work these out.

   a $\frac{3}{5} \times 30$ **c** $15 \times \frac{2}{3}$ **e** $\frac{4}{5}$ of 105 g   **g** $\frac{2}{3}$ of an hour in minutes
   b $\frac{3}{7}$ of 35   **d** $\frac{3}{4}$ of 32   **f** $\frac{5}{7}$ of 630 mℓ **h** $\frac{3}{25}$ of a metre in centimetres

3 Kevin and Steven share a bag of stickers. Kevin gets $\frac{5}{9}$ of the stickers.
There are 72 stickers in the bag. How many stickers does Steven get?

8 Decimals, fractions and percentages

4 A clothes shop is having a summer sale.
All items have $\frac{1}{3}$ off the original price.

The shop assistant is filling out these labels. Copy and complete them.

a WAS £24.00 NOW £......

b WAS £99.99 NOW £......

c WAS £49.50 NOW £......

5 Simon makes a sports drink using $\frac{1}{6}$ concentrate and $\frac{5}{6}$ water.

He makes 120 mℓ of drink. How much water does he use?

6 The three prizes in the Maths department Christmas raffle are shown on the poster.

Which prize would you prefer to win?
Explain your answer.

Raffle Prizes
A: one third of £57
B: £24 × 0.75
C: $\frac{2}{5}$ × £50

7 Work out the weight shown on each card.
Put the weights in order. Start with the lightest.

A	B	C	D
$\frac{3}{10}$ of 360 kg	$\frac{5}{9}$ of 198 kg	Two thirds of 150 kg	0.25 × 420 kg

8 Work these out. Give each answer as a mixed number.

a $\frac{1}{5} \times 8$ b $\frac{3}{7} \times 25$ c $20 \times \frac{2}{9}$ d $\frac{3}{5}$ of 43

9 Work out each of these. Give an exact number for each part.

a $\frac{2}{5}$ of 23 minutes   c $\frac{3}{5}$ of 34 m   e $\frac{5}{6}$ of 65 ℓ

b $\frac{2}{7}$ of 17 cm   d $\frac{2}{9}$ of 37 g   f $\frac{3}{8}$ of 33 kg

Explore

10 Find the value of each letter.

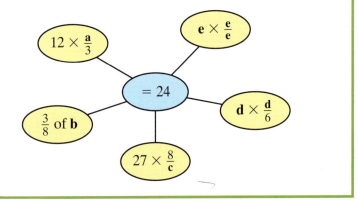

Finding a percentage of an amount — Level 5

To work out a **percentage** of an amount you change the percentage into a **decimal** and multiply the decimal by the amount.

45% of 300 g
45% = 0.45
0.45 × 300 = 135 g

To work out percentages without a calculator, use 50%, 10% and 1% as building blocks.

To find **50%** of something you **divide by 2** because 50% = $\frac{1}{2}$

To find **10%** of something you **divide by 10** because 10% = $\frac{1}{10}$

To find **1%** of something you **divide by 100** because 1% = $\frac{1}{100}$

To find **62%** of £350

| 62% |
| 50% | 10% | 1% | 1% |

Find **50%** of £350   Find **10%** of £350   Find **1%** of £350
£350 ÷ 2 = £175   £350 ÷ 10 = £35   £350 ÷ 100 = £3.50
                                                So 2% = 2 × £3.50 = £7

So **62%** of £350 = £175 + £35 + £7 = £217

To work out a new amount after a percentage **increase** find the **increase** and **add** it on to the old amount.

To work out a new amount after a percentage **decrease** find the **decrease** and **subtract** it from the old amount.

These biscuits normally weigh 200 g but now you get 10% extra.

This TV normally costs £850 but now you get 10% discount.

10% of 200 g = 200 ÷ 10 = **20 g**
The weight of the biscuits is now
200 g + 20 g = 220 g

10% of £850 = 850 ÷ 10 = **£85**
The cost of the TV is now
£850 − £85 = £765

Exercise 8:8

1 Work these out using a calculator.

  a 23% of £300
  b 87% of £900
  c 65% of 260 ℓ
  d 24% of £175
  e 29% of 750 mℓ
  f 7% of 950 g
  g 31% of £350
  h 17.5% of £1200

8 Decimals, fractions and percentages

2 In 1976 the average yearly wage was £3275.
On average, people spent 17% of £3275 on their family holiday.
How much is 17% of £3275?
Show your working.

3 a Copy this and fill it in.

10% of £400 = 400 ÷ ... = £ ....
1% of £400 = ... ÷ ... = £ ....

b Use the answers in part **a** to help you to answer these questions.

(1) 20% of £400   (3) 3% of £400   (5) 38% of £400
(2) 5% of £400   (4) 23% of £400   (6) 47% of £400

4 a Find 15% of £550. Show all of your working.

b Explain how you solved part **a**.

5 Work these out without a calculator. Show your working for each one.

a 11% of £280   c 65% of £70   e 38% of 150 cm   g 17% of 450 kg
b 61% of £2000   d 98% of 600 g   f 48% of 300 m   h 27% of 250 mg

6 These pie charts show the contents of a cereal bar and a chocolate bar.
Both bars weigh 40 g.

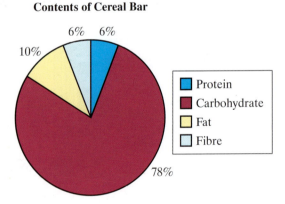
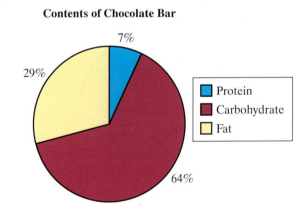

Work out the amount of protein, carbohydrate, fat and fibre in each bar.

7 Kerry calculates that 58% of 650 is 320.
Use a simple estimate to show that Kerry's answer must be wrong.

8 There are 32 pupils in Class 7T.
This table shows their Year 6 SATs results as percentages.

Level	3	4	5
Percentage (%)	25	46.875	28.125

Calculate how many pupils achieved each level.

9 Sam bought a new car for £12 000.
   After a year, the value of the car decreased by 40%.

   a Work out 40% of £12 000.

   b What is the value of the car a year after Sam bought it?

10 Work these out. Remember to give the units in your answers.

   a Increase £45 by 20%   d Decrease 2230 ℓ by 43%
   b Increase €245 by 30%   e Decrease 85 g by 11%
   c Increase 578 km by 28%   f Decrease $450 by 73%

11 a Work out 10% of 200. Add your answer to 200.

   b Work out 10% of your answer to part **a**.
      Subtract it from your answer to part **a**.

   c Explain why the answer to part **b** is not 200.

12 VAT is charged at 17.5%.
   Jenny is buying a CD player that costs £120 plus VAT.
   She says,

   'All I need to do to work out the VAT is divide £120 by 10 and jot that down.
   Then I halve my last answer and jot that down.
   Then I halve my last answer again and jot that down.
   Then I just add those three bits together.'

   a Work out the VAT that Jenny has to pay using her method.

   b Explain why Jenny's method works.

   c Write down the total cost of the CD player.

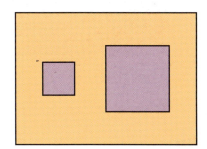

13 This rectangle is 10 cm by 8 cm.

   The sides of the larger purple square are
   twice the length of the sides of the smaller one.

   Together the squares take up 25% of the area of the rectangle.

   Work out the length of the sides of the squares.

14 Around 92% of the population of the UK
   listen to or watch a BBC channel at some time each week.
   This is about 54 000 000 people.

   Use this fact to calculate the approximate size
   of the population of the UK.

8 Decimals, fractions and percentages

Watch out ... there's a trap about

▶ When you are multiplying by 10, don't just add a zero.
0.5×10 is **not** 0.50!

Multiplying by 10 makes all the digits move one column to the left.
So $0.5 \times 10 = 5$

▶ To work out $\frac{2}{7}$ of 5 **don't** write $\frac{2}{7} \times 5 = \frac{2 \times 5}{7 \times 5} = \frac{10}{35}$

You **don't** multiply the numerator and the denominator by 5.
You work it out like this $\frac{2}{7} \times 5 = \frac{2}{7} \times \frac{5}{1} = \frac{2 \times 5}{7 \times 1} = \frac{10}{7} = 1\frac{3}{7}$

▶ 6% of 150 is **not** $0.6 \times 150 = 90$

$6\% = 6 \div 100 = 0.06$ so 6% of $150 = 0.06 \times 150 = 9$

60% of $150 = 0.6 \times 150 = 90$

▶ You know that you can find **10%** of £60 by **dividing by 10**.   10% of £60 = 60 ÷ 10 = £6

But you **don't** find 5% of £60 by dividing by 5!

$5\% = \frac{5}{100} = \frac{1}{20}$ so you find **5%** by **dividing by 20**.   5% of £60 = 60 ÷ 20 = £3

You can tell that this is the right answer because 10% of £60 is twice as big as 5% of £60.

Test yourself

1 The table shows different types of animals on farms in the UK in 2001.

a Round each percentage to the nearest whole number.

b Round each percentage to one decimal place.

c Round each percentage to two decimal places.

Livestock	%
Breeding cattle	18.559
Dairy	3.940
Beef	2.994
Pigs	10.232
Sheep	64.275

2 Write down an inverse calculation you could do to check the answer to each of these.

a $7.23 + 1.96 = 9.19$ b $64.12 - 8.9 = 55.22$ c $32.45 \times 2.6 = 84.37$

3 Copy these and fill in the gaps.

a ... × 10 = 3   c 2 ... 100 = 0.02   e ... ÷ 1000 = 3.16   g 0.43 × ... = 43

b ... × 100 = 420   d 30 ... 1000 = 0.03   f ... × 100 = 31.6   h 0.57 × ... = 570

4 Use mental methods to work these out.

    a 5.1 × 11   **c** 6.7 × 20   **e** 9 × 0.4   **g** 15.6 ÷ 6

    b 5.5 × 12   **d** 2.4 × 30   **f** 8 × 0.02   **h** 23.5 ÷ 5

5 In each part

    (1) work out the exact value

    (2) use an estimate to check your answer.

    a 15.2 × 3   **c** 61.2 × 2.3   **e** 46.8 ÷ 2   **g** 67.1 ÷ 1.1

    b 12.1 × 15   **d** 4.31 × 3.1   **f** 218.4 ÷ 12   **h** 72.48 ÷ 2.4

6 Work out each of these.

    a $\frac{2}{3} \times 18$ **b** $\frac{3}{5} \times 45$ **c** $21 \times \frac{4}{7}$ **d** $\frac{7}{9}$ of 36

7 Kieran and Dean share a bag of sweets. Kieran gets $\frac{3}{7}$ of the sweets.
There are 63 sweets in the bag. How many sweets does Kieran get?

8 Work these out. Give an exact answer for each part.

    a $\frac{3}{5}$ of 58 cm   **b** $\frac{2}{7}$ of 240 g   **c** $\frac{2}{9}$ of 34 minutes

9 Work out each of these using a calculator.

    a 21% of £180   **b** 36% of 700 g   **c** 17.5% of £150

10 a Copy the calculations and fill in the missing values.

    10% of 84 = _____

     5% of 84 = _____

    $2\frac{1}{2}$% of 84 = _____

   b The cost of a CD player is £84 plus $17\frac{1}{2}$% tax.
What is the total cost of the CD player?
You can use part **a** to help you.

11 Work out each of these without using a calculator.

    a 30% of £120   **b** 22% of 160 g   **c** 48% of 260 kg

12 A holiday brochure has this advertisement.
Marcus is going on two trips this year.
How much should he pay for his insurance?

> **Holiday Insurance**
> *Single trip cover* £12
> *Annual multi-trip cover* £30
> **BUY ONLINE AND SAVE 10%**

8 Decimals, fractions and percentages

Chapter 8 Summary

Level 5

Rounding decimals

14.872 is closer to **14.9** than **14.8**
so 14.872 rounds to 14.9 to one decimal place.

14.872 is closer to **14.87** than **14.88**
so 14.872 rounds to 14.87 to two decimal places.

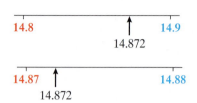

Multiplying with decimal numbers

To work out 21.6 × 3.7, you work out 216 × 37
and then divide the answer by 100.
216 × 37 = 7992 so 21.6 × 3.7 = 79.92

Use an estimate to check your answer: 20 × 4 = 80

```
        2  1  6
    ×      3  7
    6  ₁4  8  0
    1  ₁5 ₄1  2
    7   9  9  2
```

Dividing with decimal numbers

91.2 ÷ 6 = 15.2

Use an estimate to check your answer: 90 ÷ 6 = 15

To work out 91.2 ÷ 0.6 use the fact that this is
equivalent to 912 ÷ 6 = 152. So 91.2 ÷ 0.6 = 152

```
    91.2
  − 60        6 × 10
    31.2
  − 30        6 × 5
    1.2
  − 1.2       6 × 0.2
    0.0

  Answer: 15.2
```

Finding a fraction of an amount

To find $\frac{3}{5}$ of 500 g: Find $\frac{1}{5}$ of 500   500 ÷ **5** = **100**
                    Then multiply by **3**   100 × **3** = 300
                                              $\frac{3}{5}$ of 500 g = 300 g

Finding a percentage of an amount

To find **45%** of 300 g   change the **percentage** into a **decimal**   **45%** = **0.45**
                    and work out the decimal of the amount.   **0.45** × 300 = 135 g

To work out percentages without a calculator, use 50%, 10% and 1% as building blocks.
To find **50%** of something you **divide by 2** because **50%** = $\frac{1}{2}$
To find **10%** of something you **divide by 10** because **10%** = $\frac{1}{10}$
To find **1%** of something you **divide by 100** because **1%** = $\frac{1}{100}$

Increasing or decreasing by a percentage

To **increase** £35 by 23%, find 23% of £35 and **add it on**.   0.23 × £35 = £8.05
                                                £35 **+** £8.05 = £43.05

To **decrease** £35 by 23%, find 23% and **take it off**.   £35 **−** £8.05 = £26.95

9 Equations

Chapter 6 Formulae and algebraic operations
- Using BODMAS to build expressions
- Using inverse operations
- Substituting numbers into expressions and formulae

1. Function machines
2. Solving equations

Year 8
- Solving linear equations
- Solving equations using trial and improvement
- Solving simultaneous equations

You should already know:

▶ **how to use BODMAS to do calculations in the correct order**

$$\begin{array}{l}\text{Brackets}\\\text{Powers Of}\\\text{Division}\\\text{Multiplication}\\\text{Addition}\\\text{Subtraction}\end{array}$$

To work out $6 \times (5 + 3) - 10$ use BODMAS.
$$\begin{aligned}6 \times (5 + 3) - 10 &= 6 \times 8 - 10\\&= 48 - 10\\&= 38\end{aligned}$$

▶ **about inverse operations**

$7 + 3 = 10$ and $10 - 3 = 7$
So **add 3** and **subtract 3** are inverse operations.

$7 \times 4 = 28$ and $28 \div 4 = 7$
So **multiply by 4** and **divide by 4** are inverse operations.

▶ **how to substitute into expressions and formulae**

The value of the expression $3x + 7$ when $x = 5$ is $3 \times 5 + 7 = 15 + 7 = 22$

The value of p in the formula $p = 3t + 2$ when $t = 4$ is
$p = 3t + 2 = 3 \times 4 + 2 = 12 + 2 = 14$

9 Equations

1 Function machines

- **Drawing and using function machines**
- **Using inverse operations**
- **Solving equations using function machines**

Key words	
function machine	input
output	inverse
equation	unknown
solution	solve

Drawing and using function machines Level 5

A **function machine** will perform the same operation on every number that you put into it.

The number that you put in is called the **input**.

The number that you get out is called the **output**.

This function machine is adding 8.

When you draw a function machine you only need to draw the screen.

You can use more than one machine at a time. This diagram shows two machines.

```
4  →         → 8  →        → 9
7  →  × 2    → 14 →  + 1   → 15
11 →         → 22 →        → 23
input                        output
```

You multiply the **input** by 2 and then add 1 to get the final **output**. So for this machine

$$\text{input} \times 2 + 1 = \text{output}$$

Exercise 9:1

1 Copy these function machine diagrams and fill in the gaps.

a
```
2  →        → ...
5  →  × 3   → ...
10 →        → ...
input         output
```
input × ... = output

b
```
10 →        → ...
25 →  ÷ 5   → ...
45 →        → ...
input         output
```
input ÷ ... = output

2 Write down the missing function from each of these function machines.

a
8 → [...] → 11
12 → [...] → 15
17 → [...] → 20
input   output

c
9 → [...] → 5
16 → [...] → 12
19 → [...] → 15
input   output

b
3 → [...] → 6
6 → [...] → 12
12 → [...] → 24
input   output

d
20 → [...] → 5
36 → [...] → 9
52 → [...] → 13
input   output

3 a Copy this function machine diagram and fill in the gaps.

1 →
6 → [× 5] → ... → [+ 2] → ...
12 →
input   output

input × ... + ... = output

b Copy this function machine diagram and fill in the gaps.

1 →
6 → [+ 2] → ... → [× 5] → ...
12 →
input   output

(input + ...) × ... = output

c Parts **a** and **b** both use the machines [× 5] and [+ 2].

Explain what this tells you about the order of the machines in this question.

4 a Copy this function machine diagram and fill in the gaps.

3 →
6 → [× 3] → ... → [− 1] → ...
9 →
input   output

input × ... − ... = output

b Copy this function machine diagram and fill in the gaps.

3 →
6 → [− 1] → ... → [× 3] → ...
9 →
input   output

(input − ...) × ... = output

c Parts **a** and **b** both use the machines [× 3] and [− 1].

Explain what this tells you about the order of the machines in this question.

5 Look at your answers to **Questions 3** and **4**.
When you swapped the machines over you obtained different answers.
Write down a pair of machines that will give the same answers when they are swapped over.

9 Equations

Using inverse operations — Level 5

On this function machine you have the function and the **output** numbers but the **input** numbers are missing.

You need to work backwards through the machine to work out the input numbers.

You need to use the **inverse** operation of the one on the screen.

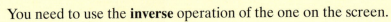

The inverse of + 12 is − 12.

The missing input numbers are 1, 12, 18, and 29.

You can do this for more than one function machine.
Look at this function machine diagram.

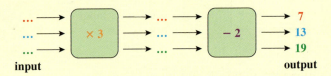

The inverse of × 3 is ÷ 3. The inverse of − 2 is + 2.

You need to work backwards through both of the machines to work out the missing numbers.

So you **add 2** and then **divide by 3** to fill in the missing values like this.

The missing input numbers are 3, 5 and 7.

Exercise 9:2

1 Copy each of these function machines and fill in the input numbers.

a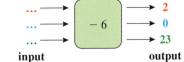

b

c

d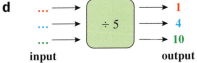

e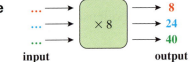

f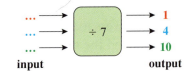

2 Copy each of these function machine diagrams and fill in the gaps.

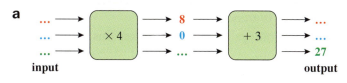

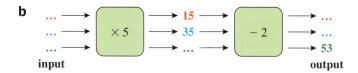

3 Copy each of these function machine diagrams and fill in the gaps.

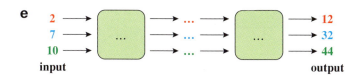

9 Equations

Solving equations using function machines — Level 5

An **equation** has an equals sign in it. $n + 6 = 30$ is an equation.
The letter n is called an **unknown**. There is only one value of n that makes this equation true.
$n = 24$ is the only value that works in this equation.
$n = 24$ is the **solution** of the equation.

You won't be able to write down the solution for most equations straight away.
But you can use function machines to **solve** equations.

Look at this equation: $\qquad 3n + 6 = 18$

In this equation the n is **multiplied by 3** and then **6 is added**.
This is the function machine for this equation.

$$n \longrightarrow \boxed{\times 3} \longrightarrow \boxed{+6} \longrightarrow 18$$

You need to draw the inverse function machine diagram.

$$\ldots \longleftarrow \boxed{\div 3} \longleftarrow \boxed{-6} \longleftarrow 18$$

Now you work out $18 - 6 = 12$ and write the answer in the middle. Then you work out $12 \div 3 = 4$.
This is the completed inverse function machine.

$$4 \longleftarrow \boxed{\div 3} \overset{12}{\longleftarrow} \boxed{-6} \longleftarrow 18$$

This gives you the solution to the equation $\qquad n = 4$

You can check your answer by substituting $n = 4$ into the original equation like this

$$3n + 6 = 3 \times 4 + 6$$
$$= 12 + 6$$
$$= 18 \checkmark$$

If you don't get the number in the original equation here, you know you've done something wrong.

Exercise 9:3

1 Connor is trying to solve the equation $2n + 7 = 35$.
He draws this function machine and inverse function machine diagram.

$$n \longrightarrow \boxed{\times 2} \longrightarrow \boxed{+7} \longrightarrow 35$$

$$\ldots \longleftarrow \boxed{\div 2} \longleftarrow \boxed{-7} \longleftarrow 35$$

$$n = \ldots$$

Copy Connor's diagrams and fill them in to find the solution of the equation.

2 Copy these equations and the function machine diagrams and fill them in.
Write down the solution to each equation.

a $3n + 8 = 44$

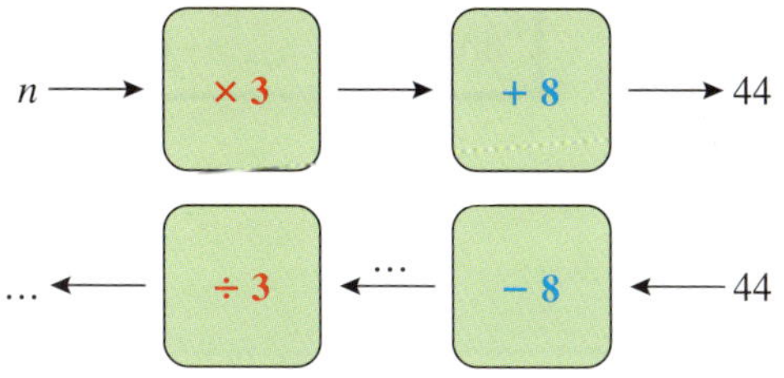

n → ×3 → +8 → 44

… ← ÷3 ← … ← −8 ← 44

$n = \ldots$

b $\dfrac{n}{5} - 3 = 52$

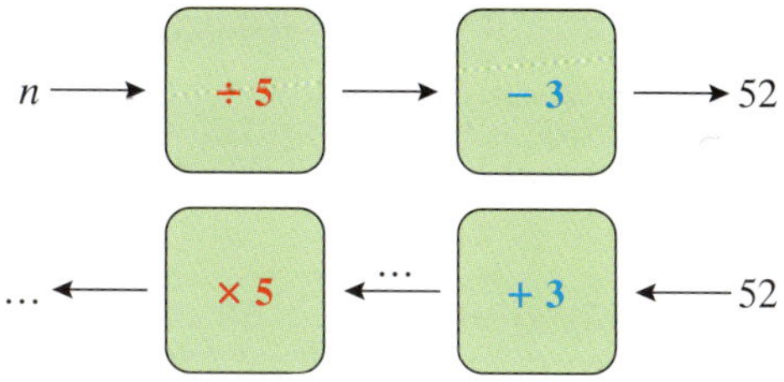

n → ÷5 → −3 → 52

… ← ×5 ← … ← +3 ← 52

$n = \ldots$

3 For each of these equations
(1) solve the equation using function machines
(2) check that your solution is correct using substitution.

a $4n + 7 = 39$
b $3n + 11 = 62$
c $5n - 3 = 67$
d $3n - 7 = 47$
e $8n - 107 = 85$
f $\dfrac{n}{4} + 8 = 19$
g $\dfrac{n}{6} + 12 = 17$
h $\dfrac{n}{7} - 5 = 11$
i $\dfrac{n}{4} - 27 = 23$
⚠ **j** $6n + 17 = 5$
⚠ **k** $12n + 57 = 33$
⚠ **l** $\dfrac{n}{7} + 12 = 6$

Think on!

4 Siobhan has solved four equations.
Here is her work.

1 $2n + 1 = 11$

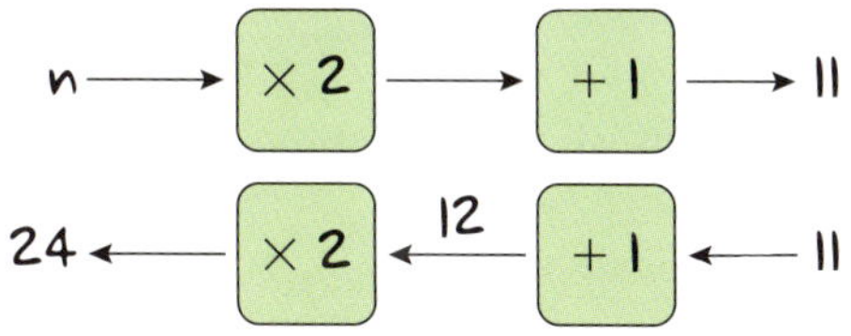

n → ×2 → +1 → 11

24 ← ×2 ← 12 ← +1 ← 11

$n = 24$

2 $4n - 2 = 34$

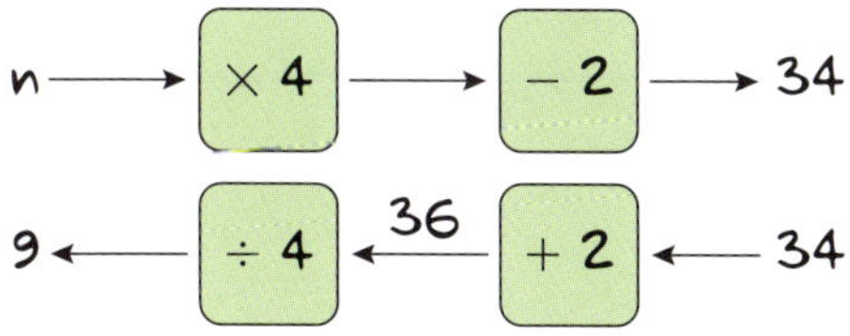

n → ×4 → −2 → 34

9 ← ÷4 ← 36 ← +2 ← 34

$n = 9$

3 $3n - 6 = 15$

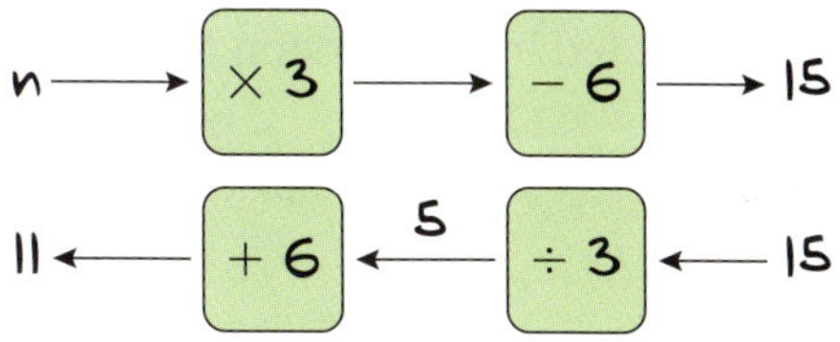

n → ×3 → −6 → 15

11 ← +6 ← 5 ← ÷3 ← 15

$n = 11$

4 $\dfrac{n}{3} + 6 = 12$

n → ÷3 → +6 → 12

2 ← ÷3 ← 6 ← −6 ← 12

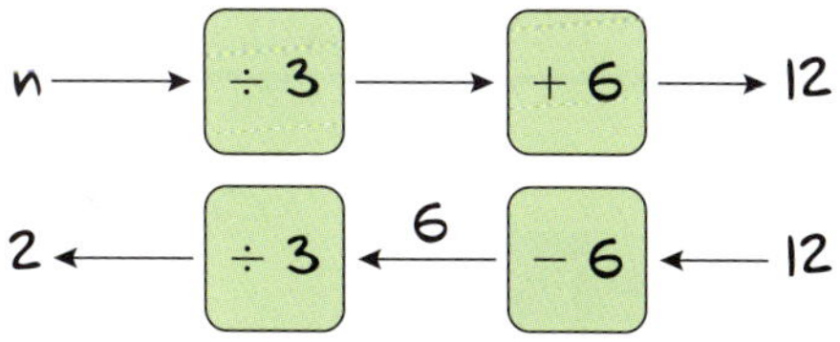

$n = 2$

a Write down which of Siobhan's solutions is correct.
b For each solution that isn't correct, explain what she has done wrong and correct her work.

9 Equations

2 Solving equations

▶ **Solving equations algebraically**

▶ **Solving equations with the unknown on the right**

▶ **Constructing and solving equations**

Key words	
equation	solve
algebraically	inverse
unknown	therefore (∴)

▶ Solving equations algebraically Level 6

Look at this **equation** $4n + 5 = 73$
n is **multiplied by 4** and then **5 is added**.

To **solve** the equation you could use a function machine like in the last exercise.
But you can solve the equation **algebraically**.

You use the **inverse** operations in the opposite order.
This is the same as how you solve equations using function machines.
But you don't draw function machine diagrams.
You show your working like this.

$$4n + 5 - 5 = 73 - 5 \quad \text{Take away 5 from both sides of the equation}$$
$$4n = 68$$
$$\frac{4n}{4} = \frac{68}{4} \quad \text{Divide both sides of the equation by 4}$$
$$n = 17$$

You should still check your answer like this.

$$\text{When } n = 17, \; 4n + 5 = 4 \times 17 + 5 = 68 + 5 = 73 \checkmark$$

Here is another equation. $\frac{n}{3} - 6 = 4$

n is **divided by 3** and then **6 is subtracted**.

$$\frac{n}{3} - 6 + 6 = 4 + 6 \quad \text{Add 6 to both sides of the equation}$$
$$\frac{n}{3} = 10$$
$$\frac{n}{3} \times 3 = 10 \times 3 \quad \text{Multiply both sides of the equation by 3}$$
$$n = 30$$
$$\text{When } n = 30, \; \frac{n}{3} - 6 = \frac{30}{3} - 6 = 10 - 6 = 4 \checkmark$$

Exercise 9:4

1 Solve each of these equations algebraically.
Check your answers.

a $n + 14 = 23$ **c** $7n = 21$ **e** $2n + 7 = 23$

b $n - 7 = 25$ **d** $\frac{n}{4} = 8$ **f** $5n - 8 = 17$

2 Solve each of these equations algebraically. Check your answers.

- **a** $7a + 8 = 22$
- **b** $5b + 9 = 34$
- **c** $4c - 3 = 21$
- **d** $6d - 12 = 60$
- **e** $\dfrac{e}{3} + 8 = 19$
- **f** $\dfrac{f}{2} + 12 = 20$
- **g** $\dfrac{g}{4} - 2 = 9$
- **h** $\dfrac{h}{8} - 5 = 7$
- **i** $3i + 15 = 60$
- **j** $12j - 32 = 112$
- **k** $\dfrac{k}{9} + 20 = 35$
- **l** $\dfrac{l}{7} - 12 = 8$

3 Solve the equation $3y + 1 = 16$. *(S 2005 part)*

4 Solve the equation $32x + 53 = 501$. *(S 2007 part)*

5 Solve these equations. They all have negative solutions.

- **a** $5a + 8 = 3$
- **b** $7b + 34 = 13$
- **c** $\dfrac{c}{3} + 5 = 4$
- **d** $\dfrac{d}{3} + 6 = 2$
- **e** $3e + 15 = {}^-6$
- **f** $9f - 3 = {}^-12$

6 Solve these equations. *(S 2006)*

- **a** $2k + 3 = 11$
- **b** $2t + 3 = {}^-11$

7 Look at this balance diagram.
The equation $2n + 13 = 33$ describes the balance.
You can solve this equation to find the value of the unknown weight.
For this example $n = 10$.

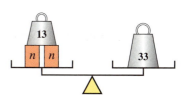

For each balance diagram
(1) write down an equation to describe the balance
(2) solve the equation to find the value of the unknown weight.

a 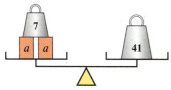 **b** 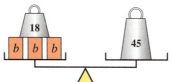 **c**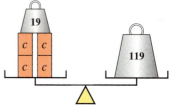

Think on!

8 Match each orange question card with the correct pink answer card.

| $4n + 6 = 20$ | $\dfrac{n}{3} - 2 = \dfrac{1}{2}$ | $n = 3\dfrac{1}{4}$ | $n = 1\dfrac{1}{2}$ |
| $4n - 2 = 11$ | $\dfrac{n}{3} + \dfrac{1}{2} = 1$ | $n = 7\dfrac{1}{2}$ | $n = 3\dfrac{1}{2}$ |

9 Equations

Solving equations with the unknown on the right — Level 6

It doesn't matter which side the **unknown** is on.

If the unknown is on the right-hand side of the equation, write the equation the other way round first.

If you're asked to solve the equation $\qquad 47 = 2n - 1$
rewrite it as $\qquad\qquad\qquad\qquad\qquad 2n - 1 = 47$
and solve it in the usual way.

The symbol ∴ means **therefore**. You can use it if you miss out some of the working because you can see how the next line follows directly from the one before.

You could write your answer for solving the equation above like this

$$47 = 2n - 1$$
$$2n - 1 = 47$$
∴ $\quad 2n = 47 + 1 \qquad$ instead of writing the line $2n - 1 + 1 = 47 + 1$
$\quad\ 2n = 48$
∴ $\quad n = \dfrac{48}{2} \qquad$ instead of writing the line $\dfrac{2n}{2} = \dfrac{48}{2}$
$\quad\ n = 24$

When $n = 24$, $2n - 1 = 2 \times 24 - 1 = 48 - 1 = 47$ ✓

Exercise 9:5

1 Solve each of these equations.

a $17 = 2a + 3$ **c** $48 = 5c - 7$ **e** $7 = \dfrac{e}{2} + 1$ **g** $19 = \dfrac{g}{6} - 1$

b $23 = 4b - 1$ **d** $73 = 8d - 47$ **f** $27 = \dfrac{f}{3} + 17$ **h** $10 = \dfrac{h}{9} - 5$

2 Solve the equation $18 = 4k + 6$.

3 Solve the equation $375 = 37 + 26y$.

4 Jordan was solving the equation $17 = 4n - 3$.
He started by rewriting the equation the other way round.
He **added 3** to both sides and then **multiplied by 4**.
His solution was $n = 80$.

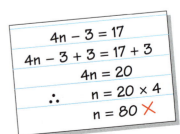

a When $n = 80$ find the value of $4n - 3$.

b Explain how this shows Jordan has made a mistake.

c Write down the correct solution to this equation.

5 Solve these equations. They all have negative solutions.

a $8 = 5a + 23$

b $14 = 26 + 6b$

c $3 = 7c + 38$

d $11 = 8d + 35$

e $2 = 4 + \dfrac{e}{3}$

f $5 = \dfrac{f}{2} + 12$

g $14 = \dfrac{g}{4} + 16$

h $6 = \dfrac{h}{5} + 12$

6 Use substitution to check the answer given for each equation. Write **True** or **False** for each part.

a $29 = 3n - 4$ $n = 10$

b $5 = 4n - 27$ $n = 8$

c $76 = 8n + 2$ $n = 9$

d $54 = 3n + 30$ $n = {}^-8$

e $18 = 5n + 3$ $n = {}^-3$

f $17 = \dfrac{n}{2} + 19$ $n = {}^-4$

7 Laura has been given these cards.

| 17 | 11 | 1 | = | $3n - 7$ | $6n - 13$ | $2n + 3$ |

She chooses a red and a blue card to make this equation.

| 11 | = | $6n - 13$ |

a Solve this equation.

b Consider the other equations she can make with one red and one blue card. Write down
   (1) the equation that gives the largest solution for n
   (2) the equation that gives the smallest solution for n.

8 Look at this equation.
You can find the value of x if $y = 2$ like this

$$28 = 2x + 3y$$
$$28 = 2x + 3 \times 2$$
$$28 = 2x + 6$$
$$2x + 6 = 28$$
$$\therefore 2x = 28 - 6$$
$$2x = 22$$
$$\therefore x = \dfrac{22}{2}$$
$$x = 11$$

Find the value of x in the equation $4y = 3x - 5$ when

a $y = 4$ b $y = 7$ c $y = {}^-5$.

9 Look at this equation. $3a + 20 = 4a + k$

a If $a = 15$, find the value of k.

b If $a = {}^-15$, find the value of k.

9 Equations

Constructing and solving equations — Level 6

Bobby thinks of a number. She **multiplies it by 4** and then **subtracts 7**. She gets 37.
Call the unknown number that Bobby thought of n.
You can find it by solving the equation $4n - 7 = 37$.

$$4n - 7 = 37$$
$$\therefore \quad 4n = 37 + 7$$
$$4n = 44$$
$$\therefore \quad n = \frac{44}{4}$$
$$n = 11$$

So Bobby thought of the number 11.

Look at this triangle.
The perimeter of the triangle is 17 cm.
You need to find the lengths of all the sides.

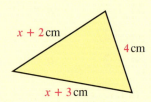

You can write this equation for the perimeter.
Collect like terms and simplify the equation.
Now you can solve the equation.

$$x + 2 + x + 3 + 4 = 17$$
$$2x + 9 = 17$$
$$\therefore \quad 2x = 17 - 9$$
$$2x = 8$$
$$\therefore \quad x = \frac{8}{2}$$
$$x = 4$$

So $x = 4$. Now you can work out the lengths of the sides of the triangle.
$x + 2 = 4 + 2 = 6$ and $x + 3 = 4 + 3 = 7$
So the triangle has sides of length 4 cm, 6 cm and 7 cm.

Exercise 9:6

1 For each part (1) write down an equation
 (2) solve your equation and find the value of n.
 a I think of a number n, **multiply it by 3** and **add 1**. The answer is 25.
 b I think of a number n, **multiply it by 6** and **subtract 7**. The answer is 47.
 c I think of a number n, **divide it by 4** and **add 2**. The answer is 27.
 d I think of a number n, **divide it by 3** and **subtract 6**. The answer is 14.

2 The perimeter of this triangle is 30 cm.
 a Write down an equation for the perimeter.
 b Collect like terms and simplify the equation.
 c Solve the equation to find the value of x.
 d Write down the lengths of the sides of the triangle.

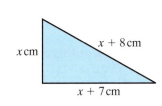

3 There are 49 gifts stacked up in four separate piles.
Let g be the number of gifts in the first pile.
The second pile has three fewer than the first pile.
The third pile has two more than the first pile.
The fourth pile has twice as many as the first pile.

  a Write down an expression to show how many gifts there are in each pile.

  b Write down and simplify an equation for the total number of gifts.

  c How many gifts are there in each pile?

4 The number in each box in the diagram is the sum of the two numbers above it.
But in this diagram you don't know all of the numbers.

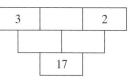

Call the number that is missing in the top row n.
You can then fill in the rest of the diagram.

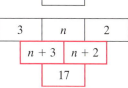

Now you can write an equation for the pink boxes.
Collect like terms and simplify the equation.
Now you can solve the equation.

$$n + 3 + n + 2 = 17$$
$$2n + 5 = 17$$
$$\therefore \quad 2n = 17 - 5$$
$$2n = 12$$
$$\therefore \quad n = \frac{12}{2}$$
$$n = 6$$

So the numbers in the boxes are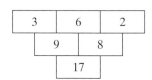

Use this method to find the missing numbers in each of these box diagrams.

  a 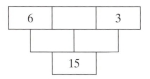   **c**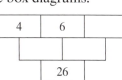

  b    **d**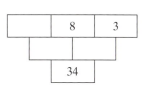

5 In the eighteenth century, Daniel **Fahrenheit** and Anders **Celsius** invented two different temperature scales. Both men lived at the same time but they never met. Celsius was born in 1701 in Sweden. Fahrenheit was born 15 years earlier in Germany.

Degrees Fahrenheit (F) and degrees Celsius (C) are connected by the formula:
$$F = 1.8C + 32$$

Write down an equation and solve it to find the value of C when

  a $F = 68$ **b** $F = 212$ **c** $F = {}^-40$.

9 Equations

Watch out ... there's a trap about

▶ When you solve an equation using inverse function machines, make sure you draw the inverse function machine diagram in the right order.

This is the function machine diagram for the equation $2n + 4 = 26$

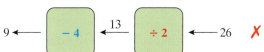

This is **not** the correct inverse function machine diagram:

The inverses must be done in the correct order. You must **subtract 4** before you **divide by 2**.

This is the correct inverse function machine diagram:

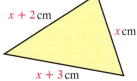

The solution of the equation $2n + 4 = 26$ is $n = 11$.

▶ When you set up and solve an equation don't forget to answer the question at the end.
The perimeter of this triangle is 26 cm.
You can write this equation for the perimeter.

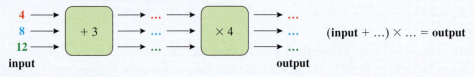

$x + 2 + x + 3 + x = 26$

When you simplify and solve the equation you get $x = 7$.

But this isn't the answer! You need to work out the lengths of the sides of the triangle.

$x + 2 = 7 + 2 = 9$ and $x + 3 = 7 + 3 = 10$

So the triangle has sides of length 7 cm, 9 cm and 10 cm.

Test yourself

1 Copy this function machine diagram and fill in the gaps.

```
4  →              →  ...  →        →  ...
8  →    + 3       →  ...  →  × 4   →  ...       (input + ...) × ... = output
12 →              →  ...  →        →  ...
input                                output
```

2 Copy each of these function machines and fill in the input numbers.

a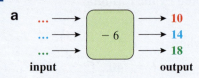

b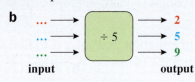

3 Copy each of these function machine diagrams and fill in the gaps.

a
```
...  →           → 10 →        → ...
...  →  × 5      → 25 →  + 2   → ...
...  →           → ... →        → 42
input                           output
```

b
```
...  →           → ... →        → 1
...  →  ÷ 3      → ... →  − 7   → 3
...  →           → ... →        → 23
input                           output
```

4 For each of these equations
(1) solve the equation using function machines
(2) check that your solution is correct using substitution.

a $3n + 9 = 42$ **b** $6n − 8 = 40$ **c** $\dfrac{n}{2} + 21 = 31$

5 Solve each of these equations algebraically. Show your working and check your answers.

a $6a − 4 = 32$ **b** $\dfrac{b}{4} + 13 = 17$ **c** $5c + 15 = 10$

6 Solve each of these equations. Show your working and check your answers.

a $55 = 7a + 6$ **b** $15 = \dfrac{b}{3} − 5$ **c** $1 = 3c + 10$

7 Use substitution to check the answer given for each equation.
Write **True** or **False** for each part.

a $4n − 12 = 20$ $n = 10$ **c** $\dfrac{n}{2} + 6 = 1$ $n = {}^-10$

b $3n + 8 = 4$ $n = {}^-4$ **d** $\dfrac{n}{3} − 4 = 14$ $n = 30$

8 For each part   (1) write down an equation
                      (2) solve your equation and find the value of n.

a I think of a number n, **multiply it by 4** and **subtract 12**. The answer is 24.

b I think of a number n, **divide it by 3** and **add 9**. The answer is 21.

9 The perimeter of this triangle is 32 cm.

a Write down an equation for the perimeter.
b Collect like terms and simplify the equation.
c Solve the equation to find the value of x.
d Write down the lengths of the sides of the triangle.

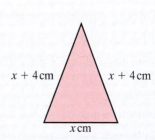

9 Equations

Chapter 9 Summary

Level 5

Drawing and using function machines

A function machine will perform the same operation on every number that you enter.
The number that you enter is called the **input**.
The number that you get out is called the **output**.

Using inverse operations

On this function machine you have the function and the **output** numbers but the **input** numbers are missing.

You need to use the **inverse** operation of the one on the screen.

The inverse of $+ 12$ is $- 12$.

The missing input numbers are **1**, **12**, **18**, and **29**.

Solving equations using function machines

You can use function machines to solve equations.

This is how you solve the equation $3n + 6 = 18$ using function machines.

The solution is $n = 4$.

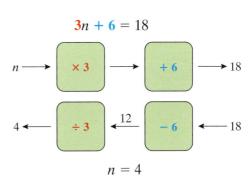

Level 6

Solving equations algebraically

You use the **inverse** operations in the opposite order.

$$7n + 12 = 47$$
$$7n + 12 - 12 = 47 - 12 \qquad \text{Take away 12 from both sides of the equation}$$
$$7n = 35$$
$$\frac{7n}{7} = \frac{35}{7} \qquad \text{Divide both sides of the equation by 7}$$
$$n = 5$$

Solving equations with the unknown on the right

If the unknown is on the right-hand side of the equation, write the equation the other way round first.
If you're asked to solve the equation $\qquad 47 = 2n - 1$
rewrite it as $\qquad 2n - 1 = 47$
and solve it in the usual way.

10 Angles – on the turn

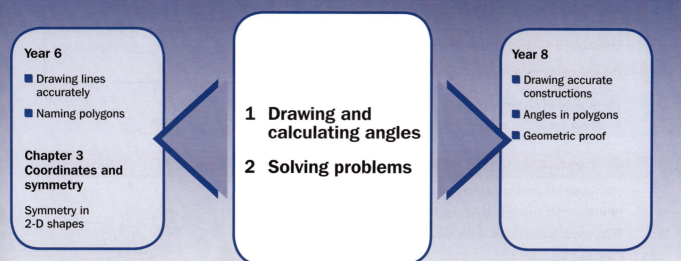

You should already know:

▶ how to measure and draw lines accurately

This line is **3.7** cm or **37** mm long.

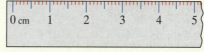

▶ how to read scales

There are **5 divisions** between 10 and 30.
The gap between 10 and 30 is 30 − 10 = 20.
So each division is worth 20 ÷ **5** = **4**.
There are **3 divisions** between the 10 and the arrow.
So the arrow is pointing to 10 + **3** × **4** = 22.

▶ the names of the different types of angles

Acute angles are **between 0° and 90°**

Obtuse angles are **between 90° and 180°**

Reflex angles are **between 180° and 360°**

There are 360° in a **full turn**
 180° in a **half turn** or **straight angle**
and 90° in a **right angle**.

10 Angles – on the turn

1 Drawing and calculating angles

- **Measuring and drawing angles**
- **Drawing triangles accurately**
- **Calculating angles**
- Finding angles between intersecting and parallel lines

Key words	
angle	degrees
protractor	angle measurer
vertically opposite	corresponding
alternate	

Measuring and drawing angles   Level 5

An **angle** measures an amount of turn.
You can call an angle by a single letter.
The red angle is angle A or Â.
You can also describe an angle using three letters.
The red angle is angle BAC, ∠BAC or BÂC.
If you follow the three letters in order, you draw out the angle.

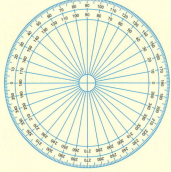

You measure angles in **degrees**
with a **protractor**
or an **angle measurer**.

You must use the scale that starts at 0°.

The turn from the red line to the blue line is 50°. You use the inside scale.

The turn from the red line to the blue line is 120°. You use the outside scale.

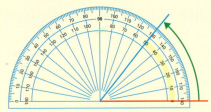

This is how to draw an angle of 50°.
Draw a starting line.

Place your protractor on one end like this.
Use the scale on the protractor that starts at 0°.
Here this is the inside scale.

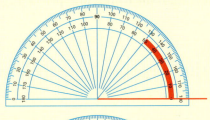

Go round the scale until you get to the angle you need.
Draw a dot on the edge of the protractor like this.

Take the protractor away and join up the angle.
Label the angle 50°.

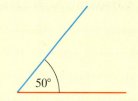

To draw a reflex angle you need to know that the angles at a point add up to 360°.
To draw an angle of 230° you need to work out 360° − 230° = 130°.
Draw an angle of 130° and then label the reflex angle 230°.

This is much easier if you have an angle measurer like this.

Draw a start line and go round from 0° to 230° on the scale that starts at 0°.

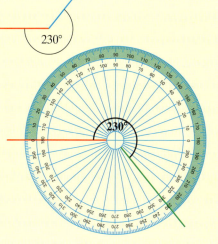

Exercise 10:1

1 Write down the three letters that describe each coloured angle.

a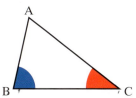

b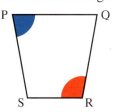

c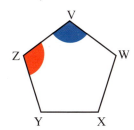

2 Look at the diagram.
Write down the letters that describe
  a an angle of 88°
  b an angle of 139°
  c an angle of 228°.

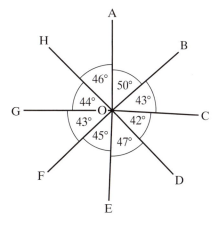

10 Angles – on the turn

3 Measure and write down the size of each angle.

a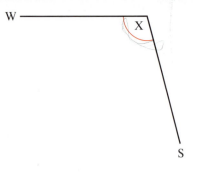

c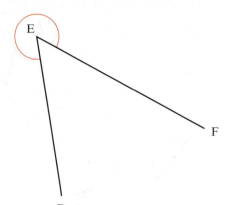

b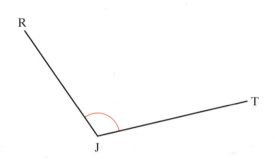

d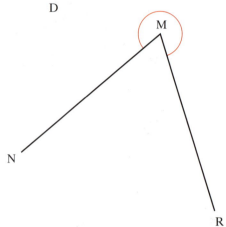

4 Measure and write down the size of ∠BCD in each shape.

a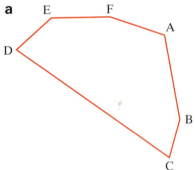

b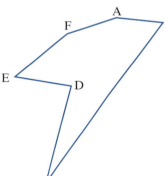

c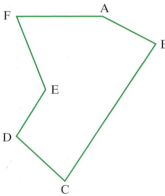

5 The diagram shows a circle centre O. Estimate and write down the size of

  a the acute angle
  b a reflex angle.

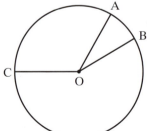

6 Make an accurate drawing of each angle. Remember to label the angle.

  a ∠AOB = 80°   c ∠GOH = 19°   e ∠NOP = 220°   g ∠VOW = 237°
  b ∠COD = 115°   d ∠KOL = 172°   f ∠ROS = 260°   h ∠XOZ = 348°

Drawing triangles accurately　　　　　　　　　　　　　　　　Level 5

Look at this triangle.

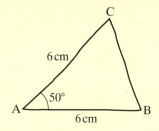

You can draw this triangle accurately like this

Draw side AB, 6 cm long.
Measure and mark the 50° angle at A.
Draw AC so that it is 6 cm long.
Mark the position of C.
Join B to C and label the triangle.

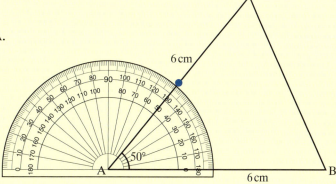

Now look at this triangle.

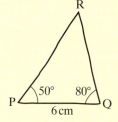

You can draw this triangle accurately like this:

Draw PQ 6 cm long.
Measure and mark the angles at P and Q.
Draw the angles at P and Q and extend
the lines until they cross.
Label this point R.

When you have drawn a triangle accurately,
you can **measure** any missing sides and missing angles.

157

10 Angles – on the turn

Exercise 10:2

1 Draw each of these triangles accurately.

a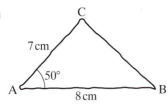
c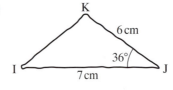
e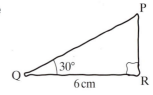

b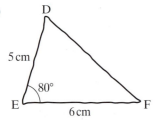
d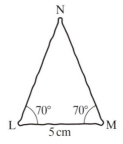
f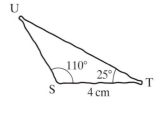

2 For each part (1) sketch triangle ABC showing the information you're given
(2) draw triangle ABC accurately
(3) measure the size of angle C in your triangle.

a AB = 8 cm, AC = 7 cm, angle A = 65°
b AB = 5 cm, AC = 6 cm, angle A = 45°
c AB = 6 cm, AC = 5.5 cm, angle A = 100°
d AB = 3 cm, angle A = 35° and angle B = 55°
e AB = 9 cm, angle A = 45° and angle B = 65°
f AB = 7 cm, angle A = 52° and angle B = 114°

3 a Draw each of these shapes accurately.

(1)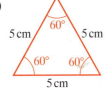
equilateral triangle

(2)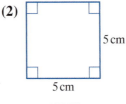
square

(3)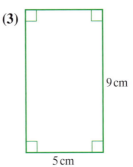
rectangle

(4)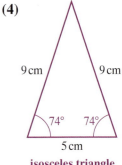
isosceles triangle

b This is a sketch of a net of a tetrahedron.
It is made using four of the **equilateral triangles** from part **a**.
Draw the net accurately.

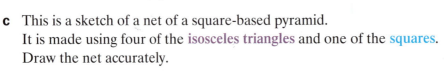

c This is a sketch of a net of a square-based pyramid.
It is made using four of the **isosceles triangles** and one of the **squares**.
Draw the net accurately.

d This is a sketch of a net of a triangular prism.
It is made using two of the **equilateral triangles** and three of the **rectangles**.
Draw the net accurately.

Calculating angles

Level 5

Angles in a triangle add up to 180°

In triangle ABC
$70° + 20° + 90° = 180°$

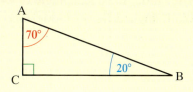

You can use this fact to work out missing angles.

In this triangle
$73° + 46° + a° = 180°$
$119° + a° = 180°$
$a° = 180° − 119°$
$a° = 61°$

In this isosceles triangle
$x° + x° + 65° = 180°$
$2x° + 65° = 180°$
$2x° = 115°$
$x° = 57.5°$

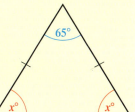

Angles on a line add up to 180°

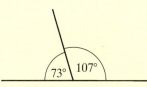

Angles at a point add up to 360°

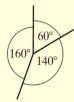

You can use these facts to work out missing angles.

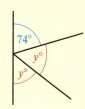

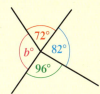

$y° + y° + 74° = 180°$
$2y° = 106°$
$y° = 53°$

$b° + 72° + 82° + 96° = 360°$
$b° + 250° = 360°$
$b° = 360° − 250°$
$b° = 110°$

Exercise 10:3

1 Work out the size of each angle marked with a letter.

a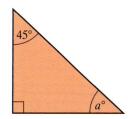

b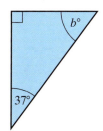

c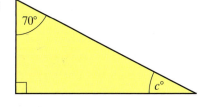

2 Angie said, 'It is possible to have two right angles in a triangle.'
Is she right? Explain your answer.

10 Angles – on the turn

3 Josh leans a ladder against a vertical wall.
The ladder makes an angle of 74° with the horizontal ground.
What angle does the ladder make with the wall?

4 Look at these isosceles triangles.
Work out the size of each angle marked with a letter.

a
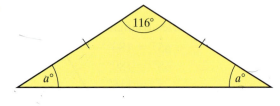

c
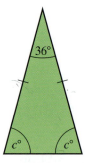

b
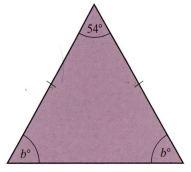

d

5 One of the angles in an isosceles triangle is 54°.
What sizes can the other angles be?
Explain your answers using diagrams.

6 Work out the size of each angle marked with a letter.

a
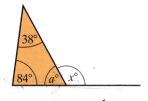

d
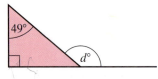

b
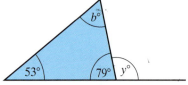

e
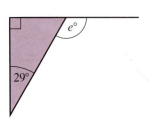

c
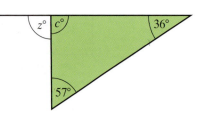

f
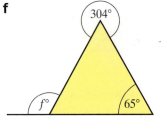

7 Work out the size of each angle marked with a letter.

a 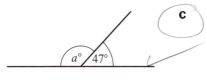   c 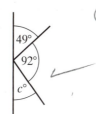   e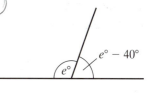

b 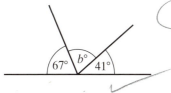   d   f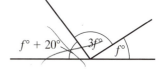

8 Work out the size of each angle marked with a letter.

a 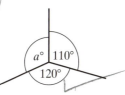   c 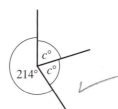   e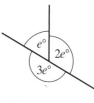

b 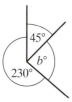   d 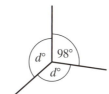   f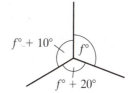

Think on!

9 Copy the diagrams.
Put one of the digits 0, 1, 2, 3, 4, 5, 6, 7, 8 and 9 in each space to make the angles correct. You can only use each digit once. You should not measure the angles.

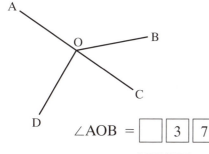

∠AOB = ☐ 3 7
∠BOC = ☐☐
∠DOA = ☐☐

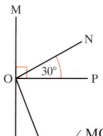

∠MOQ = 1 ☐ 3
∠MON = ☐☐
∠ROQ = ☐☐

10 Angles – on the turn

Finding angles between intersecting and parallel lines   Level 6

Where two lines intersect you get two pairs of equal angles.

The angles opposite each other are equal.
They are called **vertically opposite** angles.

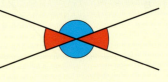

When a line crosses a pair of parallel lines you get lots of equal angles.

Angles in the same place at the two crossing points are called **corresponding angles**.

The two orange angles are equal.
They are on alternate sides of the sloping line.
They are called **alternate angles**.
The two purple angles are also alternate angles and are equal.

You can use these facts to find all the angles in a parallel line diagram.

$a° = 45°$ (vertically opposite angles)
$b° = 135°$ (on a straight line with $a°$ or $45°$)
$c° = 135°$ (vertically opposite to $b°$)
$d° = 45°$ (corresponding to $45°$ or alternate to $a°$)
$e° = 135°$ (corresponding to $b°$ or alternate to $c°$)
$f° = 135°$ (vertically opposite to $e°$)
$g° = 45°$ (vertically opposite to $d°$)

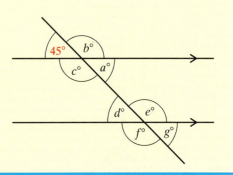

Exercise 10:4

1 Work out the size of each angle marked with a letter.

a
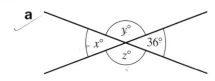

b
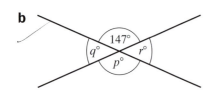

c
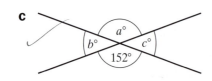

d
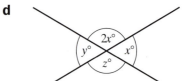

e
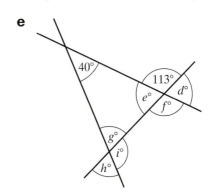

2 Work out the size of each angle marked with a letter.
For each answer, write down the rule you have used to get it.

a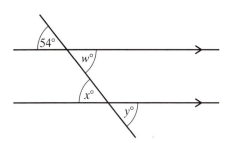

d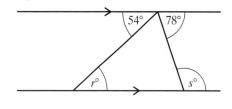

b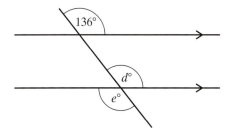

e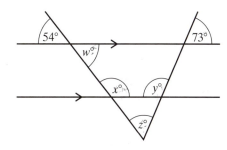

c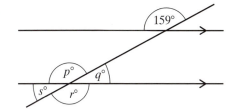

⚠ f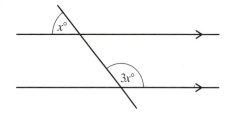

3 Write down lists of all the angles that are equal to each other in this diagram.

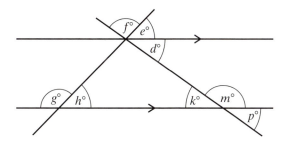

4 Cables run from the top of two towers to the foot of the opposite towers as shown.
Work out the size of each angle marked with a letter.

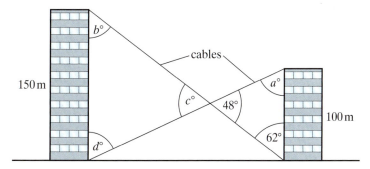

10 Angles – on the turn

2 Solving problems

- **Calculating angles in quadrilaterals**
- **Using angles and symmetry to solve problems**

Key words	
quadrilateral	square
rectangle	rhombus
parallelogram	kite
arrowhead	trapezium
reflex	geometrical

Calculating angles in quadrilaterals — Level 6

A **quadrilateral** can always be made from two triangles.

You know that the angles in a triangle add up to 180°.
The red angles add up to **180°**.
The blue angles add up to **180°**.
So the angles inside the quadrilateral add up to **360°**.

A **square** has four equal angles of 90°.   A **rectangle** has four equal angles of 90°.

    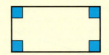

A **rhombus** has two pairs of equal angles.   A **parallelogram** has two pairs of equal angles.

A **kite** has one pair of equal angles.   An **arrowhead** has one pair of equal angles.

    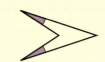

A **trapezium** may have two pairs of equal angles, one pair of equal right angles or no equal angles.

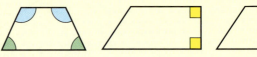

Exercise 10:5

1 Work out the size of each angle marked with a letter.

a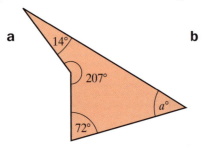

b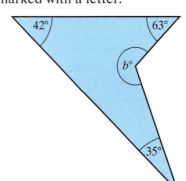

c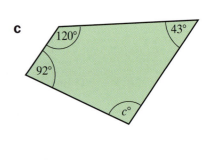

2 Work out the value of each angle marked with a letter.

a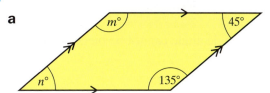

b

d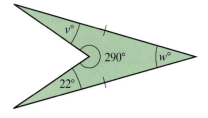

c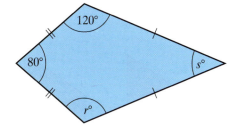

e

f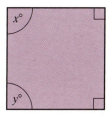

3 This drawing shows how two shapes fit together to make a **right-angled** triangle.
Work out each of the angles in shape B.

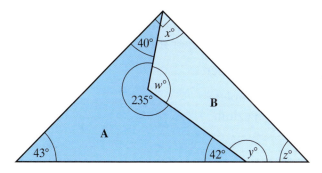

4 The diagram shows two overlapping identical rectangles.
Find the values of p and q.
Show all of your working out and give reasons for your answers.

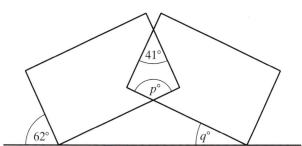

10 Angles – on the turn

> **Using angles and symmetry to solve problems** Level 6
>
> A triangle can never have a **reflex** angle inside it.
> The three angles inside a triangle add up to 180°, so a single angle cannot be bigger than 180°.
>
> A quadrilateral can contain a reflex angle.
> This is because the angles inside a quadrilateral add up to 360°.
> So you can have one angle that's bigger than 180°.
> The other three angles will make up the 360° total.
>
>
>
> You can use your knowledge of angles and symmetry
> to explain why many **geometrical** facts are true.

Exercise 10:6

1 Adam is placing these trapezia together.
Which two shapes should he combine to form a rectangle?
Explain your answer.

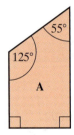 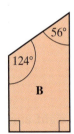 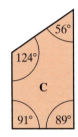 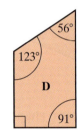 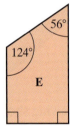

2 **You will need dotty isometric paper for this question.**
Four congruent trapezia join to make a bigger trapezium.

  a Copy this shape onto isometric paper.

  b Draw two more trapezia to complete
  the drawing of the bigger trapezium.

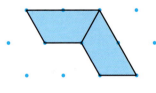

Four congruent trapezia join to make a parallelogram.

  c Copy this shape onto isometric paper.

  d Draw two more trapezia to complete
  the drawing of the parallelogram.

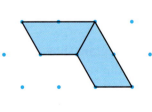

3 Write **True** or **False** for each sentence.
Explain your answers.

  a A triangle can have a reflex angle.

  b A square is the only quadrilateral with four equal angles.

  c An arrowhead is the only quadrilateral with one line of symmetry.

166

4 (1) Use the clues to sketch each shape.
(2) Name the shape you have sketched.

a It has three sides.
It has only one line of symmetry.

b It is a quadrilateral with no lines of symmetry.
Opposite angles are equal.
It has two pairs of equal sides.

c It has four equal sides.
Opposite angles are equal.
It has four lines of symmetry.

d It has one line of symmetry.
It has one pair of equal angles.
It has two pairs of equal sides.

5 Put each quadrilateral through this classification diagram.

Where does each shape come out?

a Kite
b Rhombus
c Rectangle
d Parallelogram
e Arrowhead

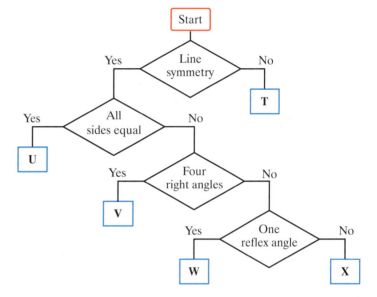

6 A square has 4 equal sides, 4 equal angles and 4 lines of symmetry.
A rectangle has opposite sides that are equal, 4 equal angles and 2 lines of symmetry.
Jessica said, 'A square is a special type of rectangle.'
Is she correct? Explain your answer.

Think on!

7 Write down the names of
a five shapes with at least one pair of parallel sides
b four shapes with two pairs of equal sides
c three shapes with exactly one line of symmetry
d two shapes with four equal sides
e one shape with a reflex angle.

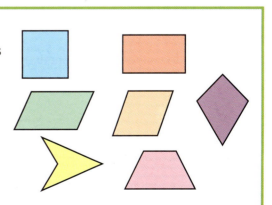

10 Angles – on the turn

Watch out ... there's a trap about

▶ Make sure you measure and draw angles using the scale that starts at 0°.

Some people might say that this angle is 50°.
They have just looked at the **50°** on the inside scale.

But this angle cannot be 50° as it is obtuse.

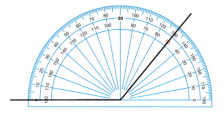

This angle is **130°**.
You must read round the outside scale here.

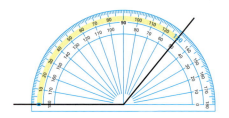

▶ Many people think that a kite has
two pairs of equal angles.
They think that the angles at the **top**
and the **bottom** have to be equal.

But the **red angles**
are the only equal angles.

If you split the kite into two isosceles triangles
the dividing line doesn't bisect the equal angles.
This means that the two parts of the angles aren't equal.
Without being given some more information
you can't work out the values of the other angles.

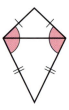

Test yourself

1 In the triangle

    a write down the three letters that describe the obtuse angle

    b measure and write down the size of angle BCA.

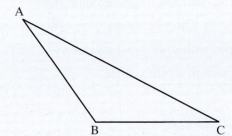

2 Work out the size of each angle marked with a letter.

a 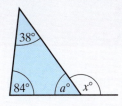 b 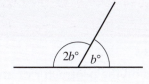 c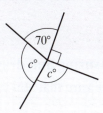

3 Work out the size of each angle marked with a letter.

a 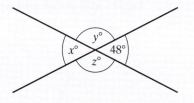 b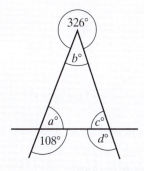

4 Work out the size of each angle marked with a letter.

a 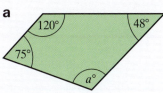 b 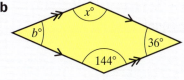 c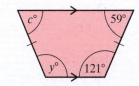

5 Copy this table.
Sort each shape into the table.
square
rectangle
rhombus
parallelogram

	Four right angles	No right angles
Four equal sides		
Two pairs of equal sides		

6 Jenny was asked to draw some shapes and show their lines of symmetry.
This is what she drew.

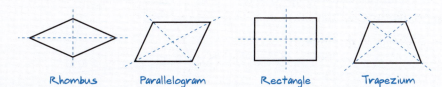

a Explain which of the blue lines Jenny has drawn are **not** lines of symmetry.

b Does a trapezium always have two pairs of equal angles? Explain your answer.

c List all the quadrilaterals that have only one pair of equal angles.

10 Angles – on the turn

Chapter 10 Summary

Level 5

Measuring and drawing angles
Make sure that you use the scale on the protractor or angle measurer that starts from 0°.

Calculating angles

Angles in a triangle add up to 180°

$64° + 56° + a° = 180°$
$120° + a° = 180°$
$a° = 180° - 120°$
$a° = 60°$

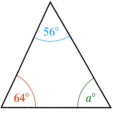

Angles at a point add up to 360°

$c° + 85° + 63° + 121° = 360°$
$c° + 269° = 360°$
$c° = 91°$

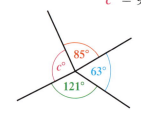

Angles on a line add up to 180°

$74° + 36° + b° = 180°$
$110° + b° = 180°$
$b° = 70°$

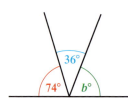

Level 6

Angles between intersecting and parallel lines
The coloured angles in each of these diagrams are equal.

vertically opposite angles   corresponding angles   alternate angles

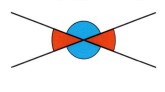  
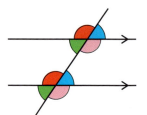 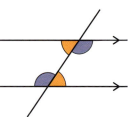

Angles in quadrilaterals
The angles in a quadrilateral add up to 360°

$73° + 116° + 98° + a° = 360°$
$287° + a° = 360°$
$a° = 360° - 287°$
$a° = 73°$

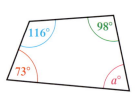

Using angles and symmetry to solve problems
You can explain why **geometrical** facts are true using facts about angles and symmetry.

11 The best chapter, probably

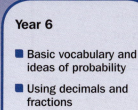

Year 6
- Basic vocabulary and ideas of probability
- Using decimals and fractions

1. Describing probabilities
2. Finding probabilities
3. Probability experiments

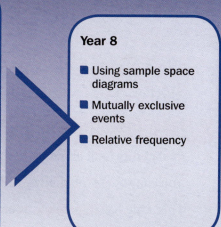

Year 8
- Using sample space diagrams
- Mutually exclusive events
- Relative frequency

You should already know:

▶ **these words to describe probability**

fair, unfair, likely, unlikely, likelihood
certain, uncertain
probable, possible, impossible
chance, good chance, poor chance, no chance
risk, doubt
equal chance, even chance, fifty-fifty chance
equally likely

▶ **how to use the above words when describing how likely something is to happen**

There is a **good chance** that I will watch TV tonight.
It is **possible** that it will snow next Christmas.
It is **probable** that I will go to the cinema this month.
It is **certain** that it will get dark tonight.
It is **impossible** that I will see Queen Victoria on my way home from school tonight.

▶ **about single fractions and decimals**

$\frac{1}{2} = 0.5 \quad \frac{1}{4} = 0.25 \quad \frac{3}{4} = 0.75$

$\frac{1}{5} = 0.2 \quad \frac{2}{5} = 0.4 \quad \frac{3}{5} = 0.6 \quad \frac{4}{5} = 0.8$

$\frac{1}{10} = 0.1 \quad \frac{3}{10} = 0.3 \quad \frac{7}{10} = 0.7 \quad \frac{5}{10} = 0.5$

11 The best chapter, probably

1 Describing probabilities

- Using probability scales
- Using numbers to describe probabilities

Key words

probability	probability scale
impossible	certain
even chance	very unlikely
unlikely	likely
very likely	event
estimate	

Using probability scales   Level 5

Probability is all about working out how likely something is to happen.

You can show probability words on a **probability scale**.

This scale has Impossible at one end and Certain at the other. Even chance is in the middle.

Impossible — Very unlikely — Unlikely — Even chance — Likely — Very likely — Certain

Things that happen in probability questions are called **events**.

You can mark the probabilities of events on a probability scale.

Impossible — Very unlikely — Unlikely — Even chance — Likely — Very likely — Certain

↑ It will snow in the UK in July   ↑ A baby being born will be a boy   ↑ More than half of a class will be right-handed

Exercise 11:1

1 a Copy this probability scale.

Impossible — Very unlikely — Unlikely — Even chance — Likely — Very likely — Certain

b Label your scale with numbered arrows to show the probabilities of these events.
   (1) You will have to do some homework today.
   (2) It will rain during the next week.
   (3) A coin thrown in the air will land on its edge.
   (4) You will get a phone call today.
   (5) A piece of toast will land butter side down if it is dropped.
   (6) A word chosen at random from this book will contain the letter *e*.

2 Copy this probability scale and label it with your own descriptions of probabilities.

...   .

3 a Copy this probability scale.

Impossible — Even chance — Certain

b Label your scale with numbered arrows to show the probabilities of these events.
  (1) You will eat some chocolate today.
  (2) You will take part in some sporting activity today.
  (3) A pupil chosen at random from your class owns a mobile phone.
  (4) A volcano will erupt in the UK this year.
  (5) A volcano will erupt somewhere in the world this week.

Using numbers to describe probabilities — Level 5

The probability of something that is **impossible** is **0**.

The probability of something that is **certain** is **1**.

All other probabilities are between 0 and 1.

The probability of an event with **even chance** is $\frac{1}{2}$

You can use fractions, decimals or percentages to write probabilities.
Here is a probability scale marked using fractions.

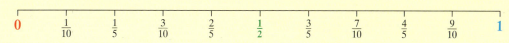

You can work out probabilities or **estimate** them.

This fair spinner has **5** equal sections in different colours.
The probability of the spinner landing on yellow is $\frac{1}{5}$

A coin has **2** outcomes: Heads and Tails.
The probability of it landing on Heads is $\frac{1}{2}$

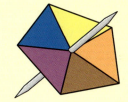

The probability that it will snow in the UK in February is very likely.

You can look back at the weather records and estimate the probability that it will snow in February.

Suppose it has snowed in the UK in February in **9** of the last **10** years.
Then you can estimate the probability that it will snow next February as $\frac{9}{10}$

You can show these probabilities on the probability scale.

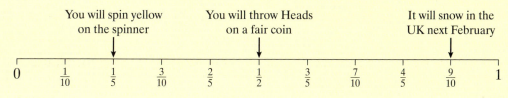

11 The best chapter, probably

Exercise 11:2

1 a Copy this probability scale.

```
|----|----|----|----|----|----|----|----|----|----|----|
0   1/10  1/5  3/10  2/5  1/2  3/5  7/10  4/5  9/10   1
```

b Label your scale with numbered arrows to show the probabilities of these events. You can calculate some of the answers but you will have to estimate others.

(1) You will get an even number when you roll an ordinary dice.
(2) A person chosen at random from your class will be a girl.
(3) A person chosen at random from your class will have blonde hair.
(4) You will listen to some music today.
(5) A counter chosen from these counters will be red.
(6) It will snow next Christmas if it has snowed once in the last 10 years.

2 These yoghurts are sold in packs of 10.
There are 4 strawberry, 3 raspberry,
2 orange and 1 lemon flavoured.

a Copy this probability scale.

```
|----|----|----|----|----|----|----|----|----|----|----|
0   0.1  0.2  0.3  0.4  0.5  0.6  0.7  0.8  0.9   1
```

b Trish chooses a yoghurt at random.
Label your scale with numbered arrows to show the probabilities of these events.

(1) Trish gets a strawberry yoghurt.
(2) Trish gets a lemon yoghurt.
(3) Trish doesn't get an orange yoghurt.
(4) Trish gets a raspberry or an orange yoghurt.

Think on!

3 Matthew has a spinner. He doesn't let Katie see it.
He spins the spinner six times and records the results.
He tells Katie that he got Red twice, Blue twice and Green twice.
Katie says that he must have a spinner that looks like this.

Do you agree with Katie? Explain your answer.

4 Matthew and Katie go to a party.
There are three types of sandwiches: ham, cheese and egg.
Katie says that because there are three types of sandwich, the probability that Matthew will choose a ham sandwich is $\frac{1}{3}$.

Is she right? Explain your answer.

2 Finding probabilities

▶ **Finding simple probabilities**

▶ Using the fact that probabilities add up to 1

▶ Drawing and using sample space diagrams

Key words

equally likely
random
outcome
sample space diagram

▶ Finding simple probabilities   Level 5

Sometimes, events are **equally likely** to happen.
When this happens you can always calculate probabilities.

When you roll a dice, all of the numbers are equally likely to happen.

If you throw this fair dice, you have a $\frac{1}{6}$ chance of getting each number.

The probability of throwing an even number is $\frac{3}{6} = \frac{1}{2}$

This is because there are **6** numbers on the dice and **3** of the numbers are even.

Not all events are equally likely.

Andy is in a PE lesson.
He is given a choice of playing football, tennis or hockey.

Although there are **3** choices, the probability that he
will choose each sport is not $\frac{1}{3}$. The events are not equally likely.

Andy likes football much more than any other sport.
The probability that he will choose football is about $\frac{99}{100}$!

Exercise 11:3

1 300 tickets were sold for a school raffle.

   a James bought one ticket. What is the probability that James will win first prize?

   b Eddie bought seven tickets. What is the probability that Eddie will win first prize?

   c Gina didn't buy any tickets. What is the probability that Gina will win first prize?

2 This ordinary fair dice is rolled once.
Write down the probability of rolling

   a a 5

   b an odd number

   c a score less than 3

   d a prime number.

11 The best chapter, probably

3 One letter is chosen at random from the word ISOSCELES.
Write down the probability of choosing

   a the letter C   b the letter S   c the letter E   d the letter T.

4 a Jo has these **4 coins**.
Jo is going to take one of these coins at random.
Each coin is equally likely to be the one she takes.
Show that the **probability** that it will be a **10p** coin is $\frac{1}{2}$.

  b Colin has **4 coins** that total **33p**.
He is going to take one of his coins at random.
What is the probability that it will be a **10p** coin?
You **must** show your working.

5 Eight counters are placed in a bag.
There are 3 red, 2 blue, 2 green and 1 yellow counter.
One counter is picked out at random.
Write down the probability that the counter is

   a red   e blue or green
   b yellow   f not blue
   c orange   g yellow or green
   d not green   h not blue or red.

6 A spinner has six equal sections each with a number.
The probability of spinning an even number is $\frac{2}{3}$.
The probability of scoring a 4 is $\frac{1}{3}$.
Write down the numbers that could be on the spinner.

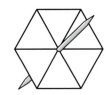

7 The National Lottery uses coloured balls numbered 1 to 49.
Balls 1 to 9 are white, 10 to 19 are blue, 20 to 29 are pink,
30 to 39 are green and 40 to 49 are yellow.

Write down the probability that the first ball drawn will be

   a white   e an even number
   b green   f an odd number
   c blue or green   g a prime number
   d not yellow   h not a square number.

8 A school sells 300 green, 200 blue and 150 red raffle tickets.

   a Explain why there isn't an equal chance of each colour winning.
   b Work out the probability of each colour winning.

9 Katy, Jane and Richard are playing a game. They each have a bag of counters.
The winner is the first player to pick a red counter out of the bag.

Jane says they all have an equal chance of winning because they all have red and blue counters in their bags.

Richard says that he has a better chance of winning than Katy because he has the most red counters.

Katy says that they should all have the same number of red and blue counters as each other to make the game fair.

a Who is correct? Explain your answer.

b How would **you** make the game fair?

10 Gordon and Alistair are playing a card game.
They shuffle these 10 cards and put them face down in a row on the table in front of them.

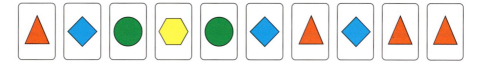

Gordon turns over the first card. It is a blue diamond.

Alistair has to guess what the next card will be.

a What is the next card most likely to be? Explain your answer.

b What is the next card least likely to be? Explain your answer.

The next card turns out to be the yellow hexagon.

Gordon has to guess what the next card will be.

c What is the probability that the next card will be a yellow hexagon? Explain your answer.

d What is the next card most likely to be? Explain your answer.

Later in the game the cards look like this.

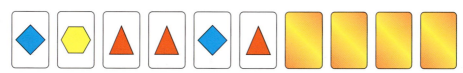

e What is the next card most likely to be? Explain your answer.

11 The best chapter, probably

> **Using the fact that probabilities add up to 1** Level 6
>
> There are 52 cards in an ordinary pack of playing cards.
> There are four suits with 13 cards in each suit.
> The suits are: clubs   ♣   hearts   ♥
>   diamonds   ♦   spades   ♠
>
> Each suit of cards has an Ace, 2, 3, 4, 5, 6, 7, 8, 9 and 10.
> Each suit also has three picture cards: **Jack**, **Queen** and **King**.
>
> If you pick one card at **random** from a pack,
> the probability that you will get a King is $\frac{4}{52} = \frac{1}{13}$
>
> You should cancel a fractional probability answer to its simplest form.
>
> The probability that the card will **not** be a King is $1 - \frac{1}{13} = \frac{12}{13}$
>
> This is because the events 'getting a King' and 'not getting a King' include all possibilities.
> So the probabilities of these events must add up to 1.
>
> The probability that something doesn't happen $= 1 -$ the probability that it does happen

Exercise 11:4

1 Fran chooses one card at random from an ordinary pack of cards.
Write down the probability that she

   a gets a heart   **f** doesn't get a club
   b gets a spade   **g** doesn't get a black card
   c gets a red card   **h** doesn't get an Ace
   d gets a 3   **i** gets a card worth at least 5
   e gets a picture card   **j** doesn't get a card worth more than 4.

2 Some games are played with a pack of cards that contains two extra cards called Jokers.
They don't count as being red or black and they don't count as picture cards.
Dale is playing a game with such a pack of cards.
Write down the probability that she

   a gets a Joker   **f** doesn't get a diamond
   b gets a club   **g** doesn't get a red card
   c gets a black card   **h** doesn't get a picture card
   d gets an Ace   **i** doesn't get a Joker
   e gets a picture card   **j** doesn't get a numbered card.

3 The weather forecast says that the chance of rain tomorrow is 65%.
What is the probability that it will not rain tomorrow?

4 The probability that Matthew's bus arrives on time is 0.64
The probability that his bus is late is 0.11
What is the probability that Matthew's bus will be early?

5 Ten coloured counters are placed in a bag.
There are 4 red, 3 blue, 2 green and 1 yellow counter.
One counter is taken from the bag at random.
Write down the probability of getting a counter that is

- **a** blue
- **b** yellow
- **c** purple
- **d** blue or red
- **e** not blue
- **f** not yellow
- **g** not purple
- **h** neither blue nor red
- **i** red, blue or green.

Drawing and using sample space diagrams   Level 6

When two events happen, you often need to list all the possible **outcomes**.
If you throw two coins in the air and look at how they land, there are four different outcomes that can happen.

There are four possible outcomes.
  Head, Head
  Head, Tail
  Tail, Head
  Tail, Tail

You can show these outcomes in a table.
This is called a **sample space diagram**.
There are four equally likely outcomes.
The probability of each outcome is $\frac{1}{4}$.

		Head	Tail
	Head	Head, Head	Head, Tail
	Tail	Tail, Head	Tail, Tail

Exercise 11:5

1 Sian throws an ordinary dice and a coin at the same time.
Copy and complete this sample space diagram to show all the possible outcomes.

		Dice					
		1	2	3	4	5	6
Coin	H		H, 2				
	T					T, 5	

11 The best chapter, probably

2 Steve spins both of these spinners and adds the two scores together.

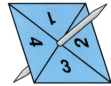

a Copy and fill in this sample space diagram to show the possible outcomes.

		Blue spinner			
		1	2	3	4
Red spinner	1	2			
	2				6
	3				

b How many possible outcomes are there?

c What is the probability of scoring more than 5?

3 Alison spins this spinner twice and adds the scores together.

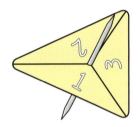

a Draw a sample space diagram to show all the possible outcomes.

b What is the probability that Alison's score will be
  (1) 3
  (2) at least 3
  (3) 7
  (4) less than 7
  (5) an odd number
  (6) a prime number.

Facts to figure

4 It was gambling on games of chance that led to the discovery of most probability theory. There was a dispute in 1654 that led to the creation of much of the modern theory of probability by two famous French mathematicians, Blaise Pascal and Pierre de Fermat.

There was a popular dice game which involved throwing a pair of dice 24 times. The widely-held belief was that it was a good bet that you would score at least one double six during your throws. You would bet an amount of money and if you did roll a double six you would win the same amount. Otherwise you lost your money. People thought that if you played this game for a while you would win overall.

However, a French nobleman, Antoine Gombaud, noticed that he kept losing, so he wrote to Pascal to ask him if he could explain why. He told Pascal that he thought that the game wasn't a good bet. Pascal wrote back to him and explained that he was right. You won't win overall if you keep on playing the game.

a Draw a sample space diagram to show the possible scores when you roll two dice.
You should have entries like 1, 1 in your table and not total scores.

b Write down the probability of scoring a double six when you roll two dice.

3 Probability experiments

> Doing probability experiments

Key words
probability   record
frequency table bias
simulation   random

> Doing probability experiments   Level 5

You are going to do some **probability** experiments in this section. Follow the instructions.
Record the results for each experiment and answer the questions as you go along.

Exercise 11:6

Experiment 1 – Guess the combination

This is for you to do in pairs.
You need some coloured counters and an envelope.
One person is the picker and the other is the guesser.
The picker puts five coloured counters into the envelope.
There should be two different colours of counters.
Make sure that the guesser doesn't know how many
counters of each colour are in the envelope.

The picker tells the guesser the two colours.
The guesser draws a **frequency table** like this and fills in the two colours in the first column.

Colour	Tally	Frequency

The picker takes a counter out of the envelope, shows it to the guesser and puts it back into the envelope.
The guesser tallies the counter in the table.
Repeat this 50 times.

Then the guesser writes down how many counters of each colour he or she thinks are in the envelope.
The picker tells the guesser if he or she is right!
Swap over and be the guesser a few times each.

Experiment 2 – Throwing a six

This is for you to do on your own. You need an ordinary dice.
Write down how many throws you will need on average before you get a six.

Now throw the dice until you get a six. Count the number of throws it takes each time.
Repeat this 20 times and record your results.

Find the mean number of throws you took to get a six.
Does this match what you expected? Explain your answer.

11 The best chapter, probably

Experiment 3 – That's odd

This is for you to do in pairs. You need two ordinary dice.

You take it in turns to throw the two dice.

You can only score points on your own throws.

Player 1 is 'Evens' and Player 2 is 'Odds'.

Player 1 throws the dice and multiplies the two numbers together.

If the product is Even then Player 1 scores 1 point.
If the product is Odd then Player 1 doesn't score a point.

Player 2 now throws the dice and multiplies the two numbers together.

If the product is Odd then Player 2 scores 1 point.
If the product is Even then Player 2 doesn't score a point.

The first player to get to 10 points is the winner.

Play the game several times.

Do you think the game is fair? Explain your answer.
If you think the game is unfair, suggest how to change the scoring system to make it fair.

Experiment 4 – Spot the bias

Copy this net of a dice with flaps onto thin card. Draw all the sides 3 cm long. Then cut it out.

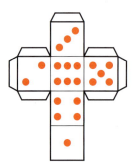

Before you glue the net together, tape a small piece of Blu-Tack® onto the inside of one of the faces. Write down the face that you have chosen in the back of your exercise book.

Put your name on the outside of your dice so you know it's yours.

Your dice is now **biased**. This means that it is not fair. Swap dice with someone else.

Do an experiment to find out which face of the dice you now have is biased.
You need to record your results carefully.

Write down which face you think the Blu-Tack® is stuck on.
Check with the owner of the dice if you've got it right.

Experiment 5 – Production line simulation

Dave works on a factory production line that makes chocolate bars.

The machinery on the production line is very old.

The probability that the bar is damaged when it comes out of the mould is $\frac{1}{20}$

The probability of the wrapper not being in the right place on the bar is $\frac{1}{6}$

Without wasting lots of chocolate, Dave wants to work out how many bars are usually made before something goes wrong. He needs to use a **simulation**. This is a probability experiment that he can use to model the problem.

a Design an experiment to simulate the chocolate mould problem.

You need a way of creating a **random** event with a probability of $\frac{1}{20}$

When this event happens, it simulates the chocolates being damaged when it comes out of the mould.

b Design an experiment to simulate the chocolate wrapper problem.

You need a way of creating a random event with a probability of $\frac{1}{6}$

Each time this event happens, it is simulating the chocolate wrapper being in the wrong place.

c Think about how to record your results.

For each chocolate bar being produced you need to be able to record if it is damaged when it comes out of the mould and also if the wrapper is in the right place.

d Design a table to record how many bars you produce before something goes wrong.

e Perform your experiment at least 20 times. You may want to work in a group for this part.

f Work out the mean number of bars produced before something goes wrong.

g Compare your results with other members of your class.

You could calculate an overall mean.

11 The best chapter, probably

Watch out... there's a trap about

▶ The probability of getting yellow when you spin this spinner is $\frac{1}{5}$

This is because there are **5** equal sections and **1** of them is yellow.

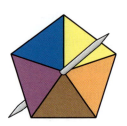

You will often hear people saying that there is a '**one** in **five**' chance of spinning a yellow.
You mustn't write your answers to probabilities like this.

You must give a probability answer as a fraction, a decimal or a percentage.

The probability of getting yellow on this spinner is $\frac{1}{5}$, 0.2 or 20%.

Test yourself

1 a Copy this probability scale.

b Label your scale with numbered arrows to show the probabilities of these events.
  (1) You will go home today.
  (2) You will eat some chips tonight.
  (3) You will one day be Prime Minister.

2 a Copy this probability scale.

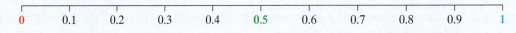

b Label your scale with numbered arrows to show the probabilities of these events.
  (1) You will get an odd number when you roll an ordinary dice.
  (2) A person chosen at random from your class wears glasses.
  (3) You will pick a red counter from a bag containing 2 red and 3 blue counters.

3 A family bag of crisps contains 4 plain, 3 salt and vinegar and 3 cheese and onion flavour packs.
Mark chooses a bag at random.
Write down the probability that Mark chooses a pack of

  a salt and vinegar crisps
  b plain or cheese and onion crisps
  c crisps that are not plain
  d prawn cocktail crisps.

4 Pardeep has these eight cards.

He shuffles them and puts them face down on the table in a row in front of him.

Pardeep turns over the first card. This is the card that he sees.

a What is the probability that the next card will match this one?

The next card that Pardeep turns over is, in fact, this one.

b What is the probability that the next card he turns over will not match either of the first two cards?

5 Hannah has the following cards.

| 6 | 13 | 8 | 14 | 5 | 17 | 2 | 19 | 9 | 7 | 8 | 11 |

She puts the cards in a bag and pulls one card out at random.

Write down the probability that Hannah pulls out a card

a with a 2
b with an 8
c with an even number
d with an odd number
e with a prime number
f with a square number
g that doesn't have an odd number
h that doesn't have a prime number
i that doesn't show a square number.

6 The weather forecaster says that the chance of it snowing tomorrow is 45%.
What is the probability that it will not snow tomorrow?

7 Gareth throws a coin and spins this spinner.

a Copy and complete this sample space diagram to show the possible outcomes.

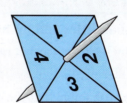

		Spinner			
		1	2	3	4
Coin	H				
	T				

b How many possible outcomes are there?

c What is the probability of getting a Head and an odd number?

11 The best chapter, probably

Chapter 11 Summary

Level 5

Probability scales

You can mark the probability of events on a probability scale.
The probability of something that is **impossible** is **0**.
The probability of something that is **certain** is **1**.
All other probabilities are between **0** and **1**.

If it has snowed in the UK in February in **9** of the last **10** years, then you can use this information to estimate the probability that it will snow next February.

Equally likely outcomes

Some events are **equally likely** to happen.
When this happens you can always calculate probabilities.
When you roll a fair dice, all of the numbers are equally likely to happen.
The probability of throwing an even number is $\frac{3}{6} = \frac{1}{2}$
This is because there are **6** numbers on the dice and **3** of the numbers are even.

Probability experiments

You can do probability experiments to estimate probabilities.
When you do an experiment more than once you won't always get the same results.
The best estimate for a probability is obtained when you repeat the experiment lots of times and combine the results.

Level 6

Probabilities add up to 1

If you pick one card at **random** from a pack, the probability that you will get a King is $\frac{4}{52} = \frac{1}{13}$

The probability that the card will **not** be a King is $1 - \frac{1}{13} = \frac{12}{13}$

The probability that something doesn't happen = 1 − the probability that it does happen

Sample space diagrams

A sample space diagram shows all the possible outcomes when two events happen.

This sample space diagram shows the 12 possible outcomes when a coin and a dice are thrown together.

		Dice					
		1	2	3	4	5	6
Coin	H	H, 1	H, 2	H, 3	H, 4	H, 5	H, 6
	T	T, 1	T, 2	T, 3	T, 4	T, 5	T, 6

12 More fractions and percentages

**Chapter 8
Decimals, fractions and percentages**

- Working out a fraction of a number
- Working out a percentage of a number

1 Fractions

2 Percentages

**Chapter 16
Ratio and proportion**

Understanding ratio and proportion

You should already know:

▶ **how to describe parts of a whole**

This shape is split into **5** equal parts.
3 of these parts are coloured **red**.

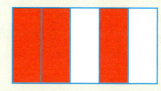

$\frac{3}{5}$ is the **proportion** of the shape that is coloured **red**.

In the **fraction** $\frac{3}{5}$,
3 is the **numerator** and **5** is the **denominator**.

▶ **about percentages**

17 out of 100 children have blue eyes.

17% have blue eyes
83% do not have blue eyes

24 out of 50 children are left-handed.

48% are left-handed
52% are right-handed

Every **percentage** is a **fraction** of 100.

30% = $\frac{30}{100}$

12 More fractions and percentages

1 Fractions

- **Cancelling fractions**
- **Comparing fractions**
- **Adding and subtracting fractions**
- **Writing one number as a fraction of another number**

Key words
fraction equivalent fractions
cancelling lowest terms
common denominator
proportion

Cancelling fractions Level 5

The colouring in this diagram can be described using more than one **fraction**.

2 of the 6 squares are red.   1 strip out of 3 is red.
$\frac{2}{6}$ of the shape is red. $\frac{1}{3}$ of the shape is red.

So $\frac{2}{6} = \frac{1}{3}$

When fractions are the same they are called **equivalent fractions**.

You simplify fractions by **cancelling**.
You divide the numerator and denominator by the same number.

$\frac{8}{14} = \frac{4}{7}$ (÷ 2) $\frac{12}{30} = \frac{2}{5}$ (÷ 6)   You can also do this in two steps like this $\frac{12}{30} = \frac{6}{15} = \frac{2}{5}$ (÷ 2, ÷ 3)

When you cannot cancel a fraction any more, the fraction is in its **lowest terms**.

Exercise 12:1

1 a Work out the HCF of 8 and 12.
   b Cancel $\frac{8}{12}$ so that it is in its lowest terms.
   c Copy this sentence and fill in the gap.
   When you cancel a fraction to its lowest terms you need to divide the numerator and denominator by their _____ .

2 Cancel each of these fractions to its lowest terms.
   a $\frac{8}{14}$ **c** $\frac{12}{48}$ **e** $\frac{12}{16}$ ⚠ **g** $\frac{245}{360}$
   b $\frac{6}{9}$ **d** $\frac{24}{32}$ **f** $\frac{45}{75}$ ⚠ **h** $\frac{140}{500}$

3 Look at this diagram. It shows you that $\frac{3}{4} = \frac{6}{8}$

It is like a cancelling diagram in reverse.

Copy these and fill in the missing parts of the equivalent fractions.

a $\frac{2}{3} = \frac{...}{9}$ (×3)

b $\frac{1}{3} = \frac{...}{15}$ (×5)

c $\frac{3}{4} = \frac{...}{24}$

d $\frac{3}{5} = \frac{18}{...}$

e $\frac{5}{12} = \frac{15}{...} = \frac{...}{72}$

f $\frac{3}{8} = \frac{...}{32} = \frac{24}{...}$

4 Each section in the diagram should contain three equivalent fractions.

One fraction in each section is in the wrong place.

Copy the diagram and put all the fractions in the right sections.

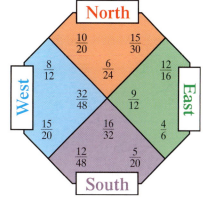

5 The fraction $\frac{7}{14}$ is called a 3-digit fraction because it has three digits!

It is equivalent to $\frac{1}{2}$.

a Write down all the other 3-digit fractions that are equivalent to $\frac{1}{2}$

b Write down all the 3-digit fractions that are equivalent to $\frac{1}{3}$

c Write down all the 3-digit fractions that are equivalent to $\frac{1}{4}$

d Explain how you know that you've found all the possible answers in parts **a** to **c**.

Facts to figure

6 The thumb and the foot were both Anglo-Saxon measures of length.

1 thumb = $\frac{1}{12}$ foot.

Copy and complete these

a 5 thumbs = $\frac{...}{12}$ foot

b ... thumbs = 1 foot

c 3 thumbs = $\frac{...}{4}$ foot

d 8 thumbs = $\frac{...}{3}$ foot

12 More fractions and percentages

Comparing fractions — Level 6

You can use a fraction wall to compare the size of fractions.

$\frac{1}{6}$ is less than $\frac{1}{5}$ This is written $\frac{1}{6} < \frac{1}{5}$

$\frac{7}{8}$ is greater than $\frac{6}{7}$ This is written $\frac{7}{8} > \frac{6}{7}$

$\frac{7}{8}$ is nearer to 1 than $\frac{6}{7}$ because $\frac{1}{8}$ is smaller than $\frac{1}{7}$

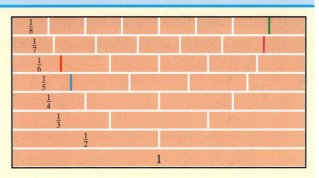

You can compare the size of fractions by writing them as fractions with a **common denominator**.

To compare $\frac{3}{8}$ and $\frac{2}{5}$ use 40 as the common denominator.

Use 40 because it's the LCM of 8 and 5.

$\frac{16}{40} > \frac{15}{40}$ so $\frac{2}{5} > \frac{3}{8}$

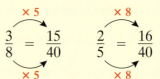

Exercise 12:2

Use a fraction wall to help you to answer questions 1 and 2.

1 Which of the fractions in each part is closer to 1?

a $\frac{2}{3}, \frac{3}{4}$ c $\frac{4}{5}, \frac{5}{6}$ e $\frac{4}{7}, \frac{3}{5}$ ⚠ g $\frac{4}{3}, \frac{3}{4}$

b $\frac{7}{8}, \frac{3}{4}$ d $\frac{6}{7}, \frac{3}{4}$ f $\frac{1}{3}, \frac{3}{7}$ ⚠ h $\frac{9}{7}, \frac{2}{3}$

2 Copy these and write > or < between each pair of fractions to make a correct statement.

a $\frac{1}{2} \ldots \frac{1}{3}$ c $\frac{1}{4} \ldots \frac{3}{8}$ e $\frac{2}{3} \ldots \frac{5}{7}$

b $\frac{2}{7} \ldots \frac{1}{5}$ d $\frac{2}{3} \ldots \frac{1}{2}$ f $\frac{3}{8} \ldots \frac{1}{3}$

3 In each part (1) write the fractions using a common denominator
              (2) write down which is the bigger fraction.

a $\frac{3}{5}, \frac{2}{3}$ c $\frac{5}{6}, \frac{4}{5}$ e $\frac{13}{20}, \frac{3}{5}$

b $\frac{3}{4}, \frac{4}{5}$ d $\frac{7}{12}, \frac{2}{3}$ ⚠ f $\frac{27}{40}, \frac{11}{16}$

4 Write the fractions in each part in order of size. Start with the smallest.

a $\frac{2}{3}, \frac{3}{4}, \frac{7}{12}$ b $\frac{3}{5}, \frac{7}{10}, \frac{13}{20}, \frac{1}{2}$ c $\frac{3}{10}, \frac{1}{3}, \frac{4}{15}$ d $\frac{17}{45}, \frac{11}{30}, \frac{2}{5}$

5 Write these fractions in order. Start with the smallest. $\frac{1}{3}, \frac{2}{5}, \frac{3}{10}, \frac{1}{4}, \frac{7}{20}, \frac{4}{15}$

Explore

6 In each part, use all the digits 2, 3, 4, 5 and 6 to make

  a the smallest possible fraction

  b the largest fraction that is less than 1

  c the largest possible fraction.

Adding and subtracting fractions — Level 6

You can use diagrams to help you to add and subtract simple fractions.

 + =

$\frac{3}{8}$ + $\frac{2}{8}$ = $\frac{5}{8}$

This is the same as

$\frac{3}{8}$ + $\frac{1}{4}$ = $\frac{5}{8}$

Before you add or subtract fractions the **denominators** must be the same.

$\frac{3}{4} - \frac{2}{3} = \frac{9}{12} - \frac{8}{12} = \frac{1}{12}$ $\frac{3}{4} \overset{\times 3}{\underset{\times 3}{=}} \frac{9}{12}$ $\frac{2}{3} \overset{\times 4}{\underset{\times 4}{=}} \frac{8}{12}$

$1 - \frac{6}{13} = \frac{13}{13} - \frac{6}{13} = \frac{7}{13}$ because $1 = \frac{13}{13}$

Exercise 12:3

1 Work these out.

  a $\frac{1}{9} + \frac{4}{9}$ d $\frac{1}{3} + \frac{1}{4}$ g $\frac{4}{5} - \frac{3}{4}$

  b $\frac{7}{12} - \frac{1}{12}$ e $\frac{3}{8} - \frac{1}{4}$ h $1 - \frac{3}{7}$

  c $\frac{2}{15} + \frac{1}{15}$ f $\frac{1}{5} + \frac{2}{3}$ i $\frac{5}{6} - \frac{2}{3}$

12 More fractions and percentages

2 This is a balance diagram.

The fractions on each side of the pivot give the same total.

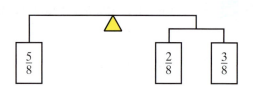

Copy and complete these balance diagrams.

a 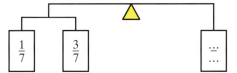   **d**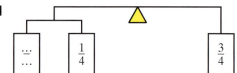

b 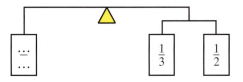   **e**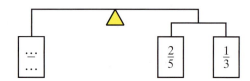

c 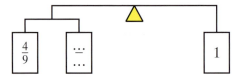   **f**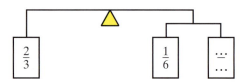

3 Work out

a $\dfrac{1}{4} + \dfrac{1}{3}$

b $\dfrac{3}{5} - \dfrac{1}{15}$

4 The fractions in the circles on each line add up to 1.

Find the missing fractions.

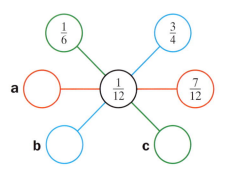

5 Write down the fraction that is halfway between the numbers shown.

a    b    c

6 $\frac{1}{3}, \frac{1}{8}, \frac{1}{5}$ are all examples of unit fractions.

The ancient Egyptians used only unit fractions.

For $\frac{3}{4}$, they wrote the sum $\frac{1}{2} + \frac{1}{4}$

a For what fraction did they write the sum $\frac{1}{2} + \frac{1}{5}$?
Show your working.

b They wrote $\frac{9}{20}$ as the sum of two unit fractions.

One of them was $\frac{1}{4}$. What was the other?
Show your working.

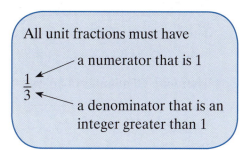

All unit fractions must have
- a numerator that is 1
- a denominator that is an integer greater than 1

$\frac{1}{3}$

7 In written music, each type of note has a different length.

Here is the number of beats for each note.

	Minim	2 beats		Semiquaver	$\frac{1}{4}$ beat
	Crotchet	1 beat		Demisemiquaver	$\frac{1}{8}$ beat
	Quaver	$\frac{1}{2}$ beat		Hemidemisemiquaver	$\frac{1}{16}$ beat

Work out how many beats are shown by each of these groups of notes.

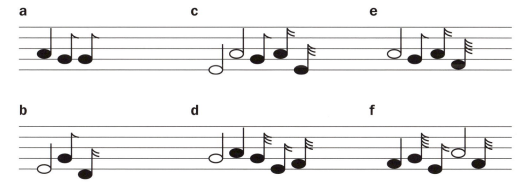

Explore

8 $\frac{1}{2} + \frac{4}{8}$

This fraction sum is made from four different digits: 1, 2, 4 and 8.

The fraction sum is 1 because $\frac{1}{2} + \frac{4}{8} = 1$.

Find five other fraction sums made from four different digits with a fraction sum of 1.

12 More fractions and percentages

Writing one number as a fraction of another number — Level 6

Use the same units when you write one quantity as a **fraction** of another.

There are **100** cents in a euro. **3** cents is $\frac{3}{100}$ of €1.

There are **1000** grams in a kilogram. **437** g is $\frac{437}{1000}$ of 1 kg.

There are **60** minutes in an hour. **27** minutes is $\frac{27}{60}$ of 1 hour.

Proportion is another way of describing a fraction of a whole.
Proportions are often used to compare two things.

This cereal has 12 g of fibre in every 100 g.

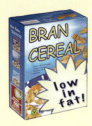

This cereal has 8 g of fibre in every 50 g.

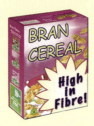

To find the proportion of fibre you need to write 12 g as a fraction of 100 g.

The proportion of fibre is $\frac{12}{100} = \frac{3}{25}$

To find the proportion of fibre you need to write 8 g as a fraction of 50 g.

The proportion of fibre is $\frac{8}{50} = \frac{4}{25}$

Exercise 12:4

1 What fraction of the large shape is the small shape in each part?

a
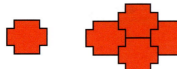

c

b
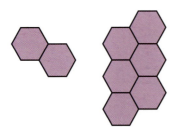

d
 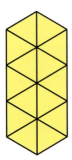

2 There are 30 pupils in Class 7X. 17 of them are girls.
  a What fraction of the class is girls?
  b What fraction of the class is boys?

3 a Write each of these as a fraction of a full turn.
  (1) 90°   **(2)** 180°   **(3)** 45°   **(4)** 36°

b Jenny always turns clockwise.
Write the fraction of a turn that takes her from facing
  (1) north to east   **(3)** east to south-east
  (2) south to east   **(4)** south to north-west.

4 Write the fraction of a turn that the minute hand of a clock turns through between these times.
  a 3:45 p.m. and 4:15 p.m.   **d** 7:45 p.m. and 8:30 p.m.
  b 11:25 a.m. and 11:55 a.m.   **e** 5:40 p.m. and 6:20 p.m.
  c 1:40 p.m. and 1:45 p.m.   **f** 3:45 p.m. and 4:10 p.m.

5 Write the first quantity as a fraction of the second quantity in each part.
Cancel your answers to their lowest terms.
  a 17 cm, 1 m   **f** 20 mins, 2 hours
  b 30 cm, 1 m   **g** 30 mins, 4 hours
  c 35 cm, 1 m   **h** 800 g, 1 kg
  d 15 mins, 1 hours   **i** 750 mℓ, 1 ℓ
  e 20 mins, 1 hours   **j** 200 mℓ, 3 ℓ

6 In a box of 48 apples, 7 are bad.
Write down the proportion of good apples.

7 Ali received some money for his birthday.
He spent £25 on a computer game and saved £15.

What proportion of the money did Ali save?

8 This chocolate bar weighs 32 g.   This chocolate bar weighs 40 g.
It has 10 g of fat in it.   It has 12 g of fat in it.

Which chocolate bar has the higher proportion of fat? Explain your answer.

12 More fractions and percentages

2 Percentages

▶ **Equivalent fractions, decimals and percentages**

▶ **Writing one number as a percentage of another number**

Key words
percentage   fraction
decimal   numerator
denominator

▶ Equivalent fractions, decimals and percentages   Level 6

You should know these simple equivalent **percentages** and **fractions**.

$50\% = \frac{1}{2}$ $25\% = \frac{1}{4}$ $10\% = \frac{1}{10}$ $20\% = \frac{1}{5}$ $1\% = \frac{1}{100}$

You should also know these simple equivalent percentages and **decimals**.

$50\% = 0.5$ $25\% = 0.25$ $10\% = 0.1$ $20\% = 0.2$ $1\% = 0.01$

You can use these facts to help you work out others like this

$20\% = \frac{1}{5}$ so $40\% = 2 \times 20\% = 2 \times \frac{1}{5} = \frac{2}{5}$

$25\% = \frac{1}{4}$ so $75\% = 3 \times 25\% = 3 \times \frac{1}{4} = \frac{3}{4}$

$1\% = 0.01$ so $3\% = 3 \times 1\% = 0.03$

$\frac{1}{5} = 0.2$ so $\frac{3}{5} = 3 \times \frac{1}{5} = 3 \times 0.2 = 0.6$

$\frac{1}{4} = 0.25$ so $\frac{1}{8} = \frac{1}{4} \div 2 = 0.25 \div 2 = 0.125$

You can write any percentage as a fraction. $36\% = \frac{36}{100} = \frac{9}{25}$ (÷4) $5\% = \frac{5}{100} = \frac{1}{20}$ (÷5)

You can write any percentage as a decimal. $36\% = 0.36$ $5\% = 0.05$

You can change any fraction into a decimal.
To do this, divide the **numerator** by the **denominator**. $\frac{3}{8} = 3 \div 8 = 0.375$

Exercise 12:5

1 Copy these and fill in the gaps. Learn these simple percentage and fraction equivalents.

a $25\% = \frac{1}{...}$ **c** $...\% = \frac{1}{2}$ **e** $75\% = \frac{...}{4}$ **g** $33\frac{1}{3}\% = \frac{1}{...}$

b $10\% = \frac{1}{...}$ **d** $20\% = \frac{1}{...}$ **f** $40\% = \frac{2}{...}$ **h** $66\frac{2}{3}\% = \frac{...}{3}$

2 Look at where the arrow is pointing, and for each part write this as
   (1) a fraction   **(2)** a decimal   **(3)** a percentage.

   a    **c**

   b    **d**

3 Write down
   (1) a fraction   **(2)** the percentage that is equivalent to each of these decimals.
   a 0.5   **c** 0.75   **e** 0.4   **g** 0.8
   b 0.25   **d** 0.2   **f** 0.6   **h** 0.1

4 Copy the diagram in each part and fill in all the missing values.
   Use decimals for the top line, percentages for the middle line and fractions for the bottom line.
   Cancel the fractions to their lowest terms.

   a    **c**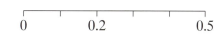

   b 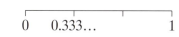   **d**

      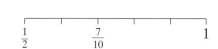

5 In each column there is one box with a fraction, decimal or percentage that is equivalent to $\frac{2}{5}$
   Starting from the left, write down the colour of these boxes.

$\frac{4}{7}$	25%	$\frac{10}{25}$	0.4	$\frac{12}{15}$
$\frac{4}{10}$	40%	$\frac{1}{40}$	0.04	$\frac{5}{8}$
$\frac{1}{4}$	4%	$\frac{6}{20}$	0.25	$\frac{16}{40}$

12 More fractions and percentages

6 a Copy this scale.

```
0                                                                    1
|___|___|___|___|___|___|___|___|___|___|
```

b Mark each of these numbers on the scale.

90%   0.5 $\frac{2}{5}$ 65%   0.05 $\frac{3}{4}$

7 Write each of these percentages as a fraction.
Cancel each fraction to its lowest terms.

a 35%   **d** 16%   **g** 72%
b 15%   **e** 9%   **h** 6%
c 70%   **f** 38%   **i** 98%

8 Copy this table and fill in the missing numbers.

Fraction	$\frac{1}{2}$		$\frac{1}{8}$			$\frac{7}{20}$	
Percentage	50%	86%			8%		
Decimal	0.5			0.24			0.075

9 These are Alan's end of term test results.

Maths 58%   Spelling $\frac{16}{20}$ French $\frac{28}{40}$

Write Alan's results in order from best to worst. Show your working.

Think on!

10 Use these cards to write down three matching sets.

Each set must contain a fraction, a decimal and a percentage.

You will have one fraction, one decimal and one percentage left over.

Work out the equivalent decimal, percentage and fraction for each of them.

Writing one number as a percentage of another number — Level 6

Tim's school has **1200** pupils. **630** of them are boys.

To work out the **percentage** of boys you need to write 630 as a percentage of 1200.

To do this

    write 630 as a fraction of 1200 $\frac{630}{1200}$

    change the fraction to a decimal using your calculator $630 \div 1200 = 0.525$

    and multiply the decimal by 100 $0.525 \times 100 = 52.5\%$

So 52.5% of the pupils in the school are boys.

Exercise 12:6

1 Write the first quantity as a percentage of the second quantity.

    a £162, £450   **b** 432 mm, 96 cm   **c** 36 minutes, 2 hours

2 A can of drink contains 330 mℓ.
120 mℓ is orange juice.

What percentage of the total is this?

3 A manufacturer makes 85 computers each day.

On average 6 computers are faulty.

What percentage of the computers is **not** faulty?

4 In 2001 the average yearly wage was £21 842.
On average people spent £1644 on their family holiday.

What percentage of the average yearly wage is that?

5 A school bus carries 48 passengers.
30 of the passengers on a Monday are girls. 8 of the girls are in Year 7.

    a Calculate the percentage of the girls that are in Year 7.

  ⚠ **b** Calculate the percentage of the passengers that are Year 7 girls.

⚠ **6**

The blue rectangle is half as long as the red one.

The green rectangle is half as long as the blue one.

What percentage of the strip is green? Give your answer to 2 d.p.

12 More fractions and percentages

Watch out ... there's a trap about

▶ Lots of people think that you add fractions by adding the numerators **and adding the denominators** like this $\frac{3}{8} + \frac{2}{8} = \frac{5}{16}$ ✗

This is wrong!

Adding **three eighths** and **two eighths** gives you **five eighths**.

It does not give you five sixteenths.

When you add or subtract fractions

- make sure that the denominators are the same
- add or subtract the numerators and leave the denominator the same $\frac{3}{7} + \frac{1}{7} = \frac{4}{7}$ ✓
- cancel the final answer to its lowest terms. $\frac{5}{9} - \frac{2}{9} = \frac{3}{9} = \frac{1}{3}$ ✓

▶ 4% is **not** the same as 0.4

4% means 4 out of 100

$\frac{4}{100} = 0.04$

so 4% = 0.04

Test yourself

1 Cancel each of these fractions to its lowest terms.
   a $\frac{10}{15}$ **b** $\frac{24}{64}$ **c** $\frac{32}{40}$

2 Write > or < between each of these pairs of fractions to make a correct statement.
   a $\frac{1}{3} \ldots \frac{1}{4}$ **b** $\frac{3}{4} \ldots \frac{4}{5}$ **c** $\frac{4}{5} \ldots \frac{5}{7}$

3 The fractions in the circles on each line add up to 1. Find the missing fractions.

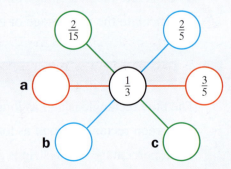

4 Write the first quantity as a fraction of the second.

  a 20 cm, 1 m
  b 25 cm, 2 m
  c 600 g, 1 kg
  d 125 g, 1 kg

5 Chris is playing cricket. The match takes 280 minutes to complete.

Chris bats for $\frac{1}{4}$ of the time and fields for $\frac{3}{8}$ of the time.

Chris is watching the other players in his team bat for the rest of the time.

  a How long does Chris bat?
  b How long does Chris field?
  c What fraction of the time is Chris watching the other players in his team bat?

6 Copy the diagram and fill in all the missing values.

Use decimals for the top line, percentages for the middle line and fractions for the bottom line.

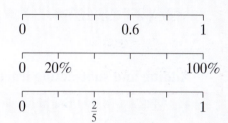

7 Copy this table and fill in the missing numbers.

Fraction	$\frac{1}{2}$		$\frac{1}{5}$			$\frac{9}{20}$	
Percentage	50%	35%			12%		
Decimal	0.5			0.36			0.06

8 In a box of 24 eggs, 3 are bad. Write down the proportion of bad eggs.

9 In Dave's class, 9 of the 27 pupils have brown eyes.

In Krishnan's class, 8 of the 25 pupils have brown eyes.

Whose class has the bigger proportion of brown-eyed pupils?
Show your working.

12 More fractions and percentages

Chapter 12 Summary

Level 5

Cancelling fractions

Simplifying fractions by **cancelling**.

Divide the numerator and the denominator by the same number.
When you can't cancel any more the fraction is in its **lowest terms**.

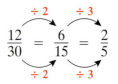

Level 6

Comparing fractions

You can compare the size of fractions by writing them as fractions with a **common denominator**.

To compare $\frac{3}{8}$ and $\frac{2}{5}$ use 40 as the common denominator.

Use 40 because it's the LCM of 8 and 5.

$\frac{16}{40} > \frac{15}{40}$ so $\frac{2}{5} > \frac{3}{8}$

Adding and subtracting fractions

- Make sure that the denominators are the same $\frac{1}{12} + \frac{1}{6} = \frac{1}{12} + \frac{2}{12}$

- Add or subtract the numerators and
  leave the denominator the same $= \frac{3}{12}$

- Cancel the final answer to its lowest terms $= \frac{1}{4}$

Writing one number as a fraction or percentage of another

Always use the same units.
There are **1000** grams in a kilogram. **437** g is $\frac{437}{1000}$ of 1 kg.

Then you change the fraction into a decimal $\frac{437}{1000} = 437 \div 1000 = 0.437$

and the decimal into a percentage. $0.437 \times 100 = 43.7\%$

Equivalent fractions, percentages and decimals

You can write any percentage as a fraction. $36\% = \frac{36}{100} = \frac{9}{25}$ $5\% = \frac{5}{100} = \frac{1}{20}$

You can write any percentage as a decimal. $36\% = 0.36$ $5\% = 0.05$

You can change any fraction into a decimal. $\frac{3}{8} = 3 \div 8 = 0.375$

13 Sequences

**Chapter 1
The language of algebra**
Writing algebra

**Chapter 6
Formulae and algebraic operations**
- Deriving formulae
- Substituting into formulae
- Using BODMAS in algebra

1. Term-to-term rules
2. Position-to-term rules
3. Non-linear sequences

Year 8
- Finding the nth term rule for a linear sequence
- Finding the nth term rule for a quadratic sequence

You should already know:

▶ **about simple sequences**

The sequence that starts at 5 and goes up in steps of 3 is   5, 8, 11, 14, 17, …

The sequence that starts at 15 and goes down in steps of 5 is   15, 10, 5, 0, −5, …

▶ **how to substitute into formulae**

The formula for the area of a rectangle is $A = lb$
When $l = 5$ cm and $b = 7$ cm $A = lb = 5 \times 7$
$A = 35$ cm²

▶ **how to write algebra correctly**

Write $n \times 5$ and $5 \times n$ as $5n$
Write $n \div 3$ as $\frac{n}{3}$
Write $n \times n$ as n^2

▶ **how to find the square numbers**

Squaring a number means multiplying it by itself.
The first five **square numbers** are
$1^2 = 1$ $2^2 = 4$ $3^2 = 9$ $4^2 = 16$ $5^2 = 25$

▶ **the order of algebraic operations**

BODMAS
The expression $6(n + 1) − 2$ means that you
add 1 to n before **multiplying by 6**
and then **subtracting 2**.

13 Sequences

1 Term-to-term rules

Finding the next term in a sequence

Key words	
sequence	infinite
term	consecutive
term-to-term rule	finite
ascending	descending
linear sequence	
non-linear sequence	
difference pattern	

Finding the next term in a sequence — Level 5

This is the **sequence** of even numbers.   2, 4, 6, 8, 10, …
The **three dots** at the end show that it carries on forever.   This is an **infinite** sequence.

Each number in a sequence is called a **term**.   The **first term** of this sequence is 2.
Terms next to each other are called **consecutive** terms.   6 and 8 are consecutive terms.

Each term is 2 more than the term before.
So the **term-to-term rule** is add 2.

10, 20, 30, …, 90 is the sequence of multiples of 10 with two digits.
The **first term** is 10 and the term-to-term rule is add 10.
You can tell that it is a **finite** sequence because there are no dots at the end.
The **three dots** in the middle show that you haven't listed all the terms.

In the sequences 10, 20, 30, …, 90 and 2, 4, 6, 8, 10, … the terms are increasing.
They are **ascending** sequences.

The terms in the sequence 34, 33, 32, … are decreasing.
It is a **descending** sequence.
The **first term** is 34 and the term-to-term rule is subtract 1.

The terms of all of these sequences increase or decrease in equal steps.
They are **linear sequences**.

Sequences that go up in unequal steps are **non-linear sequences**.

This sequence diagram shows the gap between each term and the next.

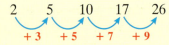

+ 3, + 5, + 7, + 9, …is called the **difference pattern**.
The difference increases by two each time.

You can also generate sequences by multiplying or dividing by the same amount each time.

In this sequence the term-to-term rule is multiply by 3.   1, 3, 9, 27, 81, …
In this sequence the term-to-term rule is multiply by −2.   2, −4, 8, −16, 32, …

Exercise 13:1

1 For each of these sequences, write down
  (1) the first term
  (2) whether the sequence is finite or infinite
  (3) whether the sequence is ascending or descending
  (4) the term-to-term rule.

  a 12, 15, 18, 21, …
  b 3, 12, 21, 30, 39, …
  c 27, 25, 23, 21, …
  d 100, 90, 80, …, 10
  e −8, −12, −16, …, −80
  f −65, −60, −55, −50, …

2 Copy these sentences and fill in the gaps.
Choose from these words.

| term | consecutive | finite |
| infinite | equal | unequal |

  a The _____ sequence 2, 4, 6, 8, … is the sequence of even numbers.
  The first _____ is 2 and the sequence increases in _____ steps.

  b The sequence 7, 12, 17, 22, 27 is a _____ sequence.
  The terms 12, 17 and 22 are _____ terms.

  c The sequence 1, 4, 9, 16, 25, … is an _____ sequence.
  It is the sequence of square numbers.
  The first square number is 1 and the sequence increases in _____ steps.

3 Continue each of these sequences by writing down the next three terms in each part.
  a 7, 13, 19, 25, …
  b 15, 28, 41, 54, …
  c 20, 11, 2, −7, …
  d 12, 9, 6, 3, …
  e −15, −12, −9, −6, …
  f 58, 47, 36, 25, …

4 Write down the special name for the numbers in each of these sequences.
  a 2, 4, 6, 8, 10, …
  b 1, 3, 5, 7, 9, …
  c 7, 14, 21, 28, 35, …
  d 3, 6, 9, 12, 15, …
  e 2, 3, 5, 7, 11, 13, 17, 19, …
  f 1, 4, 9, 16, 25, 36, …

5 Copy these. Fill in the next three terms and the term-to-term rule for each sequence.
  a 10, 100, 1000, 10 000, …, …, …   Rule × …
  b 1, 2, 4, 8, …, …, …   Rule × …
  c 3, −6, 12, −24, …, …, …   Rule × …
  d 81, 27, 9, …, …, …   Rule ÷ …
  e 8, 4, 2, 1, 0.5, …, …, …   Rule ÷ …
  ⚠ **f** 1, 5, 13, 29, …, …, …   Rule × … and then + …
  ⚠ **g** 220, 100, 40, …, …, …   Rule ÷ … and then − …

13 Sequences

6 You can use a **flow chart** to generate sequences.
This flow chart generates the sequence
2, 5, 8, 11, 14, 17, 20, 23, 26, 29, 32

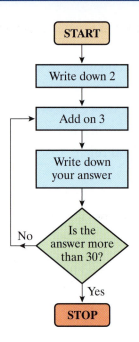

Write down the sequence generated by each of these flow charts.

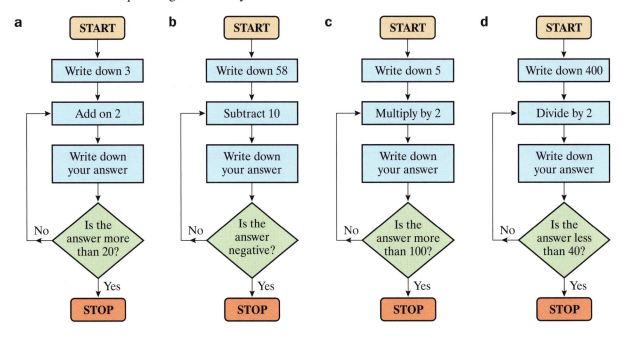

7 These sequences are non-linear. For each sequence write down
   (1) the first term
   (2) the term-to-term rule.

   a 1, 3, 9, 27, 81, …
   b 12, 24, 48, 96, 192, …
   c 400, 200, 100, 50, 25, …
   d 324, 108, 36, 12, 4, …

8 Coryn says that the fourth term of his sequence is 24.
He has used the term-to-term rule subtract 2 and then multiply by 4.
What is the first term of Coryn's sequence?

9 Draw the difference pattern and use it to write down the next three terms of each sequence.

  a 1, 2, 4, 7, 11, …
  b 1, 3, 6, 10, 15, …
  c 30, 29, 27, 24, 20, …
  d 10, 8, 5, 1, −4, …

10 a Look at the sequence 1, 2, 4, …

  Annie says that the next three terms of the sequence are 7, 11 and 16.
  Tom says that the next three terms of the sequence are 8, 16 and 32.

  Explain how Annie and Tom could both be right.

  b Look at the sequence 1, 2, 3, …

  Caitlin says that the next three terms are 4, 5 and 6.
  Brandon says that the next three terms are 5, 8 and 13.

  Explain how Caitlin and Brandon could both be right.

⚠ 11 Copy each of these sequences and fill in the missing terms.
Not all of the sequences are linear.

  a 15, …, 29, …, …, 50, …
  b 24, …, …, 9, …, −1, …
  c 0.5, …, …, 2, …, …, 3.5
  d 5, …, 8, 11, …, …, 26
  e 10, 9, 6, …, −6, …, …
  f −2.5, …, −3.1, …, −3.7, …, …
  g 3, …, 12, …, 48, …, 192
  h 160, …, 40, …, 10, …, …
  i …, …, 21, 210, …, …, 210 000
  j $\frac{1}{96}, \frac{1}{48}, \frac{...}{...}, \frac{1}{12}, \frac{...}{...}, \frac{...}{...}, \frac{2}{3}$,

Explore

12 The term-to-term rule for a sequence is add 3.
There are many sequences with this rule.
Can you find one of them in which

  a all the terms are multiples of 3
  b all the terms are odd
  c all the terms are multiples of 9
  d none of the terms is an integer?

13 The term-to-term rule for a sequence is add x.
Write down a first term and a value of x that will generate a sequence in which

  a all the terms are even
  b all the terms are odd
  c all the terms end in the same digit.

13 Sequences

2 Position-to-term rules

▶ **Finding any term in a pattern**

▶ **Generating sequences**

▶ **Finding any term in a sequence**

Key words

sequence pattern rule term
term-to-term rule term number
position-to-term formula
difference pattern
nth term rule nth term formula

▶ **Finding any term in a pattern**   Level 6

This is a **sequence** of L shapes made from counters.

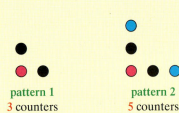 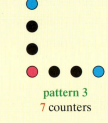 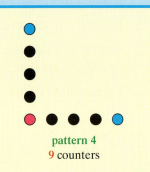

pattern 1   pattern 2   pattern 3   pattern 4
3 counters   5 counters   7 counters   9 counters

Each shape uses 2 more counters than the previous one.

The sequence of counters is 3, 5, 7, 9, …

To find the number of counters in the next **pattern** you add 2.
The number of counters in the next pattern is 9 + 2 = 11.

If you want to find the number of counters in the 50th pattern, it will take a long time!

You can often find a **rule** to work out any **term** in a sequence.

For this pattern, the rule for the number of counters is   2 × pattern number + 1
For the 50th pattern you need   2 × 50 + 1 = 101 counters

The rule has the 2 in it because you add two more counters each time.
The rule has a + 1 in it because of the pink counter in the bottom corner of the L.

It is better to write this type of rule as a formula using algebra.
You should always say what each letter in your formula represents.

Let c = number of counters and n = pattern number
then you can write the rule as a formula like this $c = 2 \times n + 1$

You have already seen that you don't write × signs in algebra.
So the formula is $c = 2n + 1$

Exercise 13:2

1 a Draw the next three patterns in this sequence.

  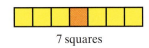

3 squares   5 squares   7 squares

b Write out the number sequence that the pattern produces.

c How many squares are there in the 15th pattern in the sequence?

2 **a** Draw the next three diagrams in this pattern.

b Write out the sequence of the numbers of dots from your diagrams.

c What is the gap between each term in the sequence?

d How many dots are there in the 12th pattern in the sequence?

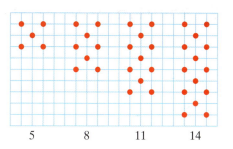

5   8   11   14

3 **a** Draw the next two patterns in the sequence.

     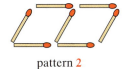   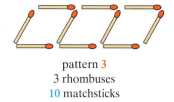

pattern **1**   pattern **2**   pattern **3**
1 rhombus   2 rhombuses   3 rhombuses
4 matchsticks   **7** matchsticks   **10** matchsticks

b Write down the sequence of the numbers of matchsticks in the patterns.

c Describe the sequence you have written down in part **b**.

d Explain how to find the number of matchsticks in the 10th pattern by following the pattern from term to term.

e The rule for finding the **number of matchsticks** from the pattern number is

3 × **pattern number** + 1

Use this rule to find the number of matchsticks in the 50th pattern.

f Can you use exactly 62 matches and make one of the patterns in this sequence? Explain your answer.

4 This is the 4th shape in a pentagon matchstick sequence.

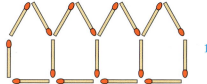

pattern **4**
17 matchsticks

a Draw the first three patterns in the sequence.

b Copy and complete the rule for finding the **number of matchsticks** from the pattern number.

… × **pattern number** + …

c Use these diagrams to explain why your rule works.

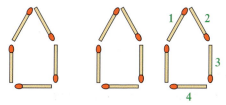

13 Sequences

5 a Draw the next two patterns in the sequence.

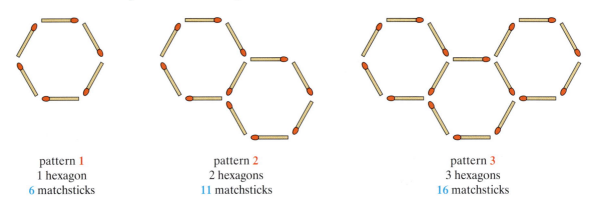

pattern 1
1 hexagon
6 matchsticks

pattern 2
2 hexagons
11 matchsticks

pattern 3
3 hexagons
16 matchsticks

b Describe the sequence of the numbers of matchsticks in the patterns.

c Explain how to find the number of matchsticks in the 10th pattern by following the pattern from term to term.

d The formula for finding the number of matchsticks, *m*, from pattern number *n* is

$$m = 5n + 1$$

Use this formula to find the number of matchsticks in the 30th pattern.

e Can you use exactly 121 matches and make one of the patterns in this sequence? Explain your answer.

1998

6 This is a series of patterns with red and blue tiles.

The series of patterns continues by adding each time.

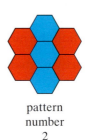

pattern number 1

pattern number 2

pattern number 3

a Copy and complete this table.

pattern number	number of blue tiles	number of red tiles
5		
16		

b Copy and complete this table by writing **expressions**.

pattern number	number of blue tiles	number of red tiles
n		

c Write an expression to show the **total** number of tiles in pattern number *n*. **Simplify** your expression.

7 Look at these triangular patterns made from counters.

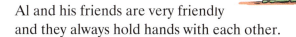

triangle **1** triangle **2** triangle **3** triangle **4**
3 counters **6** counters **9** counters **12** counters

a Write down the formula for the number of counters, *c*, in the *n*th triangle.

b Explain why the formula works.

8 The aliens are coming!

This is Al. He has 6 free hands.

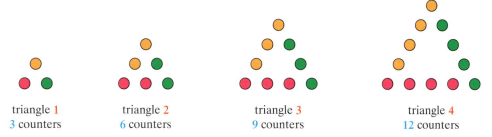

Al and his friends are very friendly and they always hold hands with each other.

So two aliens have 10 free hands

and three aliens have 14 free hands.

a Write down how many free hands you think four aliens will have. Draw the diagram for four aliens and check if you're right.

b Write out the sequence of the numbers of free hands.

c Find a formula for the number of free hands, *f*, for *n* aliens.

Think on!

9 Marshall has lots of old 1p, 2p and 3p stamps.
He works out how many ways he can use stamps to add up to different amounts.
There are 3 ways that he can make 3p.

 or + or + +

He starts to make a table of his results.

Amount	1p	2p	3p	4p	5p	6p	7p
Number of ways	1	2	3				

What should Marshall write in the table beneath 4p, 5p, 6p and 7p?

13 Sequences

Generating sequences — Level 6

You can write down the terms of a sequence if you're told one term and the **term-to-term rule**.

The **first** term of a sequence is 4.
Each term is **5 more** than the one before. The term-to-term rule is **add 5**.

The first 5 terms of the sequence are   4,   9,   14,   19,   24

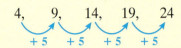

To find the 50th term you have to work out **all** the terms up to and including the 50th.
The 50th term is 249.
See if you can get to this yourself!

You can also write down the terms of a sequence using the **term number**.

The **first** term of the sequence is 4. You write this as T(1) = 4.

The **second** term of the sequence is 4 + 5 = 9. You write T(2) = 9.

T(3) = 14,   T(4) = 19   and   T(5) = 24

The rule to find any term in this sequence is 5 × term number − 1.

In algebra you write this as T(n) = $5n - 1$. This is called the **position-to-term formula**.

You use it to work out any term from its position in the sequence.

You find the **50th** term by putting $n = 50$ into the formula. T(50) = 5 × 50 − 1 = 249

Exercise 13:3

1 Work out the **50th** term for the sequence where the position-to-term rule is

    a term number + 1   **d** term number − 5   **g** 3 × term number + 2
    b term number + 15   **e** 2 × term number   **h** 2 × term number − 1
    c term number − 2   **f** 2 × term number + 1   **i** 4 × term number − 2.

2 Work out the first **five** terms for the sequence where the position-to-term rule is

    a term number + 4   **d** 2 × term number − 1.5
    b term number − 13   **e** 2 − term number
    c 3 × term number + 1   **f** 200 − 3 × term number.

3 Describe the terms of the sequence where the position-to-term rule is

    a 2 × term number   **d** 2 × term number + 2   **g** 10 × term number
    b 2 × term number − 1   **e** 3 × term number   **h** 10 × term number + 1
    c 2 × term number + 1   **f** 3 × term number + 3   **i** 110 − 10 × term number.

4 Work out the 8th term of the sequences which have these position-to-term formulae.

a $T(n) = 3n + 5$
c $T(n) = 7n - 4$
e $T(n) = 0.5n - 1$
b $T(n) = 5n - 7$
d $T(n) = 4n + 10$
f $T(n) = 20 - 2n$

5 The position-to-term formula for a sequence is $T(n) = 30 - 2n$.

Work out the first 10 terms of the sequence.

6 The position-to-term formula for a sequence is $T(n) = 5n + 3$.

Without working out any terms in the sequence, write down the gap between the terms.

7 You can also use function machines to generate sequences.

a Copy this function machine diagram and fill in the gaps.

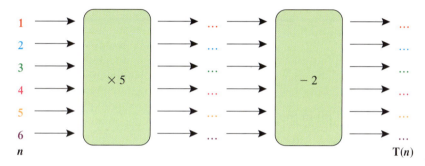

b Write the position-to-term formula for the sequence.
c Use your formula to work out the 20th term of the sequence.

8 Write down the first five terms of the sequence with the position-to-term formula

a $T(n) = 2n + 1$
d $T(n) = 10 - 2n$
g $T(n) = n + \frac{1}{2}$
b $T(n) = 3n - 1$
e $T(n) = 99 - 9n$
h $T(n) = 3n + 0.1$
c $T(n) = 2n - 5$
f $T(n) = n + 1$
i $T(n) = 0.1n$

9 a Write down the first five terms in the sequence with $T(n) = 10 - n$.
    Describe the sequence that this formula generates.

b Write down the first five terms in the sequence with $T(n) = 110 - 10n$.
    Describe the sequence that this formula generates.

10 a Describe the terms of the sequence with $T(n) = 2n + a$ for different values of a.

b Describe the terms of the sequence with $T(n) = 3n + b$ for different values of b.

c Describe the terms of the sequence with $T(n) = 10n + c$ for different values of c.

13 Sequences

Finding any term in a sequence — Level 6

You can find the formula for the *n*th term of the sequence 7, 11, 15, 19, …
(+4, +4, +4)

Look at the **difference pattern** for the sequence. The **difference** is always **4**.

This means that the *n*th term rule will start with **4 × term number**.

Next, write down the **multiples of 4** and compare them with the terms of the sequence.

Multiples of 4	4	8	12	16
	+3	+3	+3	+3
Sequence	7	11	15	19

To change the **multiples of 4** into the sequence you need to **add 3**.

The ***n*th term rule** is **4 × term number + 3**

So the ***n*th term formula** is T(*n*) = 4*n* + 3. The **70**th term is T(**70**) = 4 × **70** + 3 = 283.

Exercise 13:4

1 a Copy this diagram and fill in the difference pattern.

9, 15, 21, 27, …
+… +… +…

  b Copy and complete this sentence.
  The *n*th term rule will start with … × term number.

  c Copy and complete this diagram.

  Multiples of …: … … … …
                    +… +… +… +…
  Sequence   9   15   21   27

  d What do you have to add to the multiples to get the sequence?

  e Write down the formula for the *n*th term of the sequence.

2 Work out the formula for the *n*th term of each of these sequences.

  a 7, 13, 19, 25, 31, …
  b 11, 13, 15, 17, 19, …
  c 4, 9, 14, 19, 24, …
  d 100, 110, 120, 130, 140, …
  e 100, 107, 114, 121, 128, …
  f 4, 12, 20, 28, 36, …

3 Find a formula for the *n*th term of each of these linear sequences.

  a 2.5, 4.5, 6.5, 8.5, 10.5, …
  b 10, 5, 0, −5, −10, …
  c −7, −4, −1, 2, 5, …
  d 6, 2, −2, −6, −10, …

3 Non-linear sequences

Finding triangular numbers

Generating simple non-linear sequences

Key words
triangular numbers   difference pattern
non-linear   quadratic

Finding triangular numbers   Level 5

1, 3, 6, 10 and 15 are all **triangular numbers**.

They are called triangular numbers because you can draw triangles like this:

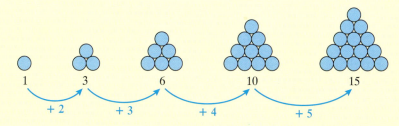

The **difference pattern** shows the gap between each triangular number and the next one. The differences increase by one each time.

Exercise 13:5

1 a Draw the next three diagrams in this pattern.

 b Write down the first six triangular numbers.

2

Use this difference pattern to write down the first 10 triangular numbers.

3 a Work out the sum of the 1st and 2nd triangular numbers.
 b Work out the sum of the 2nd and 3rd triangular numbers.
 c Work out the sum of the 3rd and 4th triangular numbers.
 d Write down what you notice. Check that the pattern continues up to the 9th and 10th triangular numbers.
 e Use diagrams like this to explain why the pattern works.

13 Sequences

4 To work out the **4**th triangular number you can multiply **4** by **5** then divide by **2**.

To work out the **5**th triangular number you can multiply **5** by **6** then divide by **2**.

You can write this as a formula. The nth triangular number $= \dfrac{n(n+1)}{2}$

Use this formula to work out the following triangular numbers.

  a 9th **b** 20th **c** 50th **d** 100th **e** 1000th

Facts to figure

5 On 10th July 1796, Carl Gauss, a German mathematician, wrote in his diary

$$\text{EYPHKA! } num = \Delta + \Delta + \Delta$$

He had discovered that every whole number can be written as the sum of **no more than** three triangular numbers.

Show that this rule works for numbers up to 30.
Write your answers like this.

$1 = 1$
$2 = 1 + 1$
$3 = 3$
$4 = 1 + 3$

Generating simple non-linear sequences Level 6

The terms of a **non-linear** sequence go up or down in unequal steps.

The sequence of square numbers is a non-linear sequence. 1, 4, 9, 16, 25 (+3, +5, +7, +9)

The **differences** are not the same.

Sequences that are based on the square numbers are called **quadratic** sequences.

The nth term formula for the sequence of square numbers is $T(n) = n^2$.

The nth term formula for the sequence   2, 5, 10, 17, 26, ...
is $T(n) = n^2 + 1$

because the terms of this sequence are all one more than the square numbers.

Exercise 13:6

1 a Copy and complete this diagram.

Square numbers ... +... ... +... ... +... ... +...
Sequence 5 8 13 20

  b What do you have to add to the square numbers to get the sequence?

  c Write down the formula for the nth term of the sequence.

2 Write down the first five terms of the sequence with nth term formula.

   a $T(n) = n^2 + 2$ **b** $T(n) = 2n^2 + 1$ **c** $T(n) = n^2 - 2$

3 Find a formula for the nth term of each of these quadratic sequences.

   a 0, 3, 8, 15, 24, …   **c** 2, 8, 18, 32, 50, …

   b 4, 7, 12, 19, 28, …   **d** $-1, -4, -9, -16, -25, …$

4 Here is a sequence of rectangular numbers.

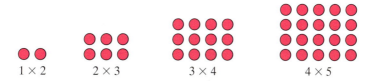

Find a formula for the nth term of this sequence.

Facts to figure

5 Fibonacci was born in 1170 in Pisa in Italy. His real name was Leonardo Pisano but he was the *figlio* (the Italian word for son) of **Bonacci**o so he was known as **Fibonacci**.

Fibonacci investigated how fast rabbits could breed.

He started with one pair of rabbits: 🟡 1 female and 🔴 1 male.

He assumed that rabbits are two months old when they first give birth.
He assumed that each breeding pair of rabbits gives birth to another pair of rabbits, one male and one female, every month.

This is the sequence he found for the number of pairs of rabbits at the end of each month.

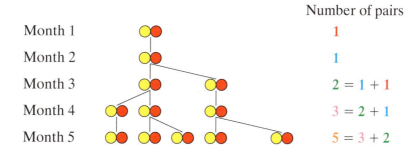

So Fibonacci's sequence is 1, 1, 2, 3, 5, …

You can find each term by adding the previous two terms.

   a Calculate how many pairs of rabbits there would be at the end of the 12th month.

   b Work out the difference pattern for Fibonacci's sequence. What do you notice?

13 Sequences

Watch out ... there's a trap about

▸ Don't make assumptions about term-to-term rules.
Look at this sequence. It has some missing terms.   2, ..., 8, ..., 32
Halfway between 2 and 8 is 5.
Halfway between 8 and 32 is 20.
But 5 and 20 are not the missing terms!

The term-to-term rule is actually multiply by 2,
so the sequence looks like this   2, 4, 8, 16, 32

▸ This is the sequence of square numbers   1, 4, 9, 16, 25, ...
The **second** term is **4**.
Using algebra you write this as T(**2**) = **4**.
Don't call it T(4)!
T(**4**) is the **fourth** term. It is **16**.

Test yourself

1 For each of these sequences, write down
   (**1**) the term-to-term rule
   (**2**) the next two terms of the sequence.

   a 4, 11, 18, 25, 32, ...   **c** 1, 3, 5, 7, 9, ...   **e** 40, 20, 10, ...
   b 8, 4, 0, −4, −8, ...   **d** 2, 4, 8, 16, 32, ...   **f** 1, 5, 25, ...

2 a Copy the sequence of patterns of counters.

 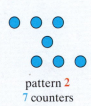 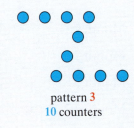

pattern **1**   pattern **2**   pattern **3**
4 counters   7 counters   10 counters

b Draw the next pattern in the sequence.
c Write down the sequence of the numbers of counters in the patterns.
d Write down the term-to-term rule.
e Explain why the pattern in your sequence happens.
f This is the formula for finding the number of counters from the pattern number.

   number of counters = 3 × pattern number + 1

Use this formula to find the number of counters in the 25th pattern.

3 Look at the following matchstick pattern.

 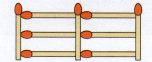 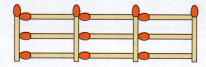

   a Write down the number of matches in the next pattern.
   b Copy and complete this formula for the number of matches, *m*, in the *n*th pattern.
   $$m = \ldots n + \ldots$$
   c Use the diagrams to explain why the formula works.
   d Can you use exactly 51 matches to make a pattern in this sequence? Explain your answer.

4 Look at these tile patterns.

   a Write down the sequence for the number of **red** tiles in this pattern.
   b Write down the next three terms of the sequence.
   c Write down a formula for the *n*th term of this sequence.
   d Work out the number of red tiles in the 50th pattern.

5 Use each rule to work out
   (1) the first five terms   **(2)** the 50th term
   for the sequence with position-to-term rule

   a **term number** + 2   c 3 × **term number**
   b 2 × **term number** − 1   d 100 − **term number**.

6 Write down the first five terms of the sequence with *n*th term formula
   a $T(n) = 5n + 1$ c $T(n) = 7 - 4n$ e $T(n) = 3 + 2n$
   b $T(n) = 2n - 2$ d $T(n) = 5 - n$ f $T(n) = 4n - 11$

7 Work out the formula for the *n*th term of each of these sequences.
   a 4, 7, 10, 13, …   b 60, 70, 80, 90, …   c 15, 17, 19, 21, …

8 What are the two smallest numbers that are **both** triangular and square?

9 Find a formula for the *n*th term of each of these quadratic sequences.
   a 3, 6, 11, 18, …   c 3, 12, 27, 48, …
   b −2, 1, 6, 13, …   d 6, 9, 14, 21, ….

13 Sequences

Chapter 13 Summary

Level 5

Sequences

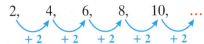

The sequence of even numbers is **infinite**.
The term-to-term rule is **add 2**.
It is a linear sequence.
It is an ascending sequence.

This sequence is finite.
The terms **go down by 1 more each time**.
It is a non-linear sequence.
It is a descending sequence.

Triangular numbers

The sequence of triangular numbers is 1, 3, 6, 10, …

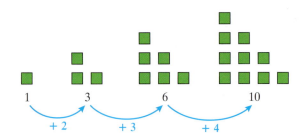

Level 6

General rules for patterns

The rule for the **number of counters** is **2 × pattern number + 1** because there are **2 more** counters in each pattern.

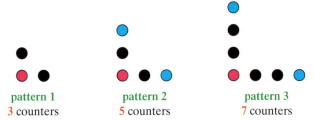

pattern 1   pattern 2   pattern 3
3 counters   5 counters   7 counters

The formula for the number of counters, c, in pattern number n is $c = 2n + 1$

The formula for the nth term

$T(1)$ is the **first** term of a sequence. $T(2)$ is the **second** term. $T(n)$ is the nth term.

The position-to-term rule for this sequence is **3 × term number + 1**.
The **formula for the nth term** is $T(n) = 3n + 1$
$T(20) = 3 × 20 + 1 = 61$ so the **20**th term is 61.

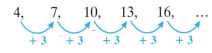

Non-linear sequences

Non-linear sequences go up or down in unequal steps.

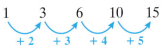

Quadratic sequences are based on the square numbers.

$T(n) = n^2$ 1, 4, 9, 16, …
$T(n) = n^2 + 1$ 2, 5, 10, 17, …

14 Area, volume and measures

Year 6
- Finding perimeters
- Using the formula for the area of a rectangle
- Recognising 2-D and 3-D shapes

Chapter 2 Multiplying and dividing
Converting metric units

1. Area and volume
2. Measures

Year 8
- Finding lengths and areas of 2-D shapes
- Finding surface areas and volumes of prisms

You should already know:

▶ **how to find perimeters**

Perimeter is the total distance around the outside of a shape.

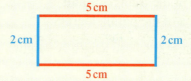

The perimeter of this rectangle is
2 cm + 5 cm + 2 cm + 5 cm = 14 cm.

▶ **the area of a rectangle**

Area is the amount of space that a shape covers. The area of the rectangle above is $5 \times 2 = 10 \text{ cm}^2$.

▶ **2-D and 3-D shapes**

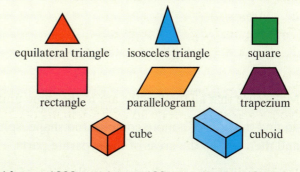

▶ **these conversion facts for metric units of length**

1 km = 1000 m   1 m = 100 cm   1 cm = 10 mm

221

14 Area, volume and measures

1 Area and volume

▶ **Using area formulae**

▶ **Calculating the surface area of cubes and cuboids**

▶ **Calculating the volume of cubes and cuboids**

Key words
area   square centimetre (cm²)
square millimetre (mm²)
square metre (m²)
parallelogram   triangle
trapezium   surface area
face   cuboid   cube   volume
cubic centimetre (cm³)

▶ Using area formulae — Level 6

Area is measured in squares. **Square centimetres** are written **cm²**.
You will also need **square millimetres** (**mm²**) and **square metres** (**m²**).

1 cm²   1 mm²

A **parallelogram** has the same area as a rectangle with the same base and height.

Area = $b$ase length × $h$eight

$A = bh$

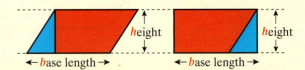

A **triangle** is half a parallelogram.

The area of the triangle is **half** of the area of the parallelogram.

Area = $\frac{1}{2}$ × $b$ase length × $h$eight

$A = \frac{1}{2}bh$

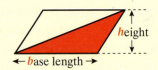

A **trapezium** has the same area as a rectangle with the same height and a width equal to the mean of the parallel sides of the trapezium.

Area = $\frac{a + b}{2} \times h$

$A = \frac{1}{2}(a + b)h$

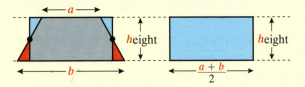

Make sure that all the lengths are in the same units before you work out the area.

To find the area of a more complicated shape, split it up and then add up the areas of the separate parts.

If a shape has a hole in it, work out the area of the surrounding shape and then subtract the area of the hole.

Exercise 14:1

1 **You need 1 cm squared paper for this question.**

   a Draw a **rectangle** that has an area of 8 cm².

   b Draw another rectangle that has an area of 8 cm². This rectangle must have a different perimeter from the rectangle in part **a**.

   c Draw a **triangle** that has an area of 4 cm².

2 The information in the box describes three different squares A, B and C.

Put squares A, B and C in order of size, starting with the smallest.

You **must** show calculations to explain how you work out your answer.

> The **area** of square A is **36 cm²**.
>
> The **side length** of square B is **36 cm**.
>
> The **perimeter** of square C is **36 cm**.

3 Find the area of each of these shapes.

Remember to give the units in your answers.

a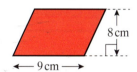

e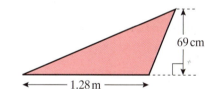

b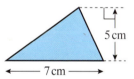

f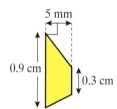

c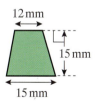

g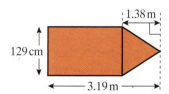

d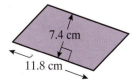

h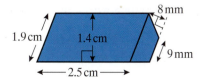

14　Area, volume and measures

4 This diagram is drawn on 1 cm dotty paper.

Find the area of the **quadrilateral** by

a using the red lines and adding up the areas of the triangles inside

b using the blue square and subtracting the areas of the triangles outside.

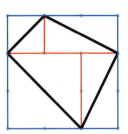

5 Find the coloured area in each of these.

a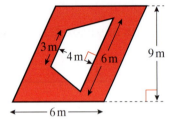

b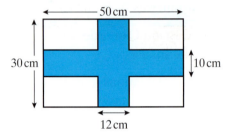

Facts to figure

6 **Pick's theorem**

Georg Alexander Pick was an Austrian mathematician. In 1899, he described a relationship that he had found between area and perimeter.

These shapes are drawn on 1 cm dotty paper.

The red shape has 6 dots on the *p*erimeter and 1 dot *i*nside. It has an *a*rea of 3 cm².

The blue shape has 6 dots on the *p*erimeter and 2 dots *i*nside. It has an *a*rea of 4 cm².

The green shape has 3 dots on the *p*erimeter and 3 dots *i*nside. It has an *a*rea of $3\frac{1}{2}$ cm².

Start by drawing shapes that all have 1 dot *i*nside and find a relationship between the *a*rea of the shape and the number of dots on the *p*erimeter.
Use the methods from **Question 4** to help you work out the areas of harder shapes.

Then look at shapes with 2 dots *i*nside and then 3 dots *i*nside and so on.

Find a relationship between the *a*rea, the number of dots on the *p*erimeter and the number of dots *i*nside for these shapes.

Calculating the surface area of cubes and cuboids Level 6

The **surface area** of a solid is the total area of all the **faces**.
You can sketch a net to help you to find the surface area.
Here is a net for this **cuboid**.

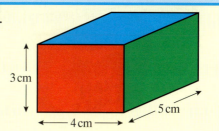

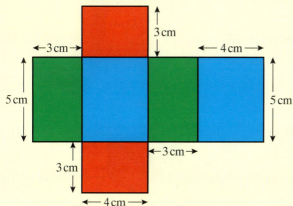

The surface area of the cuboid = 3 × 4 + 3 × 4 + 5 × 4 + 5 × 4 + 5 × 3 + 5 × 3
$$= 12 + 12 + 20 + 20 + 15 + 15$$
$$= 94 \text{ cm}^2$$

For a **cube** with sides of length l, the surface area S is given by
$$S = 6l^2$$

For a **cuboid** with length l, width w and height h, the surface area S is given by
$$S = 2lw + 2lh + 2wh$$

You can use these formulae instead of drawing the nets and adding the areas of the faces.

Exercise 14:2

1 Find the surface area of each of these cuboids by drawing a net.

a b
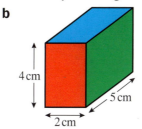

2 Find the surface area of each of these by using the appropriate formula.

a
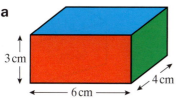

b
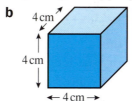

c
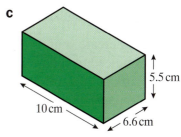

14 Area, volume and measures

3 Find the surface area of each of these boxes.

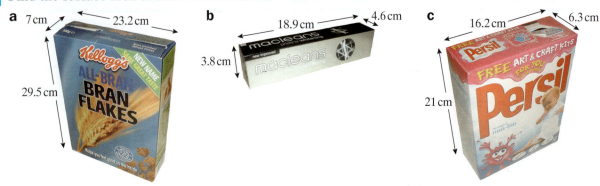

4 Find the surface area of this wooden step.

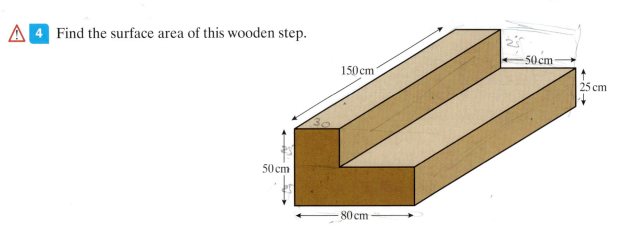

5 Find the surface area of this girder.

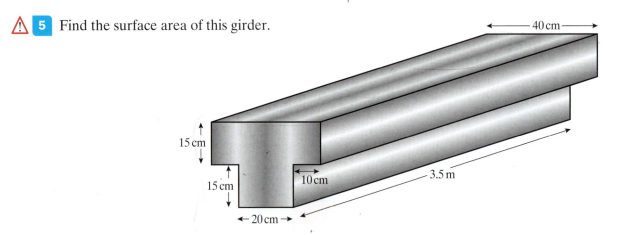

Think on!

6 The diagram shows the areas of three faces of a cuboid.
Find the length of each of the edges of the cuboid.

Now create your own question like this.
You need to choose integer values for your length, width and height.
Work out the areas of the faces of your cuboid and label them.
Swap questions with the person sitting next to you.

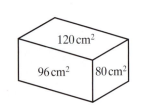

14

Calculating the volume of cubes and cuboids   Level 6

Volume is measured in cubes. **Cubic centimetres** are written **cm³**.

This is 1 cm³.

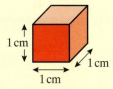

Each cube in this cuboid has a volume of 1 cm³.

There are 8 centimetre cubes in each layer.
There are 3 layers of cubes.

The volume of the cuboid is 8 × 3 = 24 cm³.

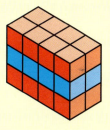

To find the **volume of a cuboid**

(1) multiply the length by the width to find the number of cubes in 1 layer.

(2) multiply your answer by the height.

You can also use the formula

    *V*olume of a cuboid = *l*ength × *w*idth × *h*eight

          V = *lwh*

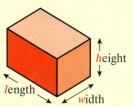

Exercise 14:3

1 Find the volume of each of these blocks of 1 cm cubes.

a   b 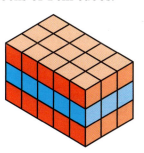   c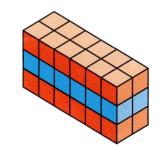

2 Find the volume of each of these cuboids by using the formula.

a 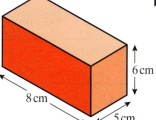   b 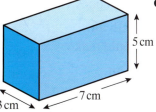   c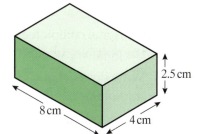

3 Find the volumes of the cuboids in Exercise 14:2 **Questions 1** to **3**.

14 Area, volume and measures

4 The squared paper shows the nets of cuboid A and cuboid B.

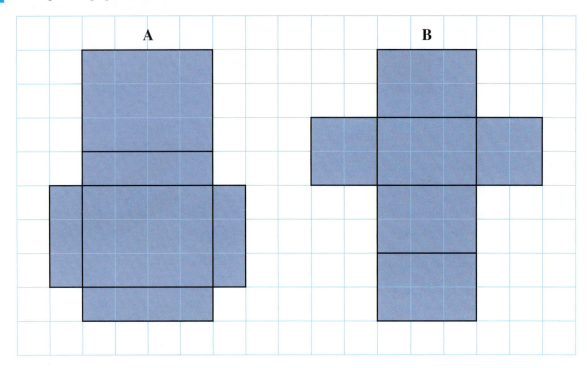

a Do the cuboids have the **same surface area**?
Show calculations to explain how you know.

b Do the cuboids have the **same volume**?
Show calculations to explain how you know.

5 This is a diagram of Fraser's new fish tank.
He needs to know the mass of the water in the tank to make sure that a shelf will support it.
He knows that $1\,cm^3$ of water has a mass of 1 gram.

Calculate the mass of the water in Fraser's fish tank.
Give your answer in kilograms.

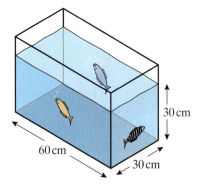

Explore

6 Imagine that you have 64 centimetre cubes.

a Copy and complete this table with all the possible cuboids that you could make.

b Write down what you notice about the volumes of the cuboids.

c Which cuboid has the smallest surface area?

Length	Width	Height	Volume	Surface area
1 cm	8 cm	8 cm		
1 cm	4 cm	16 cm		

2 Measures

- **Making sensible estimates**
- **Using metric equivalents of imperial measures**
- **Using and converting metric units**

Key words	
estimation	imperial
mile	yard
foot	inch
approximately equals (≈)	
pound (lb)	ounce (oz)
gallon	pint

Making sensible estimates   Level 5

To make an **estimation** it is useful to compare with something familiar.

When you estimate height, think of an adult man as being 2 metres tall.

This tree is about 3 times the height of the man. So the tree is roughly 6 m tall.

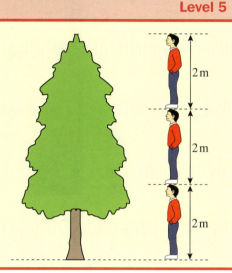

Exercise 14:4

1 Newspapers often compare the length or height of a large object with a double-decker bus. This helps readers to picture the size of the object.

In 2007 a *colossal squid* was caught.
It measured 10 metres.
Nobody knows how big *colossal squid* can grow.
This diagram shows how big they might be.

 London bus 8 m

 Sperm whale

 Colossal squid

Use the diagram to estimate
a the size of a sperm whale
b the possible size of a *colossal squid*.

14 Area, volume and measures

2 Nelson's Column in London is 52 m high.

   a Use this diagram to estimate the height of the Canary Wharf Tower in London.

   b Use this diagram to estimate the height of the CN Tower in Toronto, Canada.

52 m

3 A news web site used this diagram in a story about a new dinosaur. Scientists discovered its skeleton in Argentina.

Use the diagram to estimate the length of the dinosaur.

Facts to figure

4 In the USA, newspapers describe areas by comparing them with the size of the smallest state, Rhode Island.

Rhode Island   Wales   Belgium

Rhode Island has an area of about 4000 km². Use these diagrams to estimate the area of

   a Wales   **b** Belgium.

Using metric equivalents of imperial measures — Level 5

Many people still use **imperial** units.
You need to know approximate metric equivalents of imperial measures.

Distances are measured in **miles**, **yards**, **feet** and **inches**.

5 miles **approximately equals** (≈) 8 km

1 yard ≈ 1 m

3 feet ≈ 1 m

1 inch ≈ $2\frac{1}{2}$ cm

To change miles to km,
divide by 5 and multiply by 8
27 miles ≈ 27 ÷ 5 × 8 = 43.2 km

To change inches to cm, multiply by 2.5
5 inches ≈ 5 × 2.5 = 12.5 cm

Mass is measured in **pounds (lb)** and **ounces (oz)**.

2.2 lb ≈ 1 kg

1 oz ≈ 30 g

To change grams to ounces, divide by 30
120 g ≈ 120 ÷ 30 = 4 oz

Capacity is measured in **gallons** and **pints**.

1 gallon ≈ $4\frac{1}{2}$ ℓ

1.75 pints ≈ 1 ℓ

To change litres to pints, multiply by 1.75
18 litres ≈ 18 × 1.75 = 31.5 pints

Exercise 14:5

1 Bhupinder cycles 6 miles from his home to school.
   a How many kilometres is this?
   b He cycles to and from school five days a week.
      How many kilometres does he cycle in a week?

2 How many miles is 17 kilometres?
   Give your answer correct to 1 d.p.

3 A wine bottle holds 750 mℓ. How many pints is this?

4 1 gallon is approximately 4.5 litres. A litre of diesel costs 100.8p.
   a How much does 1 gallon cost? Give your answer to the nearest penny.
   b How many litres of diesel can I buy for £35? Give your answer to 2 d.p.
   c How many gallons of diesel can I buy for £35? Give your answer to 1 d.p.

14 Area, volume and measures

5 a A rough calculation to convert litres into pints is to double and subtract 10% from your answer.
Use this method to convert 15 litres into pints.

b The equivalent rough calculation to convert pints into litres is to halve and add 10% to your answer.
Use this method to convert 40 pints into litres.

6 Convert

- **a** 7 yards into m
- **b** 6 oz into g
- **c** 15 m into feet
- **d** 7 inches into cm
- **e** 20 kg into lb
- **f** 10 litres into pints
- **g** 330 g into oz
- **h** 128 km into miles
- **i** 110 lb into kg
- **j** 612.5 pints into litres
- **k** 16 m into feet
- **l** 450 miles into km.

7 While Catrin is on holiday in Greece she sees this sign.
It shows the maximum speed limit for the road in kilometres per hour.
What is the maximum speed in miles per hour?

8 The fuel tank on Ravi's car has a capacity of 35 litres. How many gallons is this?

9 A tonne of feathers weighs 1000 kg. How many pounds is this?

10 8 kilometres is approximately 5 miles.
In each of these formulae k is the number of kilometres and m is the number of miles.
Which is the correct formula to change kilometres into miles?

$m = 8k + 5$ $m = \frac{8}{5}k$ $m = \frac{5}{8}k$ $m = 5k + 8$

Think on!

11 Make a two-way table like this.

Sort the units on these 14 cards into your two-way table.

	Length	Mass	Capacity
Metric			
Imperial			

centimetre, foot, pint, inch, kilogram, gram, gallon, litre, mile, ounce, kilometre, yard, metre, pound

Using and converting metric units — Level 6

The sides of this square are **1 cm** long.
1 cm is the same as **10 mm**.

The area of the square is **1 cm × 1 cm = 1 cm²**,
or **10 mm × 10 mm = 100 mm²**.

So, **6 cm² = 6 × 100 mm² = 600 mm²**

1 m is the same as 100 cm

so 1 m² = 100 × 100 = 10 000 cm².

Also 1 km = 1000 m

so 1 km² = 1000 × 1000 = 1 000 000 m²

Exercise 14:6

1 Micro mosaics were very popular in the nineteenth century.
Micro tiles were used to create miniature mosaics on pieces of jewellery.
This micro tile has an area of 1 mm².

   a Write down how many micro tiles fit
      (1) along the length of this rectangle
      (2) down the side of this rectangle.

   b Write down the area of the rectangle
      (1) in cm²
      (2) in mm².

2 a A city covers an area of 1600 km².
How many square metres is this?

   b A football pitch covers an area of 5000 m².
How many football pitches would fit into an area of 1600 km²?

3 The area of the front of a CD case is 16 800 mm².
What is this area in cm²?

4 a The **perimeter** of a square is 8.4 cm. What is its **area** in mm²?

   b The **perimeter** of a square is 1.2 km. What is its **area** in m²?

   c The **area** of a square is 12.25 mm². What is its **perimeter** in cm?

14 Area, volume and measures

Watch out... there's a trap about

▶ You can enlarge a shape by stretching it.
The **red square** is stretched in two different directions to make the **blue square**.

After the stretch each side is 3 times longer but the area **isn't** 3 times bigger!

The **blue square** is **three times wider** and **three times higher** than the **red square**.

So the area of the **blue square** is $3 \times 3 = 9$ times the area of the **red square**.

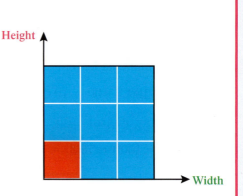

Test yourself

1 Copy this line onto squared paper.

  a Draw 3 more lines to make a rectangle with an area of 10 cm^2.

  b Draw 2 more lines to make a triangle with an area of 10 cm^2.

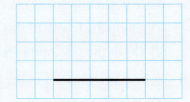

2 Find the area of each of these shapes.

Remember to give the units in your answers.

a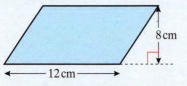

c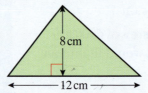

e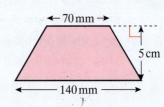

b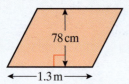

d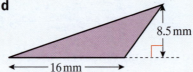

f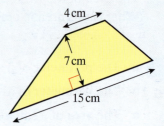

3 Find the coloured area of each of these shapes.

a 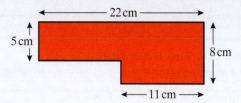   b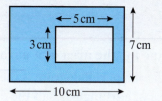

4 The picture shows the plan of a farmer's field.

a Calculate the area of the field.

The field needs to be divided into two equal parts.

b Copy the picture and show where a fence could go to divide the field into two equal parts.

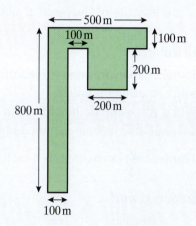

5 Use the formula for the volume of a cuboid to find the volume of each of these. Remember to give the units of your answers.

a 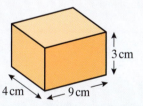   b 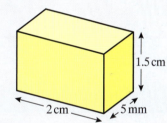   c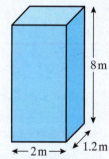

6 1 gallon is approximately 4.5 litres.
Approximately how many gallons are 90 litres?

7 Convert

a 11 yards into m
b 108 km into miles
c 15 miles into km
d 15 oz into g
e 101.2 lb into kg
f 5.5 kg into lb
g 12 litres into pints
h 77 pints into litres
i 7 gallons into litres.

8 Convert the following into cm^2.

a $5.6 \, m^2$
b $12.05 \, m^2$
c $250 \, mm^2$
d $834 \, mm^2$

14 Area, volume and measures

Chapter 14 Summary

Level 5

Formulae for the area of a parallelogram, triangle and trapezium

The **A**rea of a **parallelogram** is the **b**ase length × the **h**eight. $A = bh$

The **A**rea of a **triangle** is half the **b**ase length × the **h**eight. $A = \frac{1}{2}bh$

The **A**rea of a **trapezium**
is half the sum of the parallel sides (*a* + *b*) × the **h**eight. $A = \frac{1}{2}(a+b)h$

Estimating

To make an **estimation** it is useful to compare with something familiar.
When you estimate height, think of an adult man as being 2 metres tall.

This tree is approximately 4 metres tall.

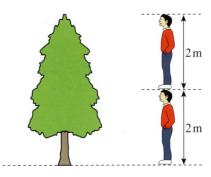

Imperial units

Distance	Mass	Capacity
5 miles ≈ 8 km	2.2 lb ≈ 1 kg	1 gallon ≈ $4\frac{1}{2}$ ℓ
1 yard ≈ 1 m	1 oz ≈ 30 g	1.75 pints ≈ 1 ℓ
3 feet ≈ 1 m		
1 inch ≈ $2\frac{1}{2}$ cm		

Level 6

Surface area and volume

For a **cube** with sides of length *l*, the surface area *S* is given by

$$S = 6l^2$$

For a cuboid with length *l*, width *w* and height *h*, the surface area *S* is given by

$$S = 2lw + 2lh + 2wh$$

Volume of a cuboid = **l**ength × **w**idth × **h**eight

$$V = lwh$$

Converting metric units

1 cm² = 10 mm × 10 mm = 100 mm²

1 m² = 100 cm × 100 cm = 10 000 cm²

1 km² = 1000 m × 1000 m = 1 000 000 m²

15 Dealing with data

**Chapter 5
Data and diagrams**
- Calculating averages
- Drawing simple diagrams

1. More diagrams
2. Writing questionnaires
3. Practical project

Year 8
- Constructing frequency polygons
- Estimating averages for grouped data

You should already know:

▶ **how to use frequency diagrams to organise data**

This frequency diagram shows the results of a survey into the distance pupils live from school.

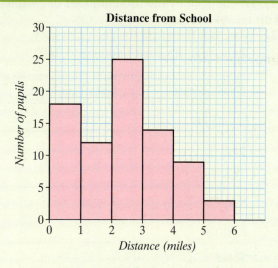

▶ **when to use different averages and the range**

The **median** is the middle value when the data values are in order.
The **mode** is the most common data value.
The **mean** is the total of all the data values divided by the number of data values.
The **range** is used to show how spread out the data is. It is the largest value take away the smallest value.

▶ **how to read information from pie charts**

This pie chart shows that more people prefer to watch football on TV than any other sport.

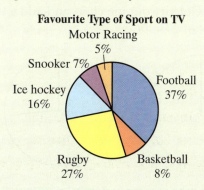

15 Dealing with data

1 More diagrams

▶ **Constructing pie charts**

▶ **Drawing scatter graphs**

▶ **Understanding correlation**

Key words
pie chart
scatter graph
correlation
positive correlation
negative correlation

Constructing pie charts — Level 6

Pie charts are used to display data that is in categories.

In a survey, **30** people were asked which newspaper they read.
To draw a pie chart of the survey results:

(1) Divide 360° by the total number of people   360° ÷ **30** = **12°** per person

(2) Work out the angle for each category.
    Check that the angles add up to **360°**.

Newspaper	Number of people	Working	Angle
Guardian	8	8 × **12°** =	96°
Mirror	7	7 × **12°** =	84°
The Times	3	3 × **12°** =	36°
Sun	6	6 × **12°** =	72°
Express	6	6 × **12°** =	72°
Total	**30**		**360°**

(3) Draw the pie chart:
  • Start by putting a dot on your paper.
  • Draw a circle with this dot as the centre.
  • Draw a vertical line from the dot to the top of the circle.
  • Measure your first angle from this line.
  • Draw in all the other angles.
  • Colour your pie chart and add a title and labels or a key.

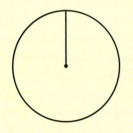 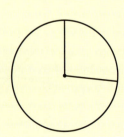  

Newspaper Survey of 30 People

Exercise 15:1

1 This table shows how Rachel spent her time yesterday.

Activity	Number of hours	Working	Angle
Sleeping	8	8 × … =	
Eating	1	1 × … =	
School	8	8 × … =	
Playing sports	2	2 × … =	
Doing homework	1	1 × … =	
Other	4	4 × … =	
Total	24		360°

a Copy the table.

b Copy and complete:
   Divide 360° by the number of hours in a day   360° ÷ 24 hours = …° per hour

c Fill in the last two columns of your table.

d Draw a pie chart to show how Rachel spent her day.
   Don't forget a title and labels.

2 Abbi has done a survey on which mobile phone networks the pupils in her year group use.
These are her results.

Network	O_2	Orange	T-Mobile	3	Other	None
Number of people	25	24	20	10	8	33

Draw a pie chart to show Abbi's results.

3 In a survey, 45 people were asked which type of chocolate they preferred.
These are the results.

Type of chocolate	Milk	Plain	White
Number of people	20	9	16

Draw a pie chart to show this data.

4 Pupils in Class 8K were asked how they travelled to school.
These are the results.

Method of travel	Bus	Walk	Car	Bike
Number of pupils	11	8	3	2

Draw a pie chart to show this data.

15 Dealing with data

5 This table shows the age of cinema-goers in a recent survey.

Age range	5 to 14	15 to 24	25 to 34	35 and over
Percentage	25%	35%	20%	20%
Angle				

a Copy the table.

b Copy this and fill in the gap.
   Divide 360° by 100%   360° ÷ 100% = …° per 1%

c Fill in the last row of your table.

d Draw a pie chart to show this data.

6 This table shows the percentages of the UK population in four age groups.

Age group	Percentage of population
Under 16	20%
16–59	62%
60–75	11%
Over 75	7%

a Draw a pie chart to show this data.
   Round the angles to the nearest degree before you draw the pie chart.

b The UK population is about 60 million.
   Work out how many people are in each group.

Explore

7 These two pie charts show music sales in 1973 and 2003.

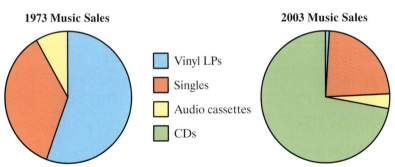

a Why do CD sales not appear in the 1973 pie chart?

b What is the best-selling format in each year?

c Were the same amount of units sold in each year?

d Draw what you think the pie chart for 2033 will look like. Explain your reasons.

Drawing scatter graphs   Level 6

Scatter graphs are used to see if there is a connection between two sets of data.

They can be used to investigate questions such as:
- Do your reaction times improve if you play a lot of computer games?
- Do pupils who do well in maths tests also do well in science?
- Does temperature affect the sales of ice cream?

This table shows the marks obtained in a **maths** test and a **science** test by 15 pupils.

Maths	67	54	23	87	56	46	43	29	56	67	51	23	36	59	64
Science	61	49	32	79	52	43	38	34	57	71	47	70	40	54	68

To draw a scatter graph, you plot the points like coordinates.

On this scatter graph, **maths** marks are on the *x*-axis and **science** marks are on the *y*-axis.

Each point represents one person.
The green point shows the person who scored 67 in maths and 61 in science.

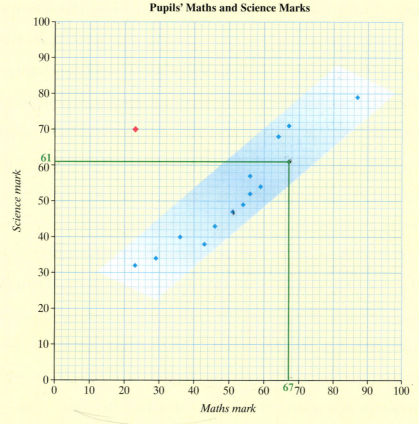

Most of the points lie in the blue strip on the diagram.

This shows that people with high maths marks also have high science marks.

There is one point that does not fit this pattern.

The pupil represented by the pink point scored 23 in maths but 70 in science.

This pupil did much better in science than in maths.

15 Dealing with data

Exercise 15:2

1 This table shows the marks obtained in a French test and a German test by 15 pupils.

French	23	32	18	28	24	31	19	32	25	28	32	13	24	35	25
German	21	35	20	27	26	34	15	31	22	34	35	17	21	29	29

    a Draw a scatter graph with French marks on the *x*-axis and German marks on the *y*-axis.

    b Do the pupils who do well in French also do well in German? Explain how you can tell.

2 This table shows the same French marks that you used in **Question 1**.

It also shows the time taken by each pupil to run 200 m. The times are to the nearest second.

French	23	32	18	28	24	31	19	32	25	28	32	13	24	35	25
200 m time (s)	32	34	35	40	29	31	37	45	36	38	35	36	33	29	42

    a Draw a scatter graph with French marks on the *x*-axis and 200 m times on the *y*-axis.

    b Do the pupils who do well in French also run the fastest? Explain how you can tell.

3 Bill owns an ice-cream van.
He keeps a record of his sales and the maximum daily temperature.
Here are his results for 15 days.

Sales (£)	67	78	75	54	67	88	24	28	38	67	65	72	92	74	65
Temp (°C)	22	26	26	22	23	30	17	19	20	21	23	26	28	27	25

    a Draw a scatter graph to show this data.

    b Describe what happens to Bill's sales as the temperature increases.

4 The ages of 10 Ford Fiestas and their current values are shown in this table.

Age (years)	3	6	5	4	2	6	5	3	6	5
Value (£)	6000	2500	2900	3500	6500	2300	3100	5800	2100	3300

    a Draw a scatter graph to show this data.

    b Describe what happens to the value of the car as it gets older.

    c A Fiesta is on sale for £2400. How old do you think it is?

15

Understanding correlation   Level 6

You have seen that scatter graphs can show a connection between two sets of data.

This connection is called **correlation**.

There are two types of correlation.

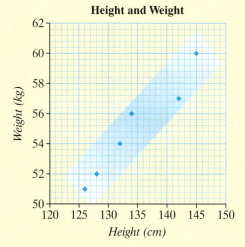

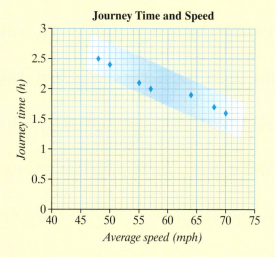

These two sets of data show **positive correlation**.
As height gets bigger, so does weight. The strip containing the points slopes upwards.

These two sets of data show **negative correlation**.
As average speed gets bigger, journey time gets smaller. The strip containing the points slopes downwards.

Exercise 15:3

1 This scatter graph shows the average body length and average foot length of different species of rodents.

What does the scatter graph tell you about the type of correlation between the body length and the foot length of these rodents?

2004 part

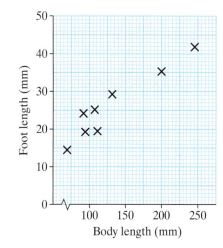

2 For each of these pairs of data, say whether you think they will show **positive**, **negative** or **no correlation**.

   a The size of a car engine and its top speed
   b The cost of a secondhand car and its age
   c The number of goals scored by a football team and its position in the league
   d The heights of pupils and their scores in a maths test
   e The cost of a taxi journey and its length

15 Dealing with data

2 Writing questionnaires

- Types of data
- Types of question
- Choosing a sample

Key words

primary	secondary
experimental	closed
open	sample

Types of data — Level 5

Statistics are used to solve problems, answer questions and to decide whether statements are correct.

Here are some examples of the sorts of problems that you can investigate using statistics.
- What is the most popular computer games console? Why is this?
- What is the reading age of this book?
- I think that the train service is much worse than it used to be.

The first stage in trying to solve a statistical problem is to decide what data you need and how you are going to collect it. There are three types of data.

Primary data   This is data that you collect using an observation sheet or questionnaire.
Secondary data   This is data that you get from other sources such as books or the internet.
Experimental data   This is data you collect by doing an experiment to test a theory. You have seen some probability experiments in Chapter 11.

Exercise 15:4

1 Read through these questions and statements.
Suggest what data you would collect to investigate each one.
  a The summers are getting hotter in the UK every year.
  b Girls have better reaction times than boys.
  c Some newspapers are easier to read than others. Why is this?
  d England is the most crowded country in Europe.
  e Is there too much traffic driving past the school?

2 Read through these questions and statements.
For each one say whether the data you would use would be:

    Primary   **Secondary**   **Experimental**
  a Pupils in our school spend too much time playing computer games.
  b Pupils in our school play less sport than pupils of 30 years ago.
  c People catch better with their writing hands.
  d How will people vote in the next general election?
  e Which is the most watched TV soap? Why is this?
  f Are more young people injured in car accidents in the winter than in the summer?

3 Colin is collecting toys from the local burger bar.
He gets a toy at random with each meal.
There are six toys to collect altogether.
Colin's mum is worried about the number of meals she is going to have to buy!

Describe how she could use a dice to do an experiment to estimate how many meals she will have to buy.

4 The National Lottery uses balls numbered 1 to 49.
Roz thinks that the numbers in the 20s come up far more than any others.

  a Describe how you could find out if this has happened in the past.

  b Describe an experiment that you could do to see if all the numbers come up roughly an equal number of times.

Types of question   Level 5

You need to plan questionnaires very carefully.

There are two basic types of question:

Closed questions   These allow a choice from a fixed number of answers.

Open questions   These allow the people to give any answer that they wish.

All questions should avoid bias. This means that they should not suggest a correct answer. Here are some examples of different styles of question.

Is The National Lottery a good way to raise money for charity? — This is a closed question with choices.

Yes ☐   No ☐   Don't know ☐

How many pieces of fruit do you eat in a week? — This is a closed question with choices in ranges.
Please circle your answer.

  0   1–5   6–10   11–15   More than 15

What do you think about the bus service in this area? — This is an open question.

Most people think you should be allowed to vote at the age of 16. Do you agree? — This is a closed question which is biased.

15 Dealing with data

Exercise 15:5

1 Read through this list of questions.
Each one needs some choices to go with it.
Suggest some suitable choices for each question.

  a How many hours a day do you spend playing computer games?

  b Do you think that diesel cars cause more or less pollution than petrol cars?

  c How many bars of chocolate do you eat on average each week?

  d How far do you travel to get to school?

  e Which mobile phone network do you use?

2 Sam is planning a questionnaire about football.
One of his questions is 'Which football team do you support?'

Explain why it might be difficult to write the choices for this question.

3 These questions are either biased or may embarrass people into giving a particular answer.
Say why each question is biased.

  a Most people think that you should be able to drive at age 16. Do you agree?

  b Do you read a quality newspaper or a tabloid newspaper?

  c Do you think it is a good idea that the unhealthy habit of smoking has been banned in public places?

  d Do you shower regularly?

  e What is your weight to the nearest kilogram?
   30 – 39 kg ☐   40 – 49 kg ☐   50 – 59 kg ☐   60 – 69 kg ☐   70 kg or more ☐

4 The problem with open questions is that it can be very difficult to analyse the results.
Every person in the survey may say something different.
Rewrite these open questions to make them easier to analyse.

  a What do you think about the timekeeping of the local trains?

  b What is your opinion about the service in the local shops?

  c How do you think the behaviour of children has changed over the last 20 years?

  d How do you think that traffic jams could be reduced?

5 Rewrite these questions so that they are not as biased.

  a Tabloid newspapers make up a lot of their stories. Do you agree?

  b Do you think GCSE maths is easier than it used to be?

6 Choose the most sensible units for the answer for each of the situations.

   a Measuring the height of Year 7 pupils
      Nearest metre   Nearest centimetre   Nearest millimetre   Nearest foot

   b Measuring the length of a journey to school
      Nearest metre   Nearest kilometre   Nearest 100 metres   Nearest minute

   c Time spent on the Internet each week
      Nearest hour   Nearest minute   Nearest 2 hours   Nearest 5 hours

Choosing a sample   Level 5

Imagine that you want to find out how many people in the UK listen to each radio station.
It is not possible to ask everybody!
In a case like this you ask a **sample** of people.

You might ask 1000 people.
You need to make sure that the sample represents the whole population of the country.

You might need to take into account:

   their gender   their age
   the type of job they do   where they live

A sample should not be too big. If it is, the data will take too long to analyse.
If there are about 1000 pupils in your school, a good sample size would be 50 or 100.

Exercise 15:6

1 Andrew is planning a survey on what the pupils in his school think about the school meals.
There are 1200 pupils in his school and he knows that he can't talk to them all.
He decides on a sample of 100.
Describe how he should choose these 100 people.

2 Sarah wants to do a survey about stress at work.
She suggests to her teacher that she goes into her local supermarket one morning
to ask people some questions.
Do you think that Sarah will get a good sample of people in the supermarket?
Explain your answer.

Explore

3 MORI is one of the biggest companies in the UK that does opinion polls.

   a Find the names of three more organisations that do opinion polls.

   b Look in a newspaper for the results of some opinion polls.

15 Dealing with data

3 Practical project

> **Doing a statistics project** Level 5

In this section you are going to do a statistics project.

You need **the Fruit and veg datasheet (1)** and **(2)**.

The Office for National Statistics organised a survey into how much fruit and veg people eat.
People were asked to give the following information:

Gender	Nationality
Age	Ethnic Group
Marital Status	Gross Income
Level of Education	Region lived in

They were then asked to answer these questions about their eating habits.

Question 1	Do you think you eat enough fruit and veg each day?
Question 2	Why do you not eat enough fruit and veg?
Question 3	What do you think is a 'portion' of satsumas?
Question 4	What do you think is a 'portion' of frozen veg?
Question 5	How many portions of fruit and veg did you eat yesterday?
Question 6	How did this amount compare to your usual intake?
Question 7	How many portions of fruit and veg do you think experts recommend that you eat a day?
Question 8	Would you like to eat more fruit and veg?

For your statistics project you are going to analyse some of this data.

There are several stages that you need to work through.

Stage 1 Decide on a question you would like to answer.

Some examples are:

> Do people in the North eat less fruit and veg than people in the South?

> Do more men than women think that they should eat more fruit and veg?

> Are younger people more aware of the recommended amounts than older people?

Stage 2   Decide what data you need from the survey and then collect it.

You could highlight the data you want on the datasheet.

You can take just the columns you need from the spreadsheet.

You can sort the spreadsheet so that your data is grouped.

You can select a smaller number of people from the whole survey as a sample.

Stage 3   Present your data using diagrams and analyse it using calculations.

You can use any of the diagrams and calculations you have learned so far.

Some examples are:

> A frequency diagram showing the numbers of people in each income category.

> A pie chart showing the answers to Question 1.

> A double bar chart showing the answers to Question 3 given by men and women.

> The mean number of portions eaten per day in each area or by each gender.

Stage 4   Write about what your analysis has shown you.

You should say something about each of your diagrams and calculations.

Some examples are:

> I can see from my pie charts that more women than men think that they eat enough fruit and veg.

> The mean number of portions of fruit and veg eaten by the men in my sample is 2.6.

> My double bar chart shows that more men than women would like to eat more fruit and veg.

Stage 5   Answer your original question.

Was the answer what you expected or were you surprised at what you found?

Write a summary. Here is an example of what you might write:

> Overall, I think that young people are more aware of what they should be eating than older people. However, when I looked at what they were actually eating, this showed that they were not having as much fruit and veg as older people. This makes me think that they know what they should be eating but they are not doing so!

15 Dealing with data

Watch out... there's a trap about

▸ If you need a sample from your class don't just choose five of your friends.
Your friends will probably think like you do, so your results will probably be biased.
This sample size is also too small.

▸ Don't choose a result that suits you.
If you are trying to show that most people watch too much TV you might calculate the mode, median and mean of your data.
If one of these is much bigger than the other two, you might be tempted to ignore the small ones.
But it isn't fair to only quote the large value.
You should always try to give a fair view of your data.

Test yourself

1 In a survey, 45 people were asked what they usually have for breakfast.
These are the results.

Breakfast	Cereal	Toast	Cooked	Nothing
Number of people	11	21	5	8

Draw a pie chart to show these results.

2 This table shows the percentage of the UK population living in each country.

Country	Percentage of population
England	83%
Scotland	9%
Wales	5%
Northern Ireland	3%

Draw a pie chart to show this data.

3 This table shows the marks obtained in a biology test and a chemistry test by 15 pupils.

Biology	54	58	65	45	50	63	46	58	59	48	57	62	49	61	50
Chemistry	29	32	38	25	28	37	26	30	36	27	29	35	27	34	30

a Draw a scatter graph with biology marks on the *x*-axis and chemistry marks on the *y*-axis.

b Do the pupils who do well in biology also do well in chemistry? Explain how you can tell.

c What type of correlation does this data show?

4 Read each of the questions below.
For each one, say whether you would use **primary**, **secondary** or **experimental** data.

 a Has it rained more in the last 10 years than in the previous 10 years?

 b How many people in my school travel by bus to school?

 c How many packets of cereal will I need to buy to get all six different toys inside the packets?

5 Read each of the questions below.
Write down if each one is open or closed.

 a What do you think about the increase in crime amongst teenagers?

 b Do you think children watch too much TV?

 Yes ☐   No ☐   Don't know ☐

 c Do you think the age at which people can buy cigarettes should be raised to 21?

 d At what age do you think people should be stopped from driving a car?
    70   75   80   85   90   Never

6 Nathaniel is writing a questionnaire on the health of teenagers.

Here are some of his questions.

 1 How old are you?
 2 Do you smoke?
 3 Do you do regular exercise?
 4 Are you a member of a gym?
 5 Do you eat healthily?
 6 Do you like sport at school?
 7 Are you in any sports teams?

Although Nathaniel has some good ideas, not all of his questions are sensible.

Rewrite Nathaniel's questions so the answers you would get would be more useful.

7 Seeta is doing a survey about swimming.
She has asked each person in her class whether or not they can swim.
Here are her results.

Boy Cannot Swim	Girl Can Swim	Boy Can Swim	Girl Can Swim	Girl Cannot Swim
Girl Cannot Swim	Boy Can Swim	Boy Cannot Swim	Boy Can Swim	Boy Can Swim
Girl Can Swim	Boy Can Swim	Boy Cannot Swim	Girl Cannot Swim	Boy Cannot Swim
Girl Can Swim	Boy Cannot Swim	Boy Can Swim	Girl Cannot Swim	Boy Can Swim
Girl Cannot Swim	Girl Can Swim	Girl Can Swim	Girl Cannot Swim	Boy Can Swim

 a Design a frequency table to organise this data.

 b Tally the data into your table.

 c Draw a diagram to show this data.

15 Dealing with data

Chapter 15 Summary

Level 5

Types of data
There are three types of data:

Primary data This is data that you collect using an observation sheet or questionnaire.
Secondary data This is data that you get from other sources such as books or the Internet.
Experimental data This is data you collect by doing an experiment to test a theory.

Types of question
There are two basic types of question:

Closed questions These allow a choice from a fixed number of answers.
Open questions These allow the people answering to give any answer that they wish.

All questions should avoid bias. This means that they should not suggest a correct answer.

Level 6

Pie charts
To draw a pie chart of the results of a survey of **30** people:
(1) Divide 360° by the total number of people   360° ÷ **30** = **12°** per person
(2) Work out the angle for each category by multiplying its frequency by **12**.
(3) Draw the pie chart:
   - Draw a circle and a vertical line from the centre to the top.
   - Measure your first angle from this line.
   - Draw in all the other angles.
   - Colour your pie chart and add a title and labels or a key.

Scatter graphs
Scatter graphs are used to see if there is a connection between two sets of data.

The data on this scatter graph shows **positive correlation**.

As maths scores get bigger, so do the science scores.

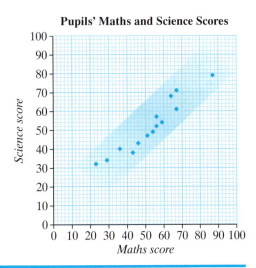

Pupils' Maths and Science Scores

16 Ratio and proportion

**Chapter 8
Decimals, fractions and percentages**

Using decimals, fractions and percentages

**Chapter 12
More fractions and percentages**

Using fractions and percentages

1 **Direct proportion**
2 **Ratio**

Year 8

- Calculating using ratios
- Problems involving comparisons
- Proportional change

You should already know:

▶ **how to cancel fractions**

Divide the numerator and the denominator by the same number.

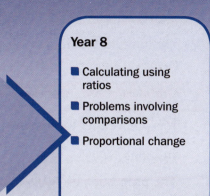

You can do the last one in two stages like this:

$$\frac{12}{30} = \frac{6}{15} = \frac{2}{5}$$

▶ **how to describe proportions using fractions and percentages**

$\frac{1}{3}$ of this flag is red.

About 60% of this flag is red.

16 Ratio and proportion

1 Direct proportion

- **Comparing proportions**
- **Using direct proportion to solve problems**
- **Working backwards using the unitary method**

Key words

compare	proportion
decimal	percentage
direct proportion	directly proportional
unitary method	working backwards

Comparing proportions — Level 5

It is often easier to **compare proportions** if you write them as **decimals** or **percentages**.

In Uzma's school, 78 out of 130 Year 7 pupils own a computer.

The proportion of Year 7 pupils in Uzma's school that owns a computer $= \dfrac{78}{130}$

Work out $78 \div 130$ and then multiply by 100 to turn the decimal answer into a **percentage** like this:

$$\dfrac{78}{130} = 78 \div 130 = 0.6 \qquad 0.6 = 0.6 \times 100\% = 60\%$$

In Caroline's school, 132 out of 240 Year 7 pupils own a computer.

The proportion of Year 7 pupils in Caroline's school that owns a computer $= \dfrac{132}{240} = 0.55 = 55\%$.

$60\% > 55\%$, so Uzma's school has the larger proportion of computer owners in Year 7.

Exercise 16:1

1 A pet shop has 27 hamsters in stock.
Fourteen of the hamsters are golden.
Work out the proportion of golden hamsters.
Write your answer as a percentage.

2 In the last year
185 days have been sunny,
97 have been wet and 83 have been overcast.
Write down the proportion of the days on which
   a it was sunny
   b it was overcast
   c it did **not** rain.

Symbol	Weather	Days
☀	Sunny	185
☁🌧	Wet	97
☁	Overcast	83

3 Stephen scored 21 out of 39 in his first maths test.
In his second maths test he scored 14 out of 27.
Compare Stephen's results. In which test did he do better?

4 Alan Shearer scored 30 goals in 63 international games.
Michael Owen has scored 40 goals in 88 international games.
Which player has the better proportion of goals per game?

5 In Chelsea's class, 23 of the 28 pupils are right-handed.
In Peter's class, 6 of the 27 pupils are left-handed.
Whose class has the bigger proportion of right-handed pupils? Show your working.

6 Danny is a quality control supervisor at a fruit wholesaler.
He compares two shipments of apples.

Farm	Weight delivered (kg)	Weight rejected (kg)
Eastfield	7850	83
Beacon	6520	69

Danny notices that Beacon Farm's delivery had fewer bad apples.
So he thinks Beacon Farm is the better supplier.
Is he right? Explain your answer.

7 The table shows the number of smoking-related deaths in four different Local Authorities.
Work out which Local Authority has the highest proportion of smoking-related deaths.

Local Authority	Population	Smoking-related deaths
Broxbourne	260 000	407
Dacorum	413 700	602
East Hertfordshire	392 100	523
Hertsmere	280 900	488

8 A garden centre sells plants for hedges.
The table shows what they sold in one week.

  a What percentage of the total number of plants sold was **Leylandii**? Show your working.

  b What percentage of the **total takings** was for Leylandii? Show your working.

Plants	Number of plants sold	Takings
Beech	125	£212.50
Leylandii	650	£2437.50
Privet	35	£45.50
Hawthorn	18	£23.40
Laurel	5	£32.25
Total	**833**	**£2751.15**

16 Ratio and proportion

Using direct proportion to solve problems — Level 5

You can use **direct proportion** to do lots of different calculations.
Two quantities are **directly proportional** if as one quantity increases by a given multiple, the other quantity increases by the same multiple.

Two chocolate bars cost 98p.
Six bars are **three times** as many so they would cost **three times** the price.

The cost of six bars would be 98p × 3 = £2.94

In a travel agency £1 will get you €1.41 for spending in Europe.

If you change £50 into euro you will get 50 × €1.41 = €70.50

A recipe uses 50 g of chocolate to make 10 cakes.
You can work out how much chocolate you need to make 15 cakes in two steps like this:

```
        ÷2  ┌ 10 cakes  need  50 g ┐  ÷2
            └ 5 cakes   need  25 g ┘
        ×3  ┌                      ┐  ×3
            └ 15 cakes  need  75 g ┘
```

Working out the cost of **5 cakes** is a good idea because **5** divides into both 10 and 15.

If you can't find a good number to use like **5**, you use the **unitary method**.
You work out the value of **1** item and then multiply by the number you need instead.

```
       ÷10  ┌ 10 cakes  need   50 g ┐  ÷10
            └ 1 cake    needs  5 g  ┘
       ×15  ┌                       ┐  ×15
            └ 15 cakes  need   75 g ┘
```

Exercise 16:2

1 A recipe for biscuits needs 60 g of oats to make 10 biscuits.
Work out the quantity of oats needed to make

 a 1 biscuit **b** 3 biscuits **c** 8 biscuits.

2 All activities use up calories.
Walking uses up 75 calories every 15 minutes.
Write down the number of calories used when you walk for

 a 30 minutes
 b 1 hour
 c $2\frac{1}{4}$ hours.

3 Look at the ingredients for shepherd's pie for four people.
Work out how much of each ingredient you need for

  a 2 people
  b 6 people
  c 10 people.

> **Shepherd's Pie**
> 250g mince   30g mushrooms
> 450g potato   100ml stock
> Serves 4

4 There are 12 inches in 1 foot.
Work out how many feet there are in

  a 36 inches   **b** 6 inches   **c** 42 inches.

5 There are 8 km in 5 miles.
Work out how many miles are equal to

  a 1 km   **b** 20 km   **c** 64 km.

6 There are 240 mℓ of lemon juice in 1.5 litres of lemon drink.
How much lemon juice will there be in 2 litres of the same drink?

7 In Europe £5 is worth €7.85
How much would

  a £123 be worth in euros?   **b** €628 be worth in pounds?

8 Britain used 'old money' until 15th February 1971.
Old money included guineas, pounds, shillings and old pence.

  a Five pounds were worth the same as 100 shillings.
  How many shillings were three pounds worth?

  b Three guineas were worth the same as 63 shillings.
  How many shillings were eight guineas worth?

  c 100 shillings had the value of 1200 old pence.
  How many old pence were in three guineas?

Explore

9 Three men dig trenches to install cables.
They dig 120 m of trenches each day between them.

  a How long will it take two men to dig 1 km of trenches?
  b How many men are needed to dig 1 km of trenches in 5 days?

16 Ratio and proportion

Working backwards using the unitary method — Level 6

This type of problem will tell you the value of something after a proportional change has happened.
You will be asked to work out the original value before the change.
This type of problem is called a **working backwards** problem.

Anne-Marie buys a pair of jeans in a sale.
They have been reduced by 25%.
They now cost £30.
She wants to know how much they were before the sale.

Because the jeans have been reduced by 25%,
the price now is 75% of the full price.   £30 = 75% of the full price
So divide by 75 to find 1% of the full price   £30 ÷ 75 = 1% of the full price
and then multiply by 100 to find the full price.   £30 ÷ 75 × 100 = 100% of the full price

The full price of the jeans was £30 ÷ 75 × 100 = £40.

Exercise 16:3

1 After a 20% reduction, a sofa costs £460.
£460 represents 100% − 20% = 80% of the full cost.
Copy and complete.

   a To find 1% of the full cost work out   £460 ÷ ... = £5.75
   b To find 100% of the full cost work out   £5.75 × ... = £....
   c The full cost of the sofa was £...

2 Alex buys a pair of trainers in a sale.
They have been reduced by 40%.
Alex paid £33 for the trainers.
To work out the full cost of the trainers Alex worked out
£33 ÷ 40 × 100 = £82.50

   a This is wrong. Explain what he should have done.
   b Calculate the full price of the trainers.

3 After a 25% decrease a mobile phone costs £135.
Work out how much it cost before the reduction.

4 12 500 people visited a science museum in July 2007.
This is a reduction of 20% on the same month last year.
Calculate how many people visited the museum in July 2006.

5 In 2007, the number of monkeys in a colony was 32.
This is a decrease of 20% since 2002.
Work out how many monkeys were in the colony in 2002.

6 In a special deal a car showroom offers a discount of 25% off the original price for cash.
Becky pays £13 980 cash for a car.
Calculate the original price of the car.

7 In a sale, all the original prices are reduced by 35%.
Gemma pays £33.80 for a hat in the sale.
Calculate the original price of the hat.

8 A shop had a sale. All prices were reduced by 15%.
A pair of shoes cost **£38.25** in the sale.
What price were the shoes before the sale?
Show your working.

9 Choose the single calculation that will undo a reduction of 25%.

× 0.25   ÷ 0.25   × 0.75   ÷ 0.75   × 1.25

10 Dominic bought an antique clock.
The same week he sold the clock for £770 making a 40% profit.
£770 represents **140**% of the original cost.
Copy and complete.

  a To find 1% of the original cost work out   £770 ÷ … = £5.50
  b To find 100% of original cost work out   £5.50 × … = £ ….
  c Dominic bought the antique clock for £…

11 The single multiplier used to calculate an increase of 25% is 1.25
Dividing by 1.25 will get back to the original amount.
Write down the calculation used to undo

  a an increase of 30%   **b** an increase of 10%.

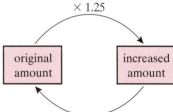

12 After a 15% increase a TV costs £920.
How much did it cost before the change?

13 After a 5% increase a bus fare cost £2.52.
Work out the price before the increase.

14 After an 8% increase the price of a house is £189 540.
Work out the price before the increase.

15 The final bill for a restaurant meal is £89.30.
Extras added on to the bill are an £8 service charge and then 17.5% VAT.
Calculate the cost of the meal before the service charge and VAT were added.

16 Ratio and proportion

2 Ratio

▶ Working with ratios
▶ Linking ratios to fractions, decimals and percentages
▶ Dividing a quantity in a given ratio
▶ Working with three-part ratios
▶ Dealing with one part of a ratio

Key words
ratio
simplify
cancel
Highest Common Factor (HCF)
simplest form
three-part ratio

Working with ratios — Level 5

Ratio is used to compare the size of different parts of a whole with each other.
In this class, there are twice as many girls as boys.
For every 2 girls there is 1 boy.

This means that the ratio of girls to boys is two to one.
You write this as 2 : 1 and say it as 'two to one'.

The order of the numbers is important. 2 : 1 and 1 : 2 are different.
The ratio of boys to girls is 1 : 2.

The ratio of orange counters to pink counters in this diagram is 5 : 3.

The ratio of orange counters to pink counters in this diagram is 10 : 6.
There are 5 orange counters for every 3 pink counters so the ratio is also 5 : 3
So 10 : 6 = 5 : 3

You can **simplify** or **cancel** ratios rather like fractions.
You can write the ratio of girls to boys in the class above as 20 : 10.
20 and 10 have a **Highest Common Factor (HCF)** of 10.
If you divide both numbers by 10 you can cancel the ratio down to 2 : 1.
So 20 : 10 = 2 : 1
To cancel a ratio, divide by the HCF of the parts of the ratio.

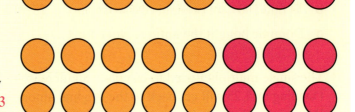

16 : 9
This ratio can't be simplified.
There is no whole number bigger than 1 that divides into 16 and 9.

27 : 6 = 9 : 2   24 : 18 = 4 : 3   16 : 9 = 16 : 9

These ratios are now in their **simplest form**. They cannot be cancelled any further.

Exercise 16:4

1 Write each of these ratios in its simplest form.
Use the diagrams to help you.

a ÷3 (21:6) ÷3 → …:…

b ÷5 (25:10) ÷5 → …:…

c ÷4 (12:16) ÷4 → …:…

2 Write each of these ratios in its simplest form.

a 6:2   3:1
b 9:3
c 12:4
d 18:6
e 16:22
f 25:10
g 12:8
h 27:18
i 35:140
j 17:13
k 3 mm : 1 cm
l 20p : £1
m 6 days : 2 weeks
n 3 min : $\frac{1}{2}$ hour
o 250 g : 1 kg

3 A baby elephant weighs 1.5 tonnes.
A male adult elephant weighs 9 tonnes.

Write down the ratio of the baby's weight to the adult's weight in its simplest form.

4 A baby snake is 90 cm long. An adult snake is 1.2 m long.

a Write the length of the adult snake in centimetres.

b Write down the ratio of the adult's length to the baby's length in its simplest form.

5 The length of a real room is 6 m.
On a scale drawing the length of the room is shown as 12 cm.

a Write down the ratio of the real room to the scale drawing.

b Write your answer in its simplest form.

Think on!

6 Look at these ratio cards. Write down

a five cards that show an equivalent ratio
b four cards that show a different equivalent ratio
c three cards that show a different equivalent ratio
d two cards that show a different equivalent ratio
e one card that is the odd one out.

27:9	24:30	15:5
14:21	7:14	28:35
9:18	21:7	10:15
6:12	12:18	24:6
9:3	8:12	33:11

16 Ratio and proportion

Linking ratios to fractions, decimals and percentages — Level 5

You can link ratios to fractions, decimals and percentages.

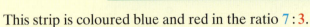

This strip is coloured blue and red in the ratio 7 : 3.
It is split into 7 + 3 = 10 parts altogether.

This means that $\frac{7}{10} = 0.7 = 70\%$ of the strip is blue and $\frac{3}{10} = 0.3 = 30\%$ of the strip is red.

Ray is topping up his car radiator with antifreeze.
The mixture is **60%** water.
This means that **40%** of the mixture is antifreeze.
The ratio of water to antifreeze is **60 : 40**.

$$\div 20 \left(\begin{array}{c} 60:40 \\ 3:2 \end{array} \right) \div 20$$

The mixture of water and antifreeze is in the ratio 3 : 2.

Exercise 16:5

1 Look at this coloured strip.

    a Write down the ratio of blue squares to red squares in its simplest form.

    b What fraction of the strip is red?

    c What percentage of the strip is blue?

    d The table shows the ratio of blue squares to red squares for two **different** strips. Copy and fill in this table.

Ratio of red : blue	Fraction of red	Percentage of red	Fraction of blue	Percentage of blue
2 : 3				
7 : 3				

2 Brett is making fruit punch.
He mixes orange juice and pineapple juice in the ratio 5 : 3.

    a What fraction of the fruit punch is orange juice?

    b What percentage of the fruit punch is pineapple juice?

3 Mark refilled his car windscreen washer bottle using a mixture of screen wash and water. The mixture is 18% screen wash and the rest is water.

    a What percentage of the mixture is water?

    b Write the ratio of screen wash to water in its simplest form.

4 A fish and chip shop sells cod and haddock.
86% of all the fish sold is cod. The remainder is haddock.

    a What percentage of the fish sold is haddock?

    b Write a ratio of cod sold to haddock sold in its simplest form.

5 The table shows the estimated proportions of red and grey squirrels at some UK locations. Copy the table and fill it in.

Location	Percentage of red squirrels	Percentage of grey squirrels	Ratio of red squirrels : grey squirrels
a	12%	88%	
b		63%	
c	50%		
d		76%	
e			2 : 23

Think on!

6 Copy the diagrams.
Use the digits 0, 1, 2, 3, 4, 5, 6, 7, 8 and 9.
Put one digit in each space to make the proportions correct.
You can only use each digit once.

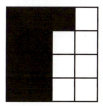  

Ratio of black : white   Ratio of black : white   Ratio of black : white

= ☐ : ☐   = ☐ : ☐   = ☐ : 1

Fraction shaded white = $\frac{7}{\square\square}$ Fraction shaded white = $\frac{5}{\square}$ Percentage coloured white = ☐☐ %

16 Ratio and proportion

Dividing a quantity in a given ratio — Level 5

You can use ratios to divide things up.

Sally and Jo share a flat. They decide to divide up the bills in the ratio of their wages. Sally earns £150 per week. Jo earns £100 per week.

$$150 : 100 \xrightarrow{\div 50} 3 : 2 \xleftarrow{\div 50}$$

The ratio of Sally's wage to Jo's wage is 150 : 100 = 3 : 2.
Their electricity bill is £65.
The ratio of 3 : 2 means that for every £3 Sally pays, Jo pays £2.

To work out how much each person should pay:
    Work out the **total number** of shares   3 + 2 = 5
    Divide the amount by the number of shares   £65 ÷ 5 = £13
    to find the value of **one share**
    Now work out what each person pays   Sally: 3 × £13 = £39
                                          Jo: 2 × £13 = £26
    Check that the two shares add up to the original amount   £39 + £26 = £65 ✓

So Sally pays £39 and Jo pays £26.

Exercise 16:6

1 Sally and Jo share their gas bill in the ratio 3 : 2.
The bill is £395.
How much does each person pay?

2 Paul and Mark share a lottery win of £1035 in the ratio 4 : 5.
How much does each person get?

3 A Breakfast tea is made by mixing Indian and Ceylon leaves in the ratio of 3 : 4.
How much of each type of leaf is needed to make 280 g of tea?

4 Share

  a £150 in the ratio 2 : 3
  b £270 in the ratio 2 : 3
  c £168 in the ratio 5 : 7
  d £231 in the ratio 6 : 5
  e £880 in the ratio 3 : 2
  f £720 in the ratio 5 : 1
  g £1700 in the ratio 9 : 8
  h £852 in the ratio 5 : 7
  i £1750 in the ratio 2 : 3
  j £16 720 in the ratio 5 : 3.

5 Dee likes a shade of pink made using red and white paint mixed in the ratio 4 : 3.
Dee used 10.5 litres of paint in total.
How many litres of white paint did she use?

6 Harry and Freddy share 49 sweets in the ratio 3 : 4.
How many sweets should Harry get?

7 A school choir is made up of boys and girls in the ratio 3 : 5.
There are 72 people in the choir altogether.
Work out how many girls are in the choir.

8 One of the angles in a triangle is a right angle.
The other two angles are in the ratio 2 : 7.
Work out the size of the other two angles.

9 Cupronickel is an alloy of copper and nickel mixed in the ratio 3 : 1.
It is easily shaped, resistant to corrosion and is used to make 'silver' coins.
A 5p coin weighs 3.25 g.
Work out the mass of copper used to make a 5p coin.

10 Paul and David are sharing a prize of £600.
They are deciding whether to split the prize between them in the ratio 7 : 18 or 13 : 37.
Which ratio would make Paul better off?
Show your working.

11 When Ali and Amy go out for a meal they always split the bill in the same proportions.
  a On Monday Ali pays £26.50 and Amy pays £13.25.
  Write a simplified ratio of the amount paid by Ali to the amount paid by Amy.
  b On Tuesday the meal costs £84.60.
  How much does each of them pay?

12 The British Heart Foundation recommends that children between the ages of 5 and 18 should spend at least one hour a day doing something active.
Their research shows that one in three of the 7.5 million children aged between 5 and 18 in this country do not get nearly enough exercise.
  a Write the ratio of the number of children aged between 5 and 18 who get enough exercise to those who don't.
  b Work out the number of children aged between 5 and 18 who do not get enough exercise.

16 Ratio and proportion

Working with three-part ratios — Level 6

These **green**, **red** and **blue** counters are in the ratio **4 : 6 : 8**
This is a **three-part ratio**.
All these numbers divide by 2, so this can be simplified to **2 : 3 : 4**
Look at the top row of counters.

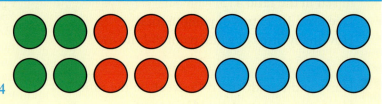

A fruit drink is made from orange, lemon and pineapple juice in the ratio **5 : 1 : 2**.
To work out how much of each flavour juice there is in 100 litres of the drink:

Work out the **total number** of shares.	$5 + 1 + 2 = 8$
Divide the amount by the number of shares to find the value of **one share**.	$100\,\ell \div 8 = 12.5\,\ell$
Work out the value of each part of the ratio.	Orange: $5 \times 12.5\,\ell = 62.5\,\ell$ Lemon: $1 \times 12.5\,\ell = 12.5\,\ell$ Pineapple: $2 \times 12.5\,\ell = 25\,\ell$

Check that the three shares add up to the original amount $62.5\,\ell + 12.5\,\ell + 25\,\ell = 100\,\ell$ ✓

So 100 ℓ of the drink contains 62.5 ℓ of orange, 12.5 ℓ of lemon and 25 ℓ of pineapple juice.

Exercise 16:7

1 Write each ratio in its simplest form.

- **a** 3 : 6 : 9
- **b** 14 : 21 : 28
- **c** 18 : 9 : 36
- **d** 30 : 14 : 26
- **e** 28 : 22 : 22
- **f** 16 : 22 : 18
- **g** 17 : 13 : 23
- **h** 38 : 19 : 57
- **i** 24 : 72 : 96
- **j** 35 : 140 : 95

2 The numbers in each part are in the ratio 1 : 3 : 5.
Copy and fill in the table.

a	2	6	
b	15		75
c			40
d		18	

3 Keema is mixing paint.
To make the colour sea green she mixes red, yellow and blue in the ratio 1 : 2 : 3.

- **a** Keema starts with 2 litres of red paint.
  How much yellow and blue paint does she add to make sea green?
- **b** How much sea green has she made altogether?
- **c** Keema needs a total of 30 litres of sea green.
  How much of each colour does she need to add?

4 Carl and Maria use this colour table to mix purple and salmon pink paint.

Colour	Red	Yellow	Blue
Purple	3	1	2
Salmon Pink	3	2	1

  a Carl has 6 litres of red paint, 5 litres of yellow paint and 4 litres of blue paint. What is the greatest amount of purple paint Carl can make?

  b Maria has 9 litres of red paint, 4.5 litres of yellow paint and 4.5 litres of blue paint. She wants to use all of her paint to make the colours purple and salmon pink. Explain how much of each colour she can make.

5 Share

  a £60 in the ratio 2 : 3 : 1
  b £70 in the ratio 2 : 3 : 2
  c £84 in the ratio 5 : 4 : 3
  d £66 in the ratio 1 : 1 : 9
  e £50 in the ratio 3 : 2 : 3
  f £120 in the ratio 2 : 3 : 5
  g £170 in the ratio 9 : 4 : 4
  h £360 in the ratio 2 : 7 : 3
  i £14.50 in the ratio 2 : 1 : 2
  j £720 in the ratio 2 : 3 : 1 : 3.

6 Fruit cake is made using raisins, currants and cherries in the ratio 7 : 1 : 2.
The total amount of fruit used is 500 g.
What weight of raisins is used to make the cake?

7 Concrete is made from sand, gravel and cement in the ratio 3 : 4 : 1.
How much sand is there in 3200 kg of concrete?

8 In an election the votes were split between the three candidates X, Y and Z in the ratio 3 : 6 : 7.
If 24 000 votes were cast, how many people voted for candidate Y?

9 A box of 32 chocolates contains milk, plain and white chocolates in the ratio 4 : 1 : 3.
  a How many plain chocolates are there?
  b How many milk chocolates are there?
  c The milk chocolates are divided between hard and soft centres in the ratio 3 : 5. How many of the milk chocolates have soft centres?

10 A gear ratio is determined by the number of teeth on a cog.
Fitting two or more cogs together makes a gear train.
The ratio of teeth in this gear train is 1 : 2 : 6.

  a How many times will the red cog turn when the blue cog turns once?
  b How many times will each cog turn before they all get back to this starting position again for the first time?

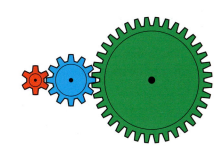

16 Ratio and proportion

Dealing with one part of a ratio — Level 6

When you know the value of one of the parts of a ratio, you can work out the total value of all the parts.
Jack gets some money for his birthday. He **spends some** and **saves £18**.
His **spending** and **savings** are in the ratio **3 : 2**.

To work out how much Jack had altogether:
  Notice that **savings** is the second part of the ratio 3 : **2**
  Divide the value given by the number of shares in that part of the ratio   £18 ÷ 2 = £9
  to get the value of **one share**
  Work out the **total number** of shares   3 + 2 = 5
  Multiply the value of **one share** by the **total number** of shares   £9 × 5 = £45

So Jack had £45 altogether.

You can also work out the value of the other parts of the ratio before you work out the total.
Here, Jack spent **3** shares worth of his money. So Jack spent **3** × **£9** = **£27**.
Notice that £27 + £18 = £45.

Exercise 16:8

1 Nicola and Sam share the winnings from a raffle in the ratio 8 : 7.
Nicola's share is £240. How much did they win altogether?

2 In a chemistry lab, Alicia mixes acid and water in the ratio 2 : 5.
She uses 50 mℓ of acid.
How much solution does she mix?

3 Sally splits her wages between money she saves and money she spends in the ratio 2 : 7.
Sally saves £328 a month.
How much does Sally get paid?

4 Gemma cast a metal statue by mixing copper and zinc in the ratio 7 : 5.
She used 161 kg of copper.
Calculate the total mass of the statue.

5 Sian and Laura invest £4000 and £7000 in a business.
They agree to share any profit in the same ratio.
Sian's share of the profit is £756.
To the nearest pound, how much profit did the business make?

6 An engine uses a special mixture of fuel.
The fuel is made using petrol and oil mixed in the ratio 20 : 1.
How much oil is mixed with 5 litres of petrol?

7 A swimming pool attendant adds chemicals to the pool every day.
He mixes chemicals labelled 'safe' and 'fresh' in the ratio 2 : 3.
He adds 0.4 litres of the chemical labelled 'safe'.
How much of the chemical labelled 'fresh' should he add?

8 The council paid £265 000 towards a new all-weather sports pitch.
A local authority grant paid for the remainder of the cost.
The costs are shared in the ratio 5 : 8.
Work out the value of the local authority grant.

9 Solder is a mixture of lead and tin in the ratio 7 : 3.

   a How much lead is mixed with 195 g of tin to make solder?

Pewter is a mixture of lead, tin and antimony in the ratio 6 : 13 : 1.

   b How much lead is mixed with 195 g of tin to make pewter?

10 Concrete is made from sand, gravel and cement in the ratio 3 : 4 : 1.
How much sand is used with 3200 kg of gravel to make concrete?

11 In an election the votes were split between the three candidates P, Q and R in the ratio 3 : 6 : 7.
Candidate Q received 12 672 votes.

   a How many people voted for candidate P?

   b How many people voted for candidate R?

   c How many votes were cast altogether?

12 A nurse diluted a drug with water in the ratio 1 : 8.

   a If 60 mℓ of the drug was used, how much water was used?

   b If 25 mℓ of the drug was used, how much solution was made up altogether?

   c A solution contains 30 mℓ of the drug and 220 mℓ of water.
      Is this solution too strong or too weak? Explain your answer.

13 Zoe shares sweets between Laura and Vicky in the ratio 3 : 4.
Vicky gets 6 more sweets than Laura. How many sweets does Vicky get?

14 A shop sells cans of cola and lemonade in the ratio 3 : 2.
The shop sells 180 cans of cola each month.
Work out how many cans the shop sells altogether in a year.

15 The ratio of total assets to total debts is used to measure how much a business is in debt.
A company has an asset to debt ratio of 2 : 1.

   a The company has £2.4 million in total assets.
      Work out the total debt of the company.

The company increases its debt by £1 million. Its assets remain unchanged.

   b What is the new asset to debt ratio of the company?

16 Ratio and proportion

Watch out... there's a trap about

▶ Don't try to compare proportions before you've converted them into decimals or percentages. 102 out of 150 doesn't have to be bigger than 77 out of 110 just because 102 is more than 77. If you want to compare 102 out of 150 with 77 out of 110, you can't just look at the red numbers. Work out the proportions:

$$\frac{102}{150} = 102 \div 150 = 0.68 = 68\% \qquad \frac{77}{110} = 77 \div 110 = 0.7 = 70\%$$

68% is less than 70%.

So 102 out of 150 is a lower proportion than 77 out of 110.

▶ Work out the total number of shares before you split an amount into a given ratio.

If you're dividing £120 in the ratio 3 : 2, some people just work out
120 ÷ 3 = 40 and 120 ÷ 2 = 60.

They would say that the two shares are £40 and £60.
This gives a total of £100 so it must be wrong.

You should work out the total number of shares	3 + 2 = 5
Divide the amount by the number of shares	£120 ÷ 5 = £24
Work out each part of the ratio	3 × £24 = £72
	2 × £24 = £48
Check that the two shares add up to the correct amount	£72 + £48 = £120 ✓

The two shares are £72 and £48.
These amounts are in the ratio 3 : 2 and they add up to give £120.

Test yourself

1 The table shows average amounts for how much water is used by each person in the UK.

  a What fraction of the total water used is needed to wash clothes?

  b What percentage of the total water used is needed for dishwashing?

Daily domestic water use	Litres of water
Bath / shower / hand basin	50
WC flushing	37
Clothes washing	21
Dishwashing	12
Garden use and car washing	10
Other	20
Total	**150**

Source: Environment Agency

2 Look at the ingredients for making four pancakes.

   a How many eggs are needed to make six pancakes?

   b How much flour is needed to make 10 pancakes?

> **Pancake mix**
> 6 dessert spoons of flour
> $\frac{1}{4}$ litre of milk
> 1 pinch of salt
> 2 eggs

3 There are 2.54 centimetres in one inch.
Work out how many centimetres there are in

   a 6 inches   **b** 15 inches   **c** 100 inches.

4 Charlotte is shopping in the January sales.
After a 70% reduction she pays £9.30 for a leather belt.
Work out how much it cost before the reduction.

5 After a 3% increase the price of a car is £23 175.
Work out the price of the car before the increase.

6 Write down how you would reverse

   a an increase of 30%   **b** a decrease of 30%.

7 Write each ratio in its simplest form.

   a 16 : 28   **b** 3 m : 20 cm

8 To make instant coffee, beans from Java and Columbia are combined in the ratio 3 : 7.

   a What percentage of the coffee beans comes from Java?

   b What fraction of the coffee beans comes from Columbia?

9 The ratio of males to females at a gym is 2 : 1.
The gym has 3231 members.
How many of the members are male?

10 Share

   a £16 000 in the ratio 1 : 2 : 5   **b** £58 500 in the ratio 2 : 3 : 4

11 A bronze statue is made from copper and tin in the ratio 9 : 1.
The mass of the tin used in the statue is 80 kg.

   a Calculate the mass of copper used.

   b Calculate the total mass of the statue.

16 Ratio and proportion

Chapter 16 Summary

Level 5

Comparing proportions
Convert proportions to decimals or percentages before you compare them.

78 out of 130 = $\frac{78}{130}$ = 0.6 = **60%**   132 out of 240 = $\frac{132}{240}$ = 0.55 = **55%** which is lower.

Using proportion to solve problems
Use the **unitary method**.
You work out the value of **1** item and then multiply by the number you need.

$\div 10$ (10 cakes need 50 g) $\div 10$
         1 cake needs   5 g
$\times 15$ (15 cakes need 75 g) $\times 15$

Cancelling ratios
To cancel a ratio,
divide by the HCF of the parts of the ratio.

$\div 6$ (24 : 18) $\div 6$
         4 : 3

24 : 18 = 4 : 3

Dividing an amount in a given ratio
To divide £63 in the ratio **4 : 3**
Work out the total number of shares   4 + 3 = 7
Divide the amount by the number of shares   £63 ÷ 7 = £9
Work out each part of the ratio   4 × £9 = £36
                                               3 × £9 = £27

Check that the two shares add up to the original amount   £36 + £27 = £63 ✓

Level 6

Working backwards using the unitary method
If something has been reduced by 25%,   Jeans cost £30 after being reduced by 25%
the price now is **75%** of the full price.   £30 = **75%** of the full price
So divide by **75** to find 1% of the full price.   £30 ÷ 75 = 1% of the full price
and then **multiply by 100** to find the full price.   £30 ÷ 75 × 100 = 100% of the full price
                                               Full price = £40

Three-part ratios
These work just the same as two-part ratios.
You cancel them down to lowest terms by dividing all three parts by their HCF.
You still work out the total number of shares first when you share something using a three-part ratio.

Dealing with one part of a ratio
Jack gets some money. He **spends some** and **saves some** in the ratio **3 : 2**. He saves **£18**.
To work out how much Jack had altogether:
   Notice that **savings** is the second part of the ratio 3 : 2.
   Divide the value by the number of shares in that part of the ratio   £18 ÷ 2 = £9
   to get the value of **one share**.
   Work out the **total number** of shares.   3 + 2 = 5
   Multiply the value of **one share** by the **total number** of shares.   £9 × 5 = £45

17 Algebraic graphs

**Chapter 3
Coordinates and symmetry**

Coordinates in all four quadrants

**Chapter 6
Formulae and algebraic operations**

Substitution into formulae

1 Plotting graphs

2 Mapping diagrams

3 Real-life graphs

Year 8

- Straight-line graphs
- Real-life graphs
- Simultaneous equations

You should already know:

▸ how to use coordinates in all four quadrants

Point A has coordinates $(-1, 3)$
Point B has coordinates $(-3, -2)$
Point C has coordinates $(2, -1)$

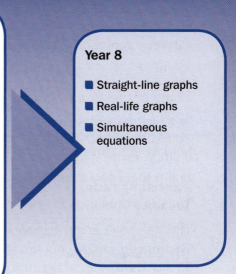

▸ how to substitute into an algebraic formula

$V = IR$ is a formula.
When $I = 4$ and $R = 6$
$V = 4 \times 6$
$ = 24$

273

17 Algebraic graphs

1 Plotting graphs

- **Generating points that follow a rule**
- **Plotting the graphs of simple functions**

Key words
sequence, x-coordinate, y-coordinate, rule, table of values, graph, straight-line graph, function, plot a graph

Generating points that follow a rule Level 6

Look at this **sequence** of points (1, 2) (2, 4) (3, 6) (4, 8) (5, 10)

In this sequence of points y-coordinate $= 2 \times x$-coordinate

You can write this as the **rule** $y = 2x$

The 10th point in this sequence has an x-coordinate of 10.
The rule for working out the y-coordinate is $y = 2x$, so y-coordinate $= 2 \times 10 = 20$.
So the coordinates of the 10th point in the sequence are (10, 20).

The rule for another sequence of points is $y = x + 6$.
Here are five points in this sequence (1, 7) (2, 8) (3, 9) (4, 10) (5, 11)

It is sometimes useful to put the coordinates into a table.
This type of table is called a **table of values**.
The x-coordinates go in the top row. The y-coordinates go in the bottom row.
This table of values shows the coordinates of some points that follow the rule $y = 3x + 1$.

x-coordinate	1	2	3	4	5
y-coordinate	4	7	10	13	16

You can also use negative coordinates.

This table of values shows coordinates of points that follow the rule $y = 2x + 1$.

x-coordinate	-3	-2	-1	0	1	2	3
y-coordinate	$2 \times -3 + 1$ $= -5$	$2 \times -2 + 1$ $= -3$	$2 \times -1 + 1$ $= -1$	$2 \times 0 + 1$ $= 1$	$2 \times 1 + 1$ $= 3$	$2 \times 2 + 1$ $= 5$	$2 \times 3 + 1$ $= 7$

Exercise 17:1

1 A coordinate pattern is made by using the rule y-coordinate $= 3 \times x$-coordinate.
Copy and complete these pairs of coordinates.

   a (1, ?) **b** (2, ?) **c** (3, ?) **d** (5, ?) **e** (10, ?)

2 A coordinate pattern is made by using the rule y-coordinate $= 2 \times x$-coordinate $+ 5$.
Copy and complete these pairs of coordinates.

   a (1, ?) **b** (2, ?) **c** (3, ?) **d** (4, ?) **e** (?, 15)

3 This function machine is used to work out *y*-coordinates from *x*-coordinates.

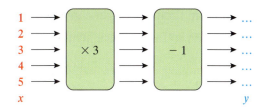

Write down the missing *y*-coordinates.

4 The rule for a sequence of points is $y = x + 4$.
Write down the point that follows this rule with

   a an *x*-coordinate of 3   **b** an *x*-coordinate of 10.

5 The coordinates of each of these points fit the rule $y = 3x - 4$.
Copy and complete each coordinate pair.

   a $(4, ?)$ **b** $(8, ?)$ **c** $(-2, ?)$ **d** $(?, 17)$ **e** $(?, 26)$

6 Complete the coordinate pairs so that they fit the given rule in each part.

	Rule	Coordinates					
a	$y = 2x + 1$	$(1, ?)$	$(4, ?)$	$(5, ?)$	$(-2, ?)$	$(2.5, ?)$	$(?, 15)$
b	$y = 10 - x$	$(1, ?)$	$(3, ?)$	$(10, ?)$	$(-1, ?)$	$(?, 12)$	$(?, 16)$

7 a Copy and complete this table for the rule $y = 2x + 8$.

x-coordinate	−4	−3	−2	−1	0	1	2	3	4
y-coordinate									

   b Write out the coordinates of the points shown in the table.

Think on!

8 For each part, select

   a five cards that fit the rule $y = 2x + 2$
   b four cards that fit the rule $y = x$
   c three cards that fit the rule $y = 3x$
   d two cards that fit the rule $y = 2 - x$
   e one card that fits the rule $y = 3x + 4$.

$(-3, -4)$ $(1, 1)$ $(-1, -3)$
$(0, 0)$ $(-2, -2)$ $(-1, 0)$
$(0, 2)$ $(2, 6)$ $(2, 2)$

17 Algebraic graphs

Plotting the graphs of simple functions — Level 6

You can plot sequences of points and join them up to get a **graph**.

All the sequences of points you have seen so far produce **straight-line graphs**.

The rules you have seen are **functions**.

Here is a table of values for the function $y = 2x + 1$

x	−2	−1	0	1	2
y	−3	−1	1	3	5

which gives you these points:

(−2, −3), (−1, −1), (0, 1), (1, 3), (2, 5).

To **plot a graph** of the function:

plot the points,
and then join them with a straight line.

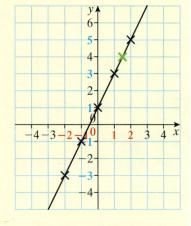

Notice that you can extend the line both ways beyond the points you have plotted.

The line is the graph of the function $y = 2x + 1$.

Any point on the line matches the function. The green point is (1.5, 4).

This matches the function $y = 2x + 1$ because $2 \times 1.5 + 1 = 4$.

Exercise 17:2

1 a Copy and complete this table for the function $y = x + 5$.

x	1	2	3	4	5	6
y	6	7				

b Copy these axes onto squared paper.
c Plot the points from your table.
d Join the points with a straight line.

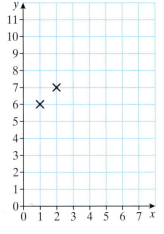

2 a Copy and complete this table for the function $y = 2x − 1$.

x	1	2	3	4	5	6
y						

b Copy these axes onto squared paper.
c Plot the points from your table.
d Join the points with a straight line.

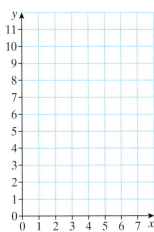

3 a Copy and complete this table for the function $y = 3x + 2$.

x	−4	−3	−2	−1	0	1	2	3	4
y									

b Draw a grid with an *x*-axis from −4 to 4 and a *y*-axis from −10 to 14.
c Draw the graph of $y = 3x + 2$ on your grid.
d Plot these points (−1.5, −3.5), (0.5, 5.5), (1.5, 6.5), (3.5, 11.5).
e Write down if the points in part **d** lie above, below or on your line.

4 The graph shows the straight line with function $y = 3x - 4$.

a Copy and complete this table.

x	−4	−2	0	2	4
y					

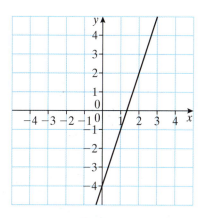

b A point on the line $y = 3x - 4$ has an *x*-coordinate of 50. What is the *y*-coordinate of this point?
c A point on the line $y = 3x - 4$ has a *y*-coordinate of 50. What is the *x*-coordinate of this point?

5 The graph shows a straight line.
The equation of the line is $y = 3x$.

Does the point (25, 75) lie on the straight line $y = 3x$? Explain how you know.

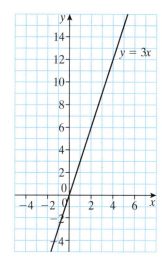

6 a Copy and complete this table for the function $y = -2x + 4$.

x	−4	−3	−2	−1	0	1	2	3	4
y									

b Draw a grid with an *x*-axis from −4 to 4 and a *y*-axis from −4 to 12.
c Draw the graph of $y = -2x + 4$ on your grid.
d Write down the coordinates of three other points that lie on your line.

17 Algebraic graphs

7 Each point on the straight line $x + y = 12$ has an x-coordinate and a y-coordinate that **add together** to make **12**.

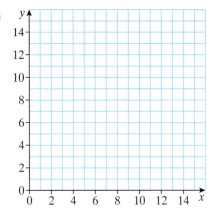

  a Copy and complete this table.

x	0	2	4	6	8	10	12
y	12	10					

  b Copy these axes onto squared paper.
  c Plot the points from your table.
  d Join the points with a straight line.

8 The graph shows a straight line.

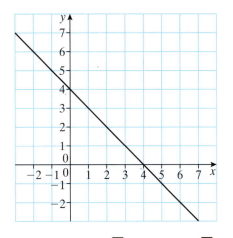

  a Copy and complete the table for some of the points on the line.

(x, y)	(,)	(,)	(,)
$x + y$			

  b Write an equation of the straight line.
  c Copy the graph. Draw the straight line that has the equation $x + y = 6$.

9 Look at this hexagon pattern.

  a Draw the next two patterns in this sequence.

  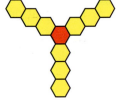

  b Copy and complete this table.

pattern number (p)	1	2	3	4	5	6
number of hexagons (n)	4					

  c Draw a grid with a p-axis from 0 to 6 and an n-axis from 0 to 20.
  d Draw a graph using the points from your table.
  e Work out the number of hexagons in the 15th pattern.

Think on!

10 a Copy the table.

  b Fill in the table using the digits 0, 1, 2, 3, 4, 5, 6, 7, 8, 9 as the coordinates of the five points.

  You can only use each digit once.

	$y = x + 3$	$y = 10 - x$
$y = 2x - 2$	(… , …)	(… , …)
$y = 6x + 3$	(… , …)	(… , …)
The point (… , …) is below the line $y = x$		

2 Mapping diagrams

Showing functions using mapping diagrams

Key words: mapping, input, output, mapping diagram, integer

Showing functions using mapping diagrams — Level 6

You have seen that $y = 3x + 1$ is a function.
You can also write a function as a **mapping**.

You write the mapping for the function $y = 3x + 1$ like this: $x \mapsto 3x + 1$
The arrow means 'is mapped to'.
So $x \mapsto 3x + 1$ means that the value of x is mapped to the value $3x + 1$.

The values of x are called the **input** values and the values of $3x + 1$ are called **output** values.

You can substitute values of x to find out where the mapping takes them.

When $x = 0$ $x \mapsto 3 \times 0 + 1 = 0 + 1 = 1$ When $x = 2$ $x \mapsto 3 \times 2 + 1 = 6 + 1 = 7$
When $x = 1$ $x \mapsto 3 \times 1 + 1 = 3 + 1 = 4$ When $x = 3$ $x \mapsto 3 \times 3 + 1 = 9 + 1 = 10$

Here is a table of values for these results

x	0	1	2	3
$3x + 1$	1	4	7	10

Now you can draw a **mapping diagram** for $x \mapsto 3x + 1$.

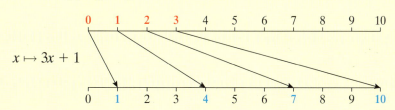

You only show the arrows that fit onto your mapping diagram.
So you don't draw the arrow from 4 as it would go to 13 which is not shown on the output scale.
You only draw mapping arrows from **integer** input values.

Exercise 17:3

1 Write down the mapping that connects the **red numbers** to the **blue numbers** in each part.

a $1 \to 4$ b $2 \to 3$ c $1 \to 8$ d $3 \to 13$
     $2 \to 5$ $4 \to 7$ $3 \to 14$ $5 \to 23$
     $3 \to 6$ $6 \to 11$ $5 \to 20$ $7 \to 33$

17 Algebraic graphs

2 a Copy the table and fill in the gaps for the mapping $x \mapsto 2x + 4$.

x	0	1	2	3
$2x+4$	4	...	...	...

b Copy this mapping diagram and fill in the missing arrows for $x \mapsto 2x + 4$.

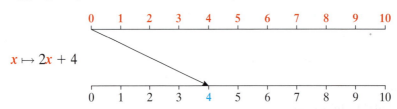

3 Copy the mapping diagram in each part and fill in the missing arrows for the mapping shown.

a $x \mapsto 3x$

d $x \mapsto 4x - 2$

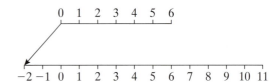

b $x \mapsto x + 1$

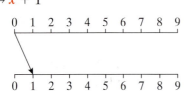

e $x \mapsto 2x - 3$

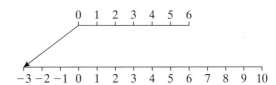

c $x \mapsto 3x + 1$

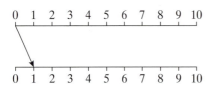

f $x \mapsto 3x - 2$

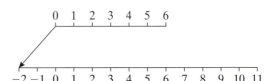

Think on!

4 Use the digits 0, 1, 2, 3, 4, 5, 6, 7, 8, 9 to fill in the gaps.
Each part shows an input value and an output value for the same function.

a 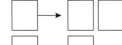   d

b 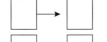   e

c   f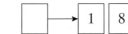

3 Real-life graphs

- Drawing and interpreting conversion graphs
- Interpreting real-life graphs

Key words

graph
conversion graph
sketch graph
explain
straight-line graph
intercept
interpret

Drawing and interpreting conversion graphs Level 6

A **graph** is a way of showing information on a diagram.
You have seen **straight-line graphs** in Section 1 when you looked at the graphs of functions.

This is another type of straight-line graph.
It is called a **conversion graph**.
This graph shows how to convert between temperatures in Celsius (°C) and Fahrenheit (°F).

For a conversion graph:
- you label both the axes in equal steps
- you don't have to use the same scale on both axes
- use the symbol ⌇ if an axis doesn't start at zero to show that part of it is missing.

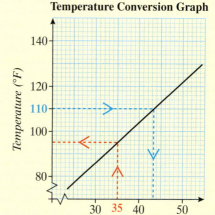

Temperature Conversion Graph

You can use this conversion graph to change from °C to °F and from °F to °C like this.

To change 35°C into °F:
Start from 35 on the °C axis
Go up to the line
Go across to the °F axis
Read off the °F value
So 35°C = 95°F

To change 110°F into °C:
Start from 110 on the °F axis
Go across to the line
Go down to the °C axis
Read off the °C value
So 110°F = 43.3°C

The 95°F is fairly easy to read off the vertical scale but the 43.3°C is more difficult.
You can see that the blue arrowed line doesn't go to exactly 43°C.
You have to do your best to judge the value of the **intercept**.

Exercise 17:4

1 a Copy these axes onto squared paper.
   b Plot the points (10, 16) and (70, 112).
   c Join the points with a straight line.

Your graph shows a conversion graph between miles and kilometres.

   d Use the graph to decide which is further, 65 miles or 100 km.

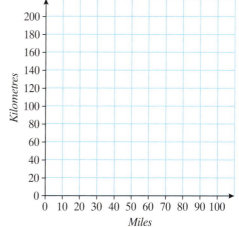

Conversion Graph for Miles and Kilometres

17 Algebraic graphs

2 This conversion graph shows the relationship between metres and feet.

  a A rope is 9 m long.
  Write down this length to the nearest foot.

  b Which is longer, 21 feet or 7 m?

  c In a triple jump competition, Cameron jumps 15 feet and Aaron jumps 4 metres. Who wins?
  Explain how you worked out your answer.

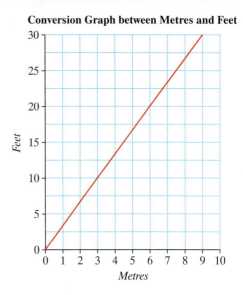

3 This conversion graph shows the relationship between grams and ounces.

  a Use the graph to convert
   (1) 2 ounces into grams
   (2) 250 grams into ounces.

  b How many ounces are there in 1 kg?
  Explain how you get your answer.

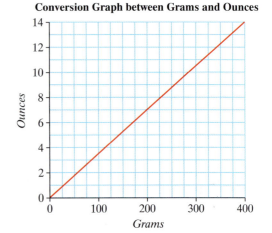

4 Different masses are placed on a spring.
The amount the spring stretches from the original length is measured each time.

This graph shows the results.

  a Write down the stretch of the spring with a mass of 250 g added.

  b Estimate the stretch of the spring with a mass of 175 g added.

  ⚠ **c** Explain why you can draw a straight line through the points.

  ⚠ **d** Explain why the line through the points can be extended to (0, 0).

  ⚠ **e** Write a sentence to describe the relationship between the mass added and the stretch of the spring.

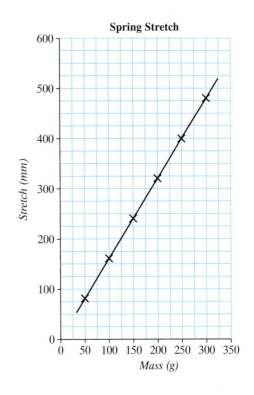

5 A cookery book shows how long it takes in minutes to roast a joint of meat.

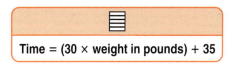

Time = (30 × weight in pounds) + 35

a Work out how long it would take to roast a 2 lb joint of meat.

b Copy and complete this table.

Weight of meat (lb)	1	2	3	4	5	6	7	8
Cooking time (minutes)	65	…	…	…	…	…	…	…

c Copy the axes, then plot the points from the table to show the cooking times for different weights of meat.

d Join the points with a straight line.

e Use the graph to work out how long it would take to roast a $2\frac{1}{2}$ lb joint of meat.

f Work out when the cooking should start to have a $5\frac{1}{2}$ lb joint of meat cooked for 1 p.m.

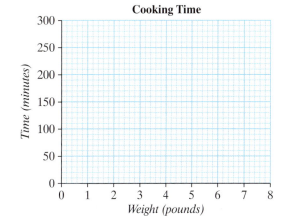

6 Ravi's car engine has an oil leak.
He fills the engine with 3.8 litres of oil.
0.4 litres of oil is leaking out every **5 hours**.

a Work out how much oil remains in the engine after 10 hours.

b Copy and complete this table.

Time (hours)	0	5	10	15	20	25	30	35
Oil level (litres)	3.8	…	…	…	…	…	…	…

c Copy the axes, then plot the points from the table to show the oil level.

d Join the points with a straight line.

e Estimate the oil level after 8 hours.

f If the oil level falls below 2 litres, the engine may be damaged. Use the graph to work out when the oil level will fall below 2 litres.

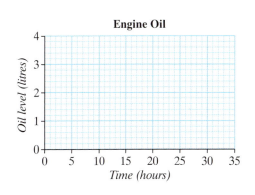

17 Algebraic graphs

> **Interpreting real-life graphs** — Level 6
>
> A flask is filled from a tap flowing at a constant rate.
>
> The **sketch graph** shows the depth of water in the flask as time passes.
>
> Notice that there are no scales or units so you can't read any exact information from the graph.
>
> You can **interpret** the graph though.
>
> This means that you can **explain** what the graph is telling you.
>
>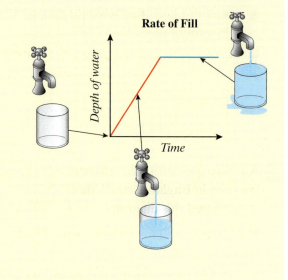
>
> The **red** part of the graph shows the flask filling up at a constant rate.
> The depth of water is increasing as time passes.
>
> The **blue** part shows that the depth doesn't change once the flask is full.
> The flask is overflowing in the blue part of the graph if the tap is still running.
>
> The points on the graph can be joined because the depth of water can be measured at any time.
>
> The graph passes through the origin (0, 0) because there is no depth of water when the time starts.

Exercise 17:5

1 Sketch a line graph to show the depth of water against time when water runs steadily from a tap into each jar. Use the same set of axes for each part.

a    b    c

2 In Uganda, forest clearance and poaching has affected the numbers of mountain gorillas.

This graph shows how the population has changed over the last 50 years.

Write a description of how the population of mountain gorillas has changed over the last 50 years.

3. This graph shows how the number of full-time secondary school teachers has changed over the last 20 years.

    a Explain what this graph tells you about the number of full-time female teachers.

    b Explain what has happened to the total number of full-time teachers over the last 20 years.

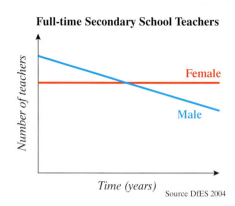

2002

4. A newspaper wrote an article about public libraries in England and Wales.
    It published this diagram.

    Use the diagram to decide whether each statement below is true or false, or whether you cannot be certain. Explain your answer in each part.

    a The number of libraries open for more than 45 hours per week **fell by more than half** from 1988 to 1998.

    b **In 2004** there will be **about 450 libraries** open in England and Wales for more than 45 hours a week.

Facts to figure

5. William Playfair was the first person to develop line graphs. He was aware of the visual impact of graphs and the impressions they can make.

    In 1768 he drew these two graphs to show how the debt of the British government changed over time.

    Both graphs show the same information.
    Between 1739 and 1784 Britain was involved in wars with France, Spain and America.

Figure 1

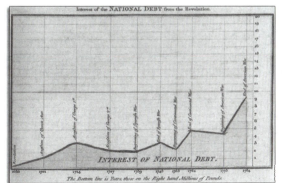
Figure 2

If you were in favour of the wars, which graph would you choose to show the data? Justify your answer.

17 Algebraic graphs

Watch out ... there's a trap about

▶ Make sure that you label the scales on your graphs correctly.

If you want to plot points with *x* values of 10, 14, 18, 23 and 30 you can't draw your scale like this!

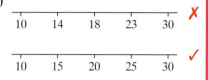

You have to draw a proper scale like this and plot your points at the correct places.

▶ This graph shows Uzma's distance away from home when she goes for a walk.

Look at the blue line.
Some people think that because there's a line on the graph, Uzma must be moving.

But the horizontal line means that her distance from home isn't changing.
She's having a rest!

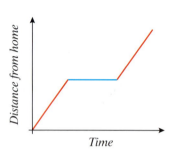

Test yourself

1 These coordinates fit the rule $y = 3x$.
Copy and complete each coordinate pair.

a (1, ?)　　b (3, ?)　　c (4, ?)　　d (−6, ?)　　e (4.5, ?)

2 These coordinates fit the rule $y = 2x + 1$.
Copy and complete each coordinate pair.

a (1, ?)　　b (5, ?)　　c (−2, ?)　　d (2.5, ?)　　e (?, 15)

3 a Copy and complete this table of values for the function $y = 2x + 3$.

x	1	2	3	4
y	5			

b Copy these axes onto squared paper.
c Plot the points from your table.
d Join the points with a straight line.

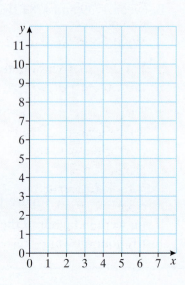

4 **a** You pay **£2.40** each time you go to a gym.
Copy and complete the table.

Number of sessions	0	10	20	30
Total cost (£)	0	24		

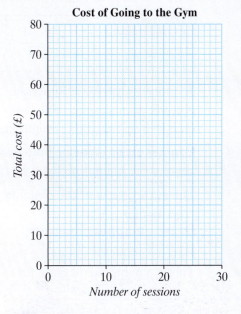

Cost of Going to the Gym

b Copy the graph.
Show this information on the graph.
Join the points with a straight line.

c A different way of paying is to pay a yearly fee of **£22**
Then you pay **£1.40** each time you go to the gym.
Complete the table.

Number of sessions	0	10	20	30
Total cost (£)	22	36		

d Now show this information on the same graph.
Join these points with a straight line.

e For how many gym sessions does the graph show that the cost is the same for both ways of paying?

5 Write down a mapping that connects the **red numbers** to the **blue numbers** in each part.

a 1 → 6
2 → 10
3 → 14

b 2 → 7
4 → 9
6 → 11

c 3 → 5
5 → 9
7 → 13

6 The graph shows my journey in a lift.
I got in the lift at floor number 10.

a The lift stopped at two different floors before I got to floor number 22.
What floors were they?

b For how long was I in the lift while it was moving?

c After I got out of the lift at floor number 22, the lift went directly to the ground floor.
It took **45 seconds**.
Copy the graph.
Show the journey of the lift from floor 22 to the ground floor.

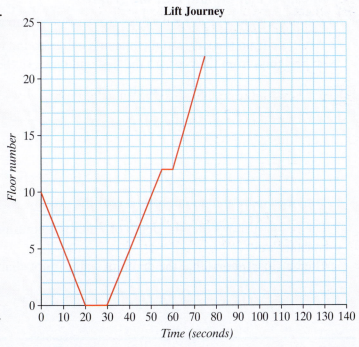

Lift Journey

17 Algebraic graphs

Chapter 17 Summary

Level 6

Plot a graph of a function

Here is a table of values for the function $y = x + 1$

x-coordinate	−2	−1	0	1	2
y-coordinate	−1	0	1	2	3

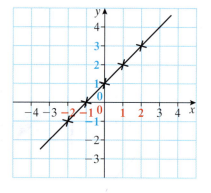

To plot a graph of the function:
plot the points in the table, and
then join them with a straight line.

You can extend the line both ways
beyond the points you have plotted.

This is the graph of the function $y = x + 1$.

Draw a mapping diagram

Here is a table of values for the mapping $x \mapsto 3x + 1$.
This is a mapping diagram for $x \mapsto 3x + 1$.

x	0	1	2	3
$3x + 1$	1	4	7	10

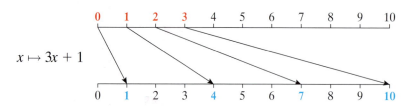

Interpret and explain real-life graphs

You need to be able to read values from a **conversion graph**.

   Go **up** from the x-axis to the line and **across** to the y-axis
or go **across** from the y-axis to the line and **down** to the x-axis.

$$35°C = 95°F \text{ and } 110°F = 43.3°C$$

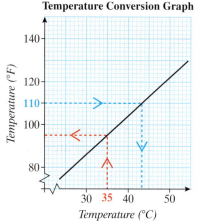

You need to be able to interpret a **real-life graph**.

The red part shows that the depth of water is increasing at a
constant rate.
The blue part shows that the depth of water is not changing.

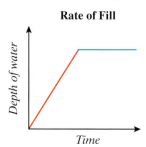

18 Transformations

Chapter 3
Coordinates and symmetry

- Identifying lines of symmetry
- Using coordinates in all four quadrants
- Identifying rotational symmetry

1. Reflections, translations and rotations
2. Enlargements

Year 8

- Enlarging a shape by a fractional scale factor
- Understanding similarity

You should already know:

- **how to identify lines of symmetry**

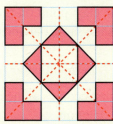

This pattern has four **lines of symmetry**.

- **how to write the coordinates of a point**

Point A has coordinates $(-1, 2)$
Point B has coordinates $(-3, -2)$
Point C has coordinates $(2, -3)$
Point D has coordinates $(3, 1)$

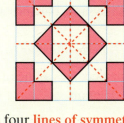

- **about rotational symmetry**

The order of rotational symmetry is the number of times that the shape looks the same as you rotate it through one full turn.

An equilateral triangle has rotational symmetry of order 3.

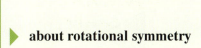

289

18 Transformations

1 Reflections, translations and rotations

▸ **Drawing and describing reflections**

▸ **Drawing and describing translations**

▸ **Drawing and describing rotations**

Key words	
transformation	reflection
translation	rotation
object	image
reflection symmetry	mirror line
perpendicular	inverse
corresponding	rotate
centre of rotation	congruent

▸ **Drawing and describing reflections**　　　　　　　　　　　　　Level 6

A **transformation** changes the position of a shape.
Reflections, **translations** and **rotations** are all transformations.

The shape that you start with is called the **object**.
The shape that you get after a transformation is called the **image**.

If A is a point on the object then the point that it moves to on the image is called A′.
You read A′ as A dashed.

You have already drawn reflections when you looked at **reflection symmetry**.

In a reflection, each point on the object moves across the **mirror line** to the point which is the same distance away from the mirror line on the other side.

The line AA′ is **perpendicular** to the mirror line.

The mirror line becomes a line of symmetry for the whole diagram.

The whole diagram has reflection symmetry in the red line.

Any point on the mirror line doesn't move.
B and B′ are exactly the same point.

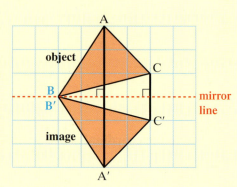

With a diagonal mirror line look at each vertex in turn.

P is diagonally 2 squares from the mirror line.

So P′ is diagonally 2 squares on the other side of the mirror line.

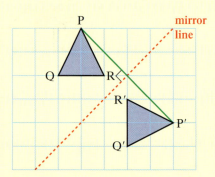

To reverse a reflection you need to do the same reflection again.
So the **inverse** of reflection in the red line is reflection in the red line.

Exercise 18:1

1 Copy and complete each diagram to show ABC being reflected in the red mirror line to give A'B'C'.

a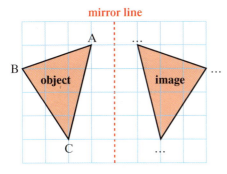

b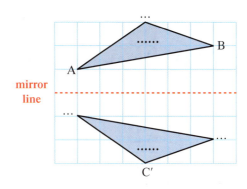

2 Copy each diagram and draw the reflection of each shape in the red mirror line. Label your diagrams properly using dash notation.

a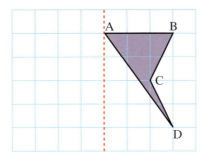

c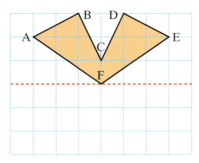

b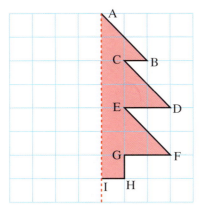

d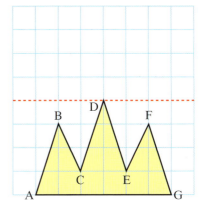

3 Explain how to transform the image back into the object after a reflection.

18 Transformations

4 Copy each diagram and draw the reflection of each shape in the red diagonal mirror line. Label your diagrams properly using dash notation.

a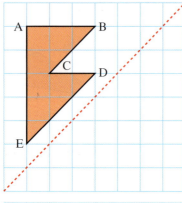

c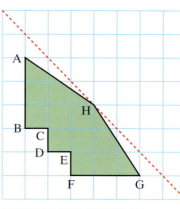

b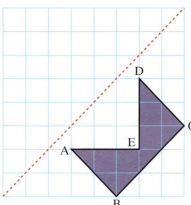

d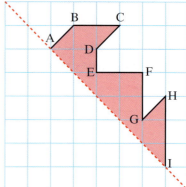

5 Each of the red dashed lines in these diagrams is a mirror line.
Copy the diagram in each part and complete it.

a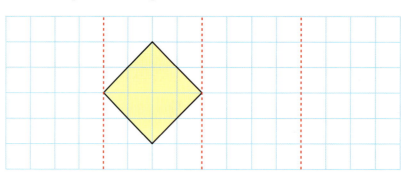

b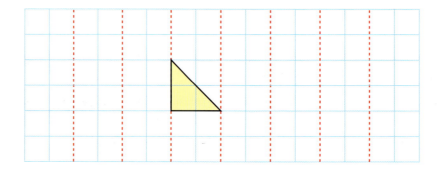

6 Naomi is drawing reflections of letters.

This is her drawing showing the reflection of the letter **A** in a vertical mirror line.

a Draw the reflection of the first 10 letters of the alphabet in a vertical mirror line.

b Write down the letters that look the same as their images.

c Explain what property a shape must possess so that it will look the same after it has been reflected in a vertical mirror line.

d Draw the reflection of the first 10 letters of the alphabet in a horizontal mirror line.

e Write down the letters that look the same as their images.

f Explain what property a shape must possess so that it will look the same after it has been reflected in a horizontal mirror line.

⚠ g Explain what property a shape must possess so that it will look the same after it has been reflected in **any** mirror line.

7 Explain why rectangle R′ is **not** the reflection of rectangle R in the line L.

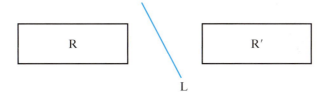

Explore

8 a Copy these diagrams.
  Draw the reflection of the word PEAR in the red mirror line in each part.

  (1) P
      E
      A
      R

  (2) P E A R

  (3) P
       E
        A
         R

b Make up some words of your own and reflect them in different mirror lines.
  Use some vertical, some horizontal and some diagonal lines.

c Nathan has drawn some words of his own and he says that all words look different when they've been reflected in a line. Investigate Nathan's claim.
  If you think he's wrong, give a counter example to show that he is wrong.

18 Transformations

Drawing and describing translations — Level 6

A **translation** is a movement of an object through a given distance in a particular direction.

This is a translation of 5 cm to the right.

AA′ is 5 cm long.

BB′ and CC′ are also 5 cm long.

Measure them and check!

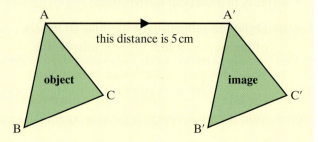

You often describe translations by saying how far right or left and how far up or down you have moved.

This is a translation of 4 squares to the right and 2 squares up.

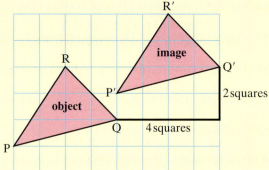

You must measure a translation using **corresponding** points on the object and the image.

You can use P and P′ or Q and Q′ or R and R′.

The inverse of a translation is a translation through the same distance in the opposite direction.

The inverse of a **translation of 5 cm to the right and 2 cm down** is a **translation of 5 cm to the left and 2 cm up**.

Exercise 18:2

1 Each diagram shows an object being translated to give an image. Describe the translation in each part.

a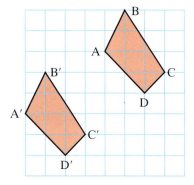

b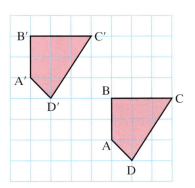

2 Each diagram shows an object being translated to give an image.
In each part (1) describe the translation   (2) write down the inverse transformation.

a 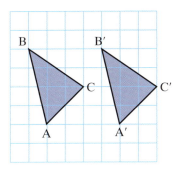 b 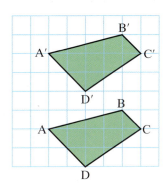 c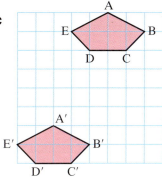

3 Maha is giving some instructions for a translation. She says,

'Move the shape 5 to the right, then 7 down, then 3 to the left and 12 up.'

Poppy says that she can make the instructions much easier.
What instructions should Poppy give?

4 Eva is giving some instructions for a translation. She says,

'Move the shape 2 across and 3 up.'

Tara says that she can't understand Eva's instructions.
What's wrong with Eva's instructions?

5 a Copy the diagram.

b Draw the image of shape PQRS after a translation of 4 units to the right and 3 units down.
Label the image P'Q'R'S'.

c Write down the coordinates of each of the points P', Q', R' and S'.

d Describe the transformation that would take P'Q'R'S' back to PQRS.

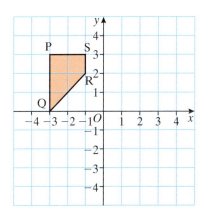

6 a Draw a set of coordinate axes with each axis from −6 to 6 on squared paper.

b (1) Plot each of these points and join them up as you go.

K(3, 6)   L(3, 4)   M(1, 4)   N(1, 6)

(2) Draw the image of KLMN after a translation of 5 to the left and 4 down.

c (1) Plot each of these points and join them up as you go.

C(−5, 6)   D(−3, 6)   E(−3, 4)   F(−5, 4)

(2) Draw the image of CDEF after a translation of 8 to the right and 7 down.

18 Transformations

7 You can show more than one transformation on the same diagram.
You use more dashes to label the images of these transformations.

   a Copy the diagram.

   b Reflect PQR in the x-axis.
   Label the image P′Q′R′.

   c Translate P′Q′R′ through 5 units to the right.
   Label the image P″Q″R″.

   d Reflect P″Q″R″ in the x-axis.
   Label the image P‴Q‴R‴.

   e Describe the transformation
   that will transform P‴Q‴R‴ to PQR.

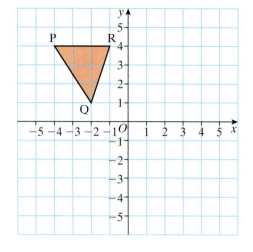

8 **a** Copy the diagram.

   b Reflect WXYZ in the y-axis.
   Label the image W′X′Y′Z′.

   c Reflect WXYZ in the x-axis.
   Label the image W″X″Y″Z″.

   d Reflect W″X″Y″Z″ in the y-axis.
   Label the image W‴X‴Y‴Z‴.

   e Describe the transformation that will
   transform W‴X‴Y‴Z‴ into W′X′Y′Z′.

   f Describe the transformation that will
   transform W‴X‴Y‴Z‴ back into WXYZ.

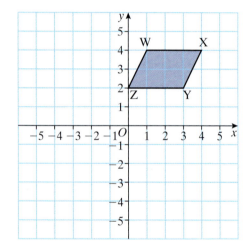

Explore

9 **a** This is a 1 by 2 right-angled triangle on a 3 by 3 grid.
There is only one possible translation of the triangle moving in
whole squares so that the image stays completely on this grid.
Describe this translation.

   b Investigate the transformations of the triangle through whole
   squares on different size grids.
   How many such transformations are there for each grid?
   Investigate what happens if you change the size of the triangle too!

Drawing and describing rotations   Level 6

The sails of the windmill **rotate**.

A **rotation** turns an object around.

There is always a point that does not move in a rotation.
This point is called the **centre of rotation**.

This triangle has been rotated around point P.
P is the centre of rotation and P does not move.
Q moves to Q′ and R moves to R′.
Every point moves except point P.

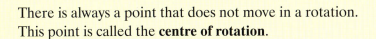

You describe a rotation by saying **how much you turn**,
which way you turn and **the centre of rotation**.
This is a rotation through **90°** **clockwise** **about P**.

For a rotation of 180° a direction is not needed because
180° clockwise and 180° anticlockwise gives the same answer.

The inverse of a rotation is a rotation about the same centre
through the same angle in the opposite direction.

The inverse of the first rotation is a rotation
through **90°** **anticlockwise** **about P**.

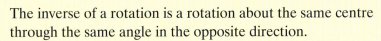

Two shapes are **congruent** if they are identical.
The object and image after a translation, a reflection or a rotation are congruent.

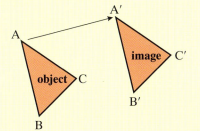 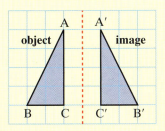 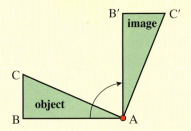

The object and the image after all of these transformations
are exactly the same size and the same shape.
The reflection has been turned over but it is still the same shape.

18 Transformations

Exercise 18:3

1 The shapes below are drawn on square grids.

The diagrams show a rectangle that is rotated, then rotated again.
The centre of rotation is marked •

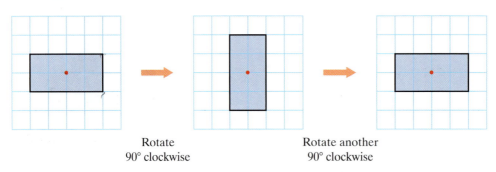

Rotate 90° clockwise   Rotate another 90° clockwise

Copy and complete the diagrams below to show the triangle when it is rotated, then rotated again.
The centre of rotation is marked •

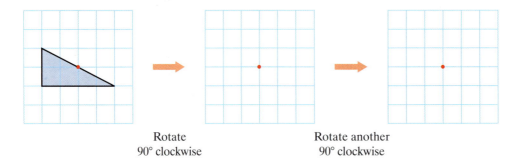

Rotate 90° clockwise   Rotate another 90° clockwise

2 Describe each of these rotations.

a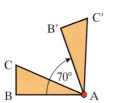

c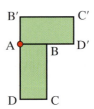

b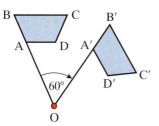

d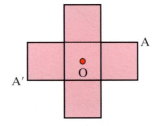

3 Write down the inverse transformation for each of the rotations in **Question 2**.

4 Follow these instructions to rotate a triangle through 90° clockwise.
You are going to use tracing paper to help you to draw the rotation.

   a Draw a triangle ABC like this one.
Your triangle does not have to be exactly this size but you can trace the triangle if you want to.

      You are going to rotate the triangle around point A.

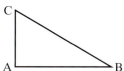

   b Trace your triangle and mark the centre of the rotation with a cross like this **+**.

      Draw over the triangle on the back of the tracing paper.

   c Now hold your pencil on the cross at A and rotate the tracing paper 90° clockwise until the cross looks the same for the first time.

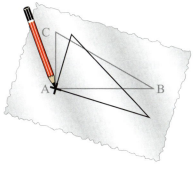

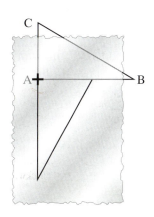

   d Now draw over the triangle to transfer the tracing underneath.
Take the tracing paper away and draw over the triangle to make it neat.

      Label the vertices of the image.

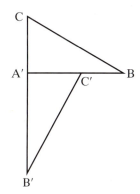

5 You need to draw a triangle like this one for each part.
Use tracing paper to draw the triangle rotated through

   a 90° **clockwise** about Q   **c** 90° **clockwise** about R

   b 90° **anticlockwise** about P   **d** 180° about P.

Label the image in each part correctly.

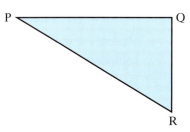

18 Transformations

6 a Copy the diagram showing triangle T.

b Rotate triangle T through 90° anticlockwise about O. Label the image T'.

c Rotate triangle T through 180° about O. Label the image T''.

d Rotate triangle T through 270° anticlockwise about O. Label the image T'''.

e Describe the single transformation that would map T''' onto T'.

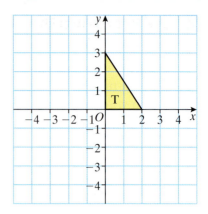

⚠ 7 a Draw a pair of coordinate axes with each axis from −8 to 8 on squared paper.

b Draw the quadrilateral PQRS where the coordinates of the vertices are:

P(2, 4), Q(7, 4), R(6, 6) and S(2, 6).

State the type of quadrilateral you have drawn.

c Rotate PQRS through 90° anticlockwise about O. Label the image P'Q'R'S'.

d Reflect P'Q'R'S' in the x-axis. Label the image P''Q''R''S''.

e Rotate P''Q''R''S'' through 270° clockwise about O. Label the image $P_3Q_3R_3S_3$.
You can still use dashes but if you do this many transformations it is easier to use numbers in subscript like this.

f Write down the single transformation that would transform PQRS into $P_3Q_3R_3S_3$.

g Rotate PQRS through 180° about the point (4, 3). Label the image $P_4Q_4R_4S_4$.

Think on!

8 Copy and complete these transformations to map triangle A onto triangle B.
You should use all of these:

    x   y   90   270   anticlockwise   clockwise

a Reflection in the x-axis,
followed by a rotation of 90° .... about O.

b Rotation of 90° .... about O,
followed by a reflection in the x-axis.

c Reflection in the ...-axis,
followed by a rotation of 270° clockwise about O.

d Rotation of ...° anticlockwise about O,
followed by a reflection in the x-axis.

e Reflection in the y-axis,
followed by a rotation of ...° clockwise about O.

f Rotation of 90° anticlockwise about O,
followed by a reflection in the ...-axis.

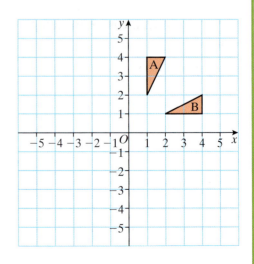

2 Enlargements

▶ **Drawing and describing enlargements**

▶ **Finding the scale factor and centre of an enlargement**

Key words
enlargement   scale factor
centre of enlargement

▶ **Drawing and describing enlargements**   Level 6

An **enlargement** changes the size of an object.

A′B′C′ is an enlargement of ABC.

Any length in A′B′C′ is **twice** the corresponding length in ABC.

The transformation from ABC to A′B′C′ is an enlargement with **scale factor** 2.

The object and the image are **not** congruent. They are the same shape but different sizes.

So   A′B′ = 2 × AB   B′C′ = 2 × BC   A′C′ = 2 × AC

$\dfrac{A'B'}{AB} = 2$ $\dfrac{B'C'}{BC} = 2$ $\dfrac{A'C'}{AC} = 2$

For every enlargement there is a point that doesn't move.

This point is called the **centre of enlargement**.

The centre of enlargement does not have to be inside the shape.

To enlarge ABC by a scale factor of 3 with centre O, measure the length of **OA**.

Multiply it by 3.

Then draw **OA′** and mark the point **A′**.

Repeat this with **B** and **C** to get **B′** and **C′**.

Join A′, B′ and C′ to get the image.

You can check that the sides of triangle A′B′C′ are three times larger than the sides of ABC by measuring them.

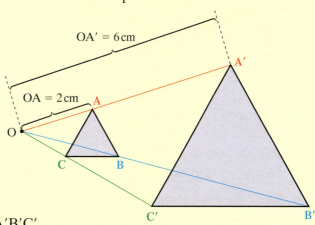

301

18 Transformations

Exercise 18:4

1 Work out the scale factor of this enlargement.

2 a Draw a rectangle that is 4 cm by 2.5 cm.

  b Draw an enlargement of your rectangle using a scale factor of 3.

3 a Copy this diagram.
  It does not have to be exactly this size but you can trace it if you want to.
  Draw the enlargement of ABCD using a scale factor of 2 and centre X.

  b Copy this diagram.
  Draw the enlargement of ABCD using a scale factor of 2 and centre Y.

  c Copy this diagram.
  Draw the enlargement of ABCD using a scale factor of 2 and centre A.

4 a Copy the diagram.

  b How far across is it from O to A?

  c How far up is it from O to A?

  d Explain how you can draw a point A' so that $OA' = 3 \times OA$ without measuring the length of OA.

  e Draw the enlargement of ABC using a scale factor of 3 and centre O.

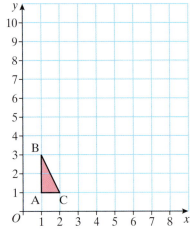

302

5 a Draw a pair of coordinate axes with each axis from −8 to 8 on squared paper.

b Draw the triangle ABC where A is the point (−2, 0), B is the point (0, 2) and C is the point (2, 0).

c Draw the enlargement of triangle ABC using a scale factor of 3 and centre (0, 0). Label the image A′B′C′.

d Draw the enlargement of triangle ABC using a scale factor of 2 and centre (−4, 2). Label the image A″B″C″.

e Draw the enlargement of triangle ABC using a scale factor of 4 and centre (0, 2). Label the image A‴B‴C‴.

6 Copy this shape onto isometric paper.
Enlarge the coloured shape by a **scale factor of 2**, using **P** as the centre of enlargement.

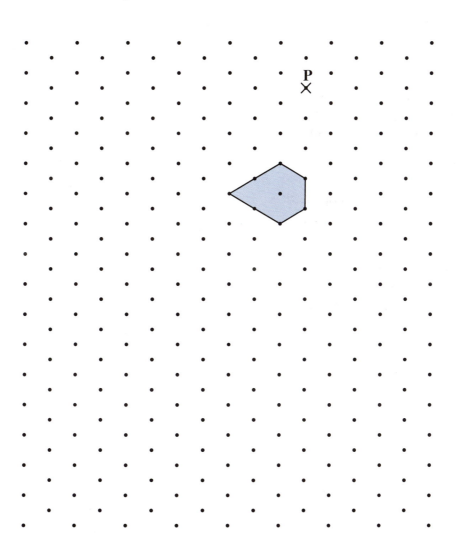

18 Transformations

Finding the scale factor and centre of an enlargement — Level 6

If you are shown an enlargement you can work out the scale factor of the enlargement by measuring two corresponding lengths.

For example, you could measure AB and A'B'.

Here AB = 1 cm and A'B' = 4 cm

Then you work out $\frac{A'B'}{AB}$ to give you the scale factor.

The scale factor of this enlargement is 4.
You can use any two corresponding lengths to work this out.

To find the centre of an enlargement, join corresponding points and extend the lines.

So, for example, join A' to A and extend the line.

Then join C' to C and extend the line.

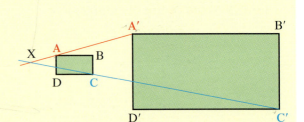

The centre of the enlargement is where these lines meet.
The centre of the enlargement here is X.

You can use any two pairs of corresponding points to find the centre.
B'B and D'D will also pass through X.

Exercise 18:5

1
  a Draw a pair of coordinate axes with each axis from −8 to 10 on squared paper.
  b Draw ABCD where A is the point (−5, −2), B is the point (−2, −2), C is the point (−1, −4) and D is the point (−4, −4).
  c Draw A'B'C'D' where A' is the point (−3, 6), B' is the point (6, 6), C' is the point (9, 0) and D' is the point (0, 0).
  d State the scale factor of the enlargement from ABCD to A'B'C'D'.
  e Find and label X, the centre of the enlargement from ABCD to A'B'C'D'.

2
  a Draw a pair of coordinate axes with each axis from −8 to 10 on squared paper.
  b Draw a shape and an enlargement of the shape on your grid.
  c Swap your grid with a friend and find the centre of enlargement and the scale factor of the enlargement of each other's diagram.

3 Look at the square grids.
Each diagram shows an enlargement of scale factor 2.

The **centre** of this enlargement is marked with a cross.

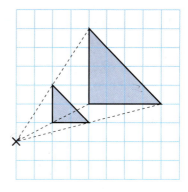

Copy each of these diagrams and mark the centre of enlargement with a cross.

a 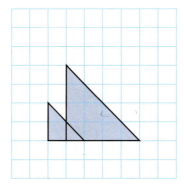　　　b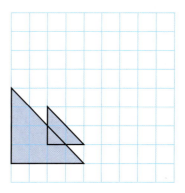

Facts to figure

4 Before the 13th century many paintings looked flat.
There was no depth to the picture.

Brunelleschi was the first artist to develop an exact method to make paintings look three-dimensional.

He discussed the problem with a mathematician, Toscanelli, who suggested that he should use a vanishing point in his paintings.

A vanishing point is like the centre of an enlargement.

He drew lines of perspective that met at the vanishing point and used these lines to construct his paintings.

Alfie drew this sketch using perspective.
Trace Alfie's sketch. You only need to trace the straight lines.

Ignore any horizontal or vertical lines as these aren't affected by perspective.
Draw pencil lines along all the other lines.
These are lines that would all be parallel in real life.
These lines all meet at the vanishing point.

Write down the vanishing point of Alfie's sketch.

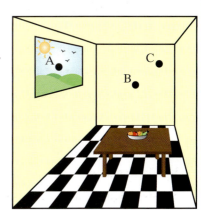

18 Transformations

Watch out... there's a trap about

▶ Be careful when the mirror line is a diagonal line.
You need to look at each vertex in turn and decide how far away it is from the mirror line.

Try turning your book so that the mirror line is vertical. Then you will see which diagram is correct.

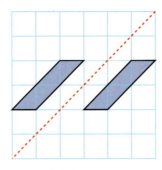
This is wrong.

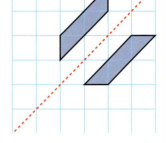
This is right.

▶ You need to describe transformations fully.
It is not enough to say that this diagram shows a 90° clockwise rotation.
You also need to say that the centre of the rotation is A.

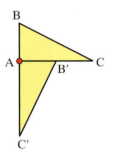

Each of these diagrams also shows a 90° clockwise rotation about the red dot.

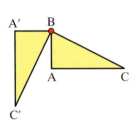 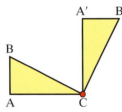 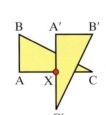 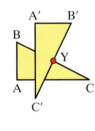

Test yourself

1 Copy each diagram and draw the reflection of each shape in the red mirror line. Label your diagrams properly using dash notation.

a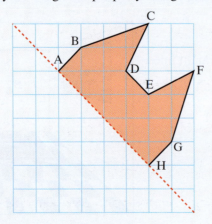

b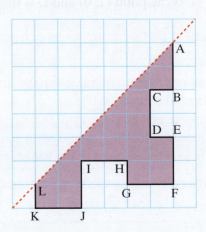

2 a Draw a set of coordinate axes with each axis from −8 to 8 on squared paper.

  b Plot each of these points and join them up as you go.
   A(3, 6)   B(3, 4)   C(1, 4)   D(1, 6)

  c Draw the image of ABCD after a translation of 7 to the left and 10 down.
   Label the image A′B′C′D′.

  d Draw the image of ABCD after a reflection in the *x*-axis.
   Label the image A″B″C″D″.

3 You need to draw a rectangle like this one for each part.
Draw the image of the rectangle after rotation through

  a 90° **clockwise** about X

  b 90° **anticlockwise** about W

  c 90° **clockwise** about Z

  d 180° about Y.

4 Write down the inverse transformation for

  a a translation of 3 left and 4 up

  b a translation of 2 right and 3 down

  c a reflection in the *x*-axis

  d a reflection in the *y*-axis

  e a rotation of 90° clockwise about (0, 0)

  f a rotation of 180° about (0, 0).

5 a Draw a pair of coordinate axes with each axis from −8 to 8 on squared paper.

  b Draw the kite ABCD where A is the point (−1, 0), B is the point (0, 1),
   C is the point (1, 0) and D is the point (0, −2).

  c Draw the enlargement of ABCD using a scale factor of 4 and centre (0, 0).
   Label the image A′B′C′D′.

  d Draw the enlargement of ABCD using a scale factor of 2 and centre (−4, −4).
   Label the image A″B″C″D″.

  e Draw the enlargement of ABCD using a scale factor of 2 and centre (2, 2).
   Label the image A‴B‴C‴D‴.

  f State the transformation that maps A‴B‴C‴D‴ onto A″B″C″D″.

  g Work out the scale factor and the centre of enlargement for the enlargement that
   transforms A″B″C″D″ into A′B′C′D′.

18 Transformations

Chapter 18 Summary

Level 6

Reflections

A reflection transforms an object by reflecting it in a mirror line.

Each point on the object moves across the **mirror line** to the point which is the same distance away on the other side.

The mirror line becomes a line of symmetry for the whole diagram.

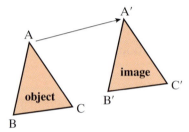

Translations

A translation transforms an object by moving it through a given distance in a particular direction.

You can describe a translation by saying how far right or left and how far up or down you have moved.

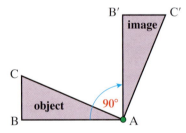

Rotations

A rotation transforms an object by turning it around a point.
The **centre of rotation** is the only point that does not move.
You describe a rotation by saying
how much you turn, **which way you turn** and **the centre of rotation**.

This is a rotation of **90°** **clockwise** **about A**.

Enlargements

An enlargement changes the size of an object.

The **centre of enlargement** is the only point that does not move.
You describe an enlargement by giving the **scale factor** of the enlargement and the centre of enlargement.

This is an enlargement with scale factor 3. The centre of enlargement is O.

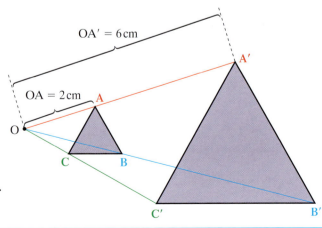

Break Away and Functional Maths

The next six pages are different from the rest of the book.
They use maths in the real world and have projects for you to carry out.
We hope you find them interesting and fun!

Water   310

Investigate how
water is used

Grow your own   312

Explore how
vegetables grow

On the buses   314

Solve problems using a
bus timetable

Water

Background

When you turn on a tap, clean water comes out of it. This water is safe for us to drink because it has been treated and tested to make sure it is free from bacteria. In many countries people do not have running water in their homes. They must collect water from somewhere else. In some places this may mean using river water, which is likely to be dirty and not very safe to drink. Some charities provide safe drinking water for people by creating wells. A well brings clean water from underground to the surface.

Get together!

Work in pairs.
Discuss how much water you think you use each day.
Use this frequency table to help you.

Activity	Average water usage (litres)	Frequency	Total water usage (litres)
Bath	80		
Shower	50		
Flushing the toilet	9		
Washing your hands or face	4		
Brushing teeth with the tap running	10		
Brushing teeth with the tap off	1		
Washing machine	80		
Dishwasher	15		
Washing dishes by hand	6		

Go it alone!

1. **How many litres of water do you use every day?**
   Work out how much water you use for each activity in a day.
   Draw a bar chart to show your water use for a day.

2. **How could you reduce the amount of water you use?**
   Investigate what you could do to save water.
   Make a list of things you could do to save water.
   How much water would you now use for each activity?
   Draw a bar chart and a pie chart to show your daily water usage now.
   Compare your charts and write a short report to explain how your water use has changed.

3. **How many buckets of water do you use every day?**
   Imagine that you had to collect water in buckets because no water came out of your taps at home.
   How many buckets of water do you need to collect each day?

4. **How long would it take you to collect the water?**

   Assume that:
   - the nearest source of water is 1 kilometre away
   - it takes you 30 minutes to walk 1 kilometre
   - you can carry two buckets at a time.

   How long will it take you to collect all the water that you need for a day?

5. **How much time would you have left to go to school?**
   What fraction of a day do you have left to go to school?
   Remember that you need to sleep too!

Explore

Why do you think many people in the world use less than 50 litres of water each day?

Imagine you are living in Africa where you can only use at most 50 litres of water per day. How will you use your daily allowance?

Grow your own

Background

The fruit and vegetables you see in supermarkets have been grown by farmers in Britain and around the world. This means that the food you eat has sometimes been transported thousands of miles. Why do you think it is better to buy food that has been produced closer to where you live?

Get together!

Work in pairs. Decide if these vegetables grow

underground, on the ground or **above the ground**.

potatoes	peas	cauliflowers
runner beans	carrots	leeks
lettuces	pumpkins	cabbages

Draw a table and sort the vegetables into the three groups.

Think of some fruits and add them to your table. What do you notice?

Go it alone!

Work on your own. You are going to think about growing your own vegetables.

1   Your vegetable plot

Here are some sketches of vegetable plots:

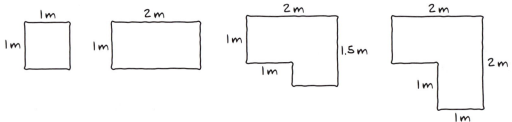

Use a sensible scale to draw an accurate plan of each of these plots.
You will need 1 cm squared A4 paper to do this.

2   **Which vegetables will you grow?**
    Look at the planting instructions below to help you to choose three or four vegetables that you would like to include in your vegetable plot. You could choose the vegetables you like the most or the ones you would like to try growing and eating.

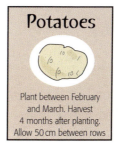

3   **How will you organise your vegetable plot?**
    Plants need to be given enough room to grow so it is important to look carefully at the planting instructions to find out how much space a particular plant needs to grow.
    Choose one of the vegetable plots from **part 1**.
    Design a key for your plan and use your chosen symbols to mark on your plan where you would grow your vegetables.
    If you have chosen peas or potatoes think carefully about which plot you choose or else you might not have any room to grow your other vegetables!

4   **When will you plant each vegetable?**
    Decide in which month you need to plant each of your vegetables so that they will all be ready in the same month.

Explore

Potatoes should be planted 30 cm apart.
Imagine you have space to plant them in a row that is 3 metres long.
You plant one potato at each end of the row.
How many potatoes can you plant in total in the row?
Can you explain how to find the number of potato plants you can grow in a row of length x cm?

On the buses

Background

The timetable for the number 18 and 18A buses is shown below.

Route map: Tinshill 18 and Ireland Wood 18A → Eden Drive → Burley Road → Leeds → York Road → Whitkirk → Garforth 18 and Colton 18A

18: TINSHILL – LEEDS Bond Street – GARFORTH
18A: IRELAND WOOD – LEEDS Bond Street – COLTON

Mondays to Fridays

Service Number	18	18A	18	18A	18	18A	18	18A	18	18A
Ireland Wood	—	1558	—	1622	—	1642	—	1702	—	1722
Tinshill	1548	—	1612	—	1632	—	1652	—	1712	—
Eden Drive	1600	1611	1624	1635	1644	1655	1704	1715	1724	1735
Burley Road	1612	1623	1636	1647	1657	1707	1717	1727	1737	1747
Bond Street	1625	1637	1650	1700	1710	1721	1732	1742	1752	1802
York Road	1634	1646	1659	1709	1719	1730	1741	1751	1801	1811
Whitkirk	1644	1657	1709	1720	1729	1741	1751	1802	1811	1822
Colton	—	1702	—	1725	—	1747	—	1807	—	1827
Old George	1653	—	1722	1729	1742	1751	1803	1812	1823	1832
Ninelands	—	—	—	1742	—	1804	—	1825	—	1845
Garforth	1703	—	1732	—	1755	—	1816	—	1833	—

18: GARFORTH – LEEDS Infirmary Street – TINSHILL
18A: COLTON – LEEDS Infirmary Street – IRELAND WOOD

Mondays to Fridays

Service Number	18A	18	18A	18	18A	18	18A	18	18A	18
Garforth	—	1548	—	1608	—	1628	—	1648	—	1708
East Road	—	1601	—	1621	—	1641	—	1701	—	1721
Colton	1551	—	1611	—	1631	—	1651	—	1711	—
Whitkirk	1553	1605	1613	1625	1633	1645	1653	1705	1713	1725
York Rd	1605	1615	1625	1635	1645	1655	1705	1715	1725	1735
Infirmary Street	1620	1630	1640	1650	1700	1710	1720	1730	1740	1750
Burley Road	1630	1640	1650	1700	1710	1722	1732	1742	1752	1800
Eden Drive	1640	1650	1700	1710	1722	1734	1744	1754	1804	1810
Tinshill	—	1707	—	1727	—	1755	—	1815	—	1830
Ireland Wood	1658	—	1718	—	1740	—	1804	—	1822	—

Questions

1 There is a bus from Tinshill to Garforth at 16:52.
What time is it due to arrive in Garforth?

2 How often do buses run from Garforth to Tinshill on Thursday afternoons?

3 A number 18 bus leaves Eden Drive at 17:54.
How long does it take to reach Tinshill?

4 Bhanu catches the 16:31 from Colton.
The bus runs on time.
How many minutes does it take Bhanu to get to Eden Drive?

5 Zoë is going to watch a television programme being filmed at the television studios on Burley Road.
She needs to arrive before five o'clock in the afternoon.
What is the latest bus that Zoë can catch from Ireland Wood?

6 Tom and Joe are meeting in Eden Drive.
Tom arrives at the bus stop in Tinshill at 4.40 p.m.
Joe gets to the bus stop in York Road at 4.40 p.m.
Both buses are running on time.

  a Who gets to Eden Drive first?

  b How long does he then have to wait for his friend to reach Eden Drive?

7 The nearest bus stop to the railway station is five minutes walk away in Infirmary Street.
Lee's train is due into the station at 16:43.
The train arrives 45 minutes late.
What is the first bus that Lee can get home to Tinshill?

8 Bus passengers can buy the following types of pass.

Off Peak Day Pass	All Day Pass	Weekly Pass
Journeys after 09:30 One day £2.50	Use any time One day £3.50	Use any time Seven days £14.00

  a Dylan catches the bus six days each week.
He takes the 9.40 a.m. bus to work.
How much does he save by buying a weekly pass instead of day passes?

  b Gina catches the bus four days each week.
Her journey always starts at nine o'clock in the morning.
Is it cheaper for her to buy a pass each day or a weekly pass?
Explain your answer.

Test yourself answers

Chapter 1

1
- **a** $q + 5$
- **b** $24 - m$
- **c** $8a$
- **d** $\dfrac{12}{v}$
- **e** x^2
- **f** $3x + 6$
- **g** $\dfrac{y}{4} - 5$
- **h** $2(x + 7)$
- **i** $\dfrac{n + 4}{3}$
- **j** $5m + 7$
- **k** $\dfrac{n}{2} + 6$
- **l** xy

2
- **a** $3n$
- **b** $5p$
- **c** $2j + 3k$
- **d** $3l + 4m$
- **e** $3p + q$
- **f** $r + 4s$

3
- **a** $6n$ means multiply n by 6
  $n + 6$ means add 6 to n
- **b** $7(n + 1)$ means add 1 to n then multiply the result by 7
  $7n + 1$ means multiply n by 7 then add 1
- **c** $2x$ means multiply x by 2 (or add x to itself)
  x^2 means multiply x by itself

4 $3e^2$, $-5f$ and $+7$ (or 7)

5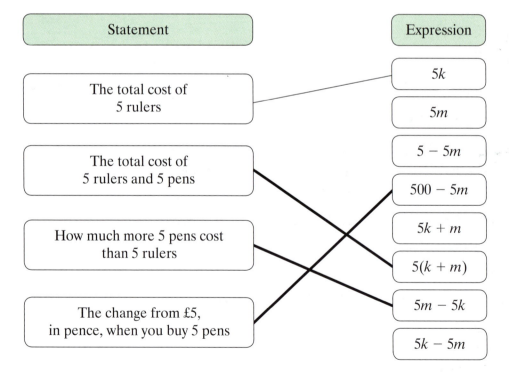

6
- **a** $6n + 7$ means multiply n by 6 then add 7
- **b** $2n - 4$ means multiply n by 2 then subtract 4
- **c** $\dfrac{n}{2} + 9$ means divide n by 2 then add 9
- **d** $8(n - 1)$ means subtract 1 from n then multiply the answer by 8

Test yourself answers

7 a *9a*
    b *9bc*
    c $11uv + 7$
    d $10p^2q$
    e $15x^2y$
    f $5a^2b$

8 a $5a + 5b$
    b $8c - 4d$
    c $14e - 35f$
    d $3g - 9h$
    e $24i + 6j$
    f $40k - 32l$

9 $6x + 6 + 30 + 10x = 16x + 36$

10 a $6a + 8b$
     b $6a - 9$
     c $12ab$
     d $2ab - 3ac$
     e $9a + 11b$
     f $16a + 2b$

Chapter 2

1 a $7 \times 14 = 7 \times 10 + 7 \times 4 = 70 + 28 = 98$
    b $9 \times 15 = 9 \times 10 + 9 \times 5 = 90 + 45 = 135$
    c $5 \times 32 = 10 \times 16 = 160$
    d $12 \times 99 = 12 \times 100 - 12 \times 1 = 1200 - 12 = 1188$
    e $40 \times 50 = 40 \times 5 \times 10 = 200 \times 10 = 2000$
    f $1400 \div 70 = 1400 \div 10 \div 7 = 140 \div 7 = 20$
    g $4^3 = 4 \times 4 \times 4 = 64$
    h $\sqrt{81} = 9$

2 a 7672   b 16 800   c 30 624   d 29 684

3 $1460 \times 13 = 18\,980$

4 a (1) 7 R3   (2) $7\frac{3}{4}$ (3) 7.75
    b (1) 6 R4   (2) $6\frac{4}{5}$ (3) 6.8
    c (1) 3 R8   (2) $3\frac{8}{16} = 3\frac{1}{2}$ (3) 3.5
    d (1) 3 R3   (2) $3\frac{3}{12} = 3\frac{1}{4}$ (3) 3.25

5 a $144 \div 16 = 144 \div 2 \div 8 = 72 \div 8 = 9$
    b $192 \div 6 = 192 \div 2 \div 3 = 96 \div 3 = 32$
    c $555 \div 15 = 555 \div 5 \div 3 = 111 \div 3 = 37$
    d $1872 \div 9 = 1872 \div 3 \div 3 = 624 \div 3 = 208$

6 a $220 \div 16 = 220 \div 2 \div 2 \div 2 \div 2 = 110 \div 2 \div 2 \div 2 = 55 \div 2 \div 2 = 27.5 \div 2 = 13.75$
     The teacher needs 14 packs.
    b $220 \times 48 = 10\,560\,\text{g}$
     $10\,560\,\text{g} = 10.56\,\text{kg}$

7 a 5 g = **5000** mg   c 5.5 km = **5500** m   e 2500 mℓ = **2.5 ℓ**
    b 6 kg = **6000** g   d 85 cm = **850** mm   f 15 m = **1500** cm

Test yourself answers

8 **a** 7.6 cm + 3 mm = 76 mm + 3 mm = 79 mm (or 7.9 cm)
   b 4 m + 17 cm + 12 mm = 4000 mm + 170 mm + 12 mm = 4182 mm (or 418.2 cm or 4.182 m)
   c 2.67 kg − 450 g = 2670 g − 450 g = 2220 g (or 2.22 kg)
   d 7.325 kg − 225 000 mg = 7 325 000 mg − 225 000 mg = 7 100 000 mg (or 7.1 kg)

9 **a** metres   **b** litres   **c** seconds   **d** kilograms

10 BODMAS
   a 15 − 7 × 2 = 15 − 14 = 1
   b 3 × (8 − 3) = 3 × 5 = 15
   c 18 − (13 − 4) = 18 − 9 = 9
   d 4 × (3 + 9) ÷ 3 = 4 × 12 ÷ 3 = 16
   e (15 − 8) × (1 + 2) = 7 × 3 = 21

11 2   6 x^2 − 1 9 6   1 2 1 =

12 **a** £24.50   **b** 24 m 50 cm   **c** 24 hours and 30 minutes

Chapter 3

1 **a**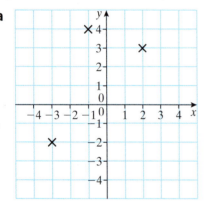

   b (0, −3)

2 (35, 10). The x-coordinate has to be half of 70 and the y-coordinate has to be half of 20.

3 **a** 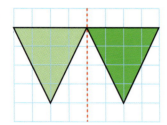   **b**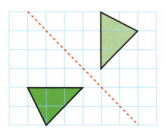

4 **a**   **b** Order 2

5 a $j = 6\,\text{cm}, k = 6\,\text{cm}, l = 5\,\text{cm}$
angle $m = 65°$, angle $n = 65°$, angle $P = 50°$

b, c

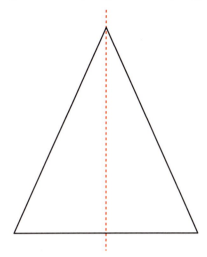

d It only has two equal angles instead of three.
It only has two equal sides instead of three.
It only has one line of symmetry instead of three.
It only has rotational symmetry of order 1 instead of 3.

6 a Scalene triangle **b** Square **c** Parallelogram

7 a Arrowhead **Q** **c** Kite **T** **e** Rhombus **R**
 b Isosceles trapezium **P** **d** Parallelogram **S**

Chapter 4

1 a 8, 16, 24, 32, 40, 48 **b** 12, 24, 36, 48, 60, 72 **c** 24, 48 **d** 24

2 Multiples of 6 : 6, 12, 18, 24
Multiples of 8 : 8, 16, 24
LCM is 24.

3 a 1, 2, 4, 8, 16 **b** 1, 2, 3, 4, 6, 9, 12, 18, 36 **c** 1, 2, 4 **d** 4

4 2, 3, 4, 5, 6, 8, 9 and 10 are all factors of 360.

5 a 2, 3, 5, 7, 11, 13, 17, 19, 23, 29 **b** 41 and 43

6 a 1, 2, 3, 6, 7, 14, 21, 42 **b** 2, 3, 7

7 $350 = 2 \times 5 \times 5 \times 7$

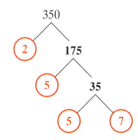

Test yourself answers

8 $112 = 2 \times 2 \times 2 \times 2 \times 7$

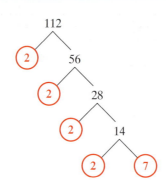

9 $^{-}7°C, ^{-}6°C, ^{-}1°C, 0°C, 1°C, 2°C$

10 **a** $2 > ^{-}1$ **b** $^{-}2 > ^{-}4$ **c** $^{-}2 < 4$ **d** $^{-}2 < 1$

11
a $^{-}7 + {^+}4 = ^{-}7 + 4 = ^{-}3$
b $^{-}5 + 2 = ^{-}3$
c $^{-}3 - {^+}5 = ^{-}3 - 5 = ^{-}8$
d $^{-}7 - 3 = ^{-}10$
e $8 - {^-}6 = 8 + 6 = 14$
f $^{-}4 - {^-}10 = ^{-}4 + 10 = 6$
g $^{-}5 + 15 = 10$
h $^{-}14 + {^-}6 = ^{-}14 - 6 = ^{-}20$

12

×	$^{-}1$	4	$^{-}2$	$^{-}3$
$^{-}2$	2	$^{-}8$	4	6
$^{-}5$	5	$^{-}20$	10	15
$^{-}6$	6	$^{-}24$	12	18
3	$^{-}3$	12	$^{-}6$	$^{-}9$

13
a $^{-}4 \times 7 = ^{-}28$
b $^{-}2 \times {^-}6 = 12$
c $^{-}15 \div 3 = ^{-}5$
d $16 \div {^-}8 = ^{-}2$
e $6 \times {^-}5 = ^{-}30$
f $0 \times {^-}3 = 0$
g $^{-}16 \div {^-}4 = 4$
h $12 \div {^-}6 = ^{-}2$

Chapter 5

1 30.4 s

2 **a** 65 minutes ($50 + 70 + 0 + 120 + 30 + 150 + 35 = 455$ and $455 \div 7 = 65$)
  b Because each value appears once.
  c Range: $150 - 0 = 150$

3 **a** Mean: 6.2
  Median: 6.5
  Mode: 7
  b The mode is best since this is an actual shoe size. It tells you the shoe size that best represents the 10 people in the question.

Test yourself answers

4

Number of eggs	Number of days	Total number of eggs
15	15	225
16	7	112
17	4	68
18	4	72
19	1	19
Totals	31	496

Mean number of eggs laid by the chickens in July = 496 ÷ 31 = 16

5 79% (70 × 4 − 67 × 3)

6
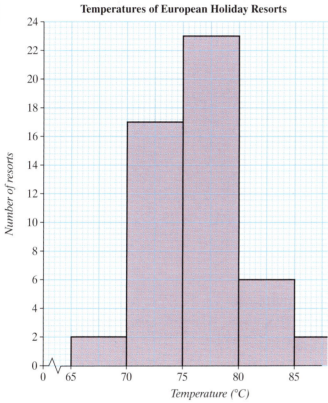

7 a Because weight can take any value within a certain range.

  b Because you can only have whole numbers of sweets.

8

Year	Births (millions)	Deaths (millions)
1921	**1.0**	0.6
1931	**0.8**	0.6
1941	**0.8**	0.6
2001	**0.7**	0.6
2021	**0.7**	0.6
2041	**0.7**	0.8

Test yourself answers

Chapter 6

1
a $7 + 6 = 13$
b $21 - 3 = 18$
c $6 \times 7 = 42$
d $\frac{12}{3} = 4$
e $4 \times 6 + 2 = 24 + 2 = 26$
f $15 - 9 + 4 = 10$
g $2 \times 5 - 5 \times 0 - 2 \times 1 = 10 - 0 - 2 = 8$
h $3 \times 12 - 4 \times 5 = 36 - 20 = 16$
i $2(3 + 4) = 2 \times 7 = 14$
j $4(10 - 4 \times 2) = 4 \times 2 = 8$
k $5(4 + 2 \times 1) = 5 \times 6 = 30$
l $3(2 \times 3 - 3 \times 2) = 3(6 - 6) = 0$

2
a £12 $t = 3.5 \times 2 + 5 = 7 + 5 = 12$
b £40 $t = 3.5 \times 10 + 5 = 35 + 5 = 40$
c £22.50 $t = 3.5 \times 5 + 5 = 17.5 + 5 = 22.5$

3
a £38 $t = 11 \times 2 + 8 \times 2 = 22 + 16 = 38$
b £65 $t = 11 \times 3 + 8 \times 4 = 33 + 32 = 65$

4 a

Shape number (s)	1	2	3	4
Number of blue counters	3	6	9	12
Number of red counters	1	1	1	1
Total number of counters (t)	4	7	10	13

b The number of blue counters increases by 3.
c The number of red counters is always 1.
d $s \times 3 + 1 = t$

5
a $6n - 3$ means multiply n by 6 and then subtract 3.
   $6(n - 3)$ means subtract 3 from n and then multiply the answer by 6.
b $\frac{n}{5} + 3$ means divide n by 5 and then add 3.
   $\frac{n + 3}{5}$ means add 3 to n and then divide the answer by 5.
c $\frac{n}{4}$ means divide n by 4.
   $\frac{4}{n}$ means divide 4 by n.
d $n - 8$ means subtract 8 from n.
   $8 - n$ means subtract n from 8.

6
a subtract 8
b add 5
c divide by 4
d $+ 12$
e $\div 6$
f $\times 8$
g double
h square

7
a 5 $(5 \times 4 + 2 = 22)$
b 2 $((2 + 10) \times 5 = 60)$
c 7 $(7 \times 3 - 9 = 12)$
d 25 $((25 - 5) \div 2 = 10)$
e 27 $(27 \div 3 - 4 = 5)$

Chapter 7

1 a 6 balls of modelling clay   **b** 9 straws

2 The third drawing is wrong. The diagonal plane is not a plane of symmetry.

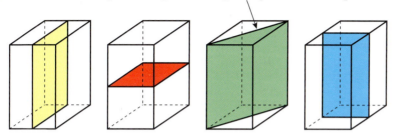

A cuboid only has three planes of symmetry.

3

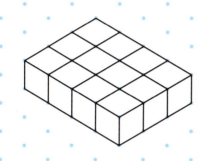 or

4 a 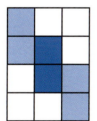   **b** 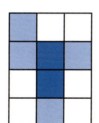   **c**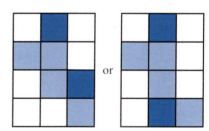

5 a BD   **b** AB   **c** B and F

6 a 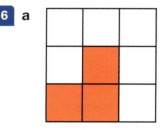   **b** 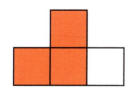   **c**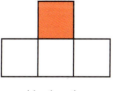

    plan view   front elevation   side elevation

Test yourself answers

Chapter 8

1

Livestock	a	b	c
Breeding cattle	19%	18.6%	18.56%
Dairy	4%	3.9%	3.94%
Beef	3%	3.0%	2.99%
Pigs	10%	10.2%	10.23%
Sheep	64%	64.3%	64.28%

2 a $9.19 - 1.96$ to see if it's 7.23
or $9.19 - 7.23$ to see if it's 1.96

b $55.22 + 8.9$ to see if it's 64.12

c $84.37 \div 2.6$ to see if it's 32.45

3 a $0.3 \times 10 = 3$ **c** $2 \div 100 = 0.02$ **e** $3160 \div 1000 = 3.16$ **g** $0.43 \times \mathbf{100} = 43$
b $4.2 \times 100 = 420$ **d** $30 \div 1000 = 0.03$ **f** $\mathbf{0.316} \times 100 = 31.6$ **h** $0.57 \times \mathbf{1000} = 570$

4 a $(5.1 \times 10) + (5.1 \times 1)$ **c** $6.7 \times 10 \times 2$ **e** $9 \times 4 \div 10$ **g** $15.6 \div 3 \div 2$
$\quad = 51 + 5.1 \quad = 67 \times 2 \quad = 36 \div 10 \quad = 5.2 \div 2$
$\quad = 56.1 \quad = 134 \quad = 3.6 \quad = 2.6$

b $(5.5 \times 10) + (5.5 \times 2)$ **d** $2.4 \times 10 \times 3$ **f** $8 \times 2 \div 100$ **h** $23.5 \div 10 \times 2$
$\quad = 55 + 11 \quad = 24 \times 3 \quad = 16 \div 100 \quad = 2.35 \times 2$
$\quad = 66 \quad = 72 \quad = 0.16 \quad = 4.7$

5 a (1) 45.6 **c** (1) 140.76 **e** (1) 23.4 **g** (1) 61
(2) $15 \times 3 = 45$ ✓ (2) $61 \times 2 = 122$ ✓ (2) $50 \div 2 = 25$ ✓ (2) $67 \div 1 = 67$ ✓

b (1) 181.5 **d** (1) 13.361 **f** (1) 18.2 **h** (1) 30.2
(2) $10 \times 15 = 150$ ✓ (2) $4 \times 3 = 12$ ✓ (2) $200 \div 10 = 20$ ✓ (2) $70 \div 2 = 35$ ✓

6 a $12 \ (18 \div 3 \times 2)$ **b** $27 \ (45 \div 5 \times 3)$ **c** $12 \ (21 \div 7 \times 4)$ **d** $28 \ (36 \div 9 \times 7)$

7 Kieran gets $\frac{3}{7}$ of the sweets.
$63 \div 7 = 9$ and $9 \times 3 = 27$
so Kieran gets 27 sweets.

8 a $\dfrac{3 \times 58}{5 \times 1} = \dfrac{174}{5} = 34\frac{4}{5}$ cm **b** $\dfrac{2 \times 240}{7 \times 1} = \dfrac{480}{7} = 68\frac{4}{7}$ g **c** $\dfrac{2 \times 34}{9 \times 1} = \dfrac{68}{9} = 7\frac{5}{9}$ minutes

9 a £37.80 (0.21×180) **b** 252 g (0.36×700) **c** £26.25 (0.175×150)

10 a
$\div 2$ { 10% of 84 = **8.4** } $\div 2$ ($84 \div 10$)
$\quad\quad\ \ $ 5% of 84 = **4.2** $\quad\quad$ ($8.4 \div 2$ or $84 \div 20$)
$\div 2$ { $2\frac{1}{2}$% of 84 = **2.1** } $\div 2$ ($4.2 \div 2$ or $84 \div 40$)

b Total cost of CD player = £84 + £8.40 + £4.20 + £2.10
$\quad\quad\quad\quad\quad\quad\quad\quad\quad\quad\ \ = $ £98.70

Test yourself answers

11 a To find 30% of £120, first find **10%** of £120 which is 120 ÷ 10 = **£12**
So **30%** of £120 = **3 × 12**
= £36

b To find 22% of 160 g, first find **10%** which is 160 ÷ 10 = **16 g**
So **20%** is **2 × 16** = **32 g**. This also means that **2%** is **32 ÷ 10** = **3.2 g**
Finally 22% of 160 g = **20%** of 160 g + **2%** of 160 g
= **32 g + 3.2 g**
= 35.2 g

c To find 48% of 260 kg, find **50%** of 260 kg which is 260 ÷ 2 = **130 kg**
Then find **1%** of 260 kg which is 260 ÷ 100 = **2.6 kg**
This means that **2%** of 260 kg is **2.6 × 2 = 5.2 kg**
Finally 48% of 260 kg = **50%** of 260 kg − **2%** of 260 kg
= **130 kg − 5.2 kg**
= 124.8 kg

12 £21.60 because he should buy two single trip policies online.
(10% of £24 = £2.40 and £24 − £2.40 = £21.60
If Marcus buys multi-trip cover online, he would pay £30 − £3 = £27)

Chapter 9

1 4 → [+3] → 7 → [×4] → 28
8 → 11 → 44
12 → 15 → 60
input   output   (input + **3**) × **4** = output

2 a 16 → [−6] → 10
20 → 14
24 → 18
input   output

b 10 → [÷5] → 2
25 → 5
45 → 9
input   output

3 a 2 → [×5] → 10 → [+2] → 12
5 → 25 → 27
8 → 40 → 42
input   output

b 24 → [÷3] → 8 → [−7] → 1
30 → 10 → 3
90 → 30 → 23
input   output

4 a (1) $3n + 9 = 42$

n → [×3] → [+9] → 42

11 ← [÷3] ← 33 ← [−9] ← 42

$n = 11$

(2) $3n + 9 = 3 × 11 + 9 = 33 + 9 = 42$ ✓

325

Test yourself answers

b (1) $6n - 8 = 40$

$n \to \boxed{\times 6} \to \boxed{- 8} \to 40$

$8 \leftarrow \boxed{\div 6} \xleftarrow{48} \boxed{+ 8} \leftarrow 40$

$n = 8$

(2) $6n - 8 = 6 \times 8 - 8 = 48 - 8 = 40 \checkmark$

c (1) $\dfrac{n}{2} + 21 = 31$

$n \to \boxed{\div 2} \to \boxed{+ 21} \to 31$

$20 \leftarrow \boxed{\times 2} \xleftarrow{10} \boxed{- 21} \leftarrow 31$

$n = 20$

(2) $\dfrac{n}{2} + 21 = \dfrac{20}{2} + 21 = 10 + 21 = 31 \checkmark$

5 a $6a - 4 = 32$
$\therefore\ 6a = 32 + 4$
$6a = 36$
$\therefore\ a = \dfrac{36}{6}$
$a = 6$
$6a - 4 = 6 \times 6 - 4 = 32 \checkmark$

b $\dfrac{b}{4} + 13 = 17$
$\therefore\ \dfrac{b}{4} = 17 - 13$
$\dfrac{b}{4} = 4$
$\therefore\ b = 4 \times 4$
$b = 16$
$\dfrac{b}{4} + 13 = \dfrac{16}{4} + 13$
$= 4 + 13 = 17 \checkmark$

c $5c + 15 = 10$
$\therefore\ 5c = 10 - 15$
$5c = {}^-5$
$\therefore\ c = \dfrac{{}^-5}{5}$
$c = {}^-1$
$5c + 15 = 5 \times {}^-1 + 15$
$= {}^-5 + 15 = 10 \checkmark$

6 a $55 = 7a + 6$
$7a + 6 = 55$
$\therefore\ 7a = 55 - 6$
$7a = 49$
$\therefore\ a = \dfrac{49}{7}$
$a = 7$
$7a + 6 = 7 \times 7 + 6$
$= 49 + 6 = 55 \checkmark$

b $15 = \dfrac{b}{3} - 5$
$\dfrac{b}{3} - 5 = 15$
$\therefore\ \dfrac{b}{3} = 15 + 5$
$\dfrac{b}{3} = 20$
$\therefore\ b = 20 \times 3$
$b = 60$
$\dfrac{b}{3} - 5 = \dfrac{60}{3} - 5$
$= 20 - 5 = 15 \checkmark$

c $1 = 3c + 10$
$3c + 10 = 1$
$\therefore\ 3c = 1 - 10$
$3c = {}^-9$
$\therefore\ c = \dfrac{{}^-9}{3}$
$c = {}^-3$
$3c + 10 = 3 \times {}^-3 + 10$
$= {}^-9 + 10 = 1 \checkmark$

Test yourself answers

7 a False $(4n - 12 = 4 \times 10 - 12 = 28)$ **c** True $\left(\dfrac{n}{2} + 6 = \dfrac{^-10}{2} + 6 = 1\right)$

  b False $(3n + 8 = 3 \times {}^-4 + 8 = {}^-4)$ **d** False $\left(\dfrac{n}{3} - 4 = \dfrac{30}{3} - 4 = 6\right)$

8 a (1) $4n - 12 = 24$ (2) $n = 9$ **b** (1) $\dfrac{n}{3} + 9 = 21$ (2) $n = 36$

9 a $x + x + 4 + x + 4 = 32$
  b $3x + 8 = 32$
  c $x = 8$
  d 8 cm, 12 cm, 12 cm

Chapter 10

1 a angle ABC   **b** 27° ± 2°

2 a Angles in a triangle add up to 180°
    $a° + 84° + 38° = 180°$ $a° = 58°$
    Angles on a straight line add up to 180°
    $x° + 58° = 180°$ $x° = 122°$

  c Angles at a point add up to 360°
    $2c° + 90° + 70° = 360°$
    $2c° = 200°$
    $c° = 100°$

  b Angles on a straight line add up to 180°
    $3b° = 180°$
    $b° = 60°$

3 a Vertically opposite angles are equal
    $x° = 48°$
    Angles on a straight line add up to 180°
    $y° = 180° - 48°$
    $y° = 132°$
    Vertically opposite angles are equal
    $z° = 132°$

  b Angles on a straight line add up to 180°
    $a° = 180° - 108°$
    $a° = 72°$
    Angles at a point add up to 360°
    $b° = 360° - 326°$
    $b° = 34°$
    Angles in a triangle add up to 180°
    $c° = 180° - 72° - 34°$
    $c° = 74°$
    Angles on a straight line add up to 180°
    $d° = 180° - 74° = 106°$

4 a Angles in a quadrilateral add up to 360°
    $a° = 360° - 75° - 120° - 48°$
    $a° = 117°$

  b A parallelogram has two pairs of equal angles.
    $b° = 36°$
    $x° = 144°$

  c An isosceles trapezium has two pairs of equal angles.
    $c° = 59°$
    $y° = 121°$

5

	Four right angles	No right angles
Four equal sides	square	rhombus
Two pairs of equal sides	rectangle	parallelogram

Test yourself answers

6 a The blue lines drawn on the trapezium and parallelogram are not lines of symmetry.
A parallelogram has no lines of symmetry.
An isosceles trapezium only has one vertical line of symmetry.

b No. Only an isosceles trapezium has two pairs of equal angles.
This trapezium has no equal angles for example.

c A kite, an arrowhead and a trapezium with two right angles

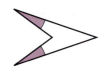
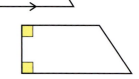

Chapter 11

1 a You should have copied the scale in the question.

b You should have numbered arrows pointing to the scale as follows:

(1) should be pointing to **Certain** if you're going home today or **Impossible** if you know you're not going home today.

(2) depends on whether you eat chips. For lots of people the arrow should point to Very likely or **Certain** but you can put it anywhere depending on you.

(3) arrow close to **Impossible** and no further across than Very unlikely.

2 a You should have copied the scale in the question.

b

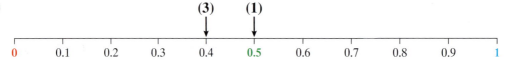

(2) You need to work out the number of people in your class who have glasses divided by the number of people in your class. Then mark and label an arrow at this point on the scale.

3 a $\frac{3}{10}$ — There are **3** packs of salt and vinegar and **10** packs altogether.

b $\frac{7}{10}$ — There are 7 packs of plain or cheese and onion crisps out of 10 packs altogether.

c $\frac{6}{10}\left(=\frac{3}{5}\right)$ — There are 6 packs that are not plain out of the 10 packs.

d 0 — There are no packs of prawn cocktail crisps.

4 a $\frac{2}{7}$ — There are **2** more blue star cards. There are **7** cards left.

b $\frac{1}{6}$ — The card has to be the red one. There is only **1** red card out of **6** cards left.

5 a $\frac{1}{12}$ — There is **1** card with a 2 on it and **12** cards altogether.

b $\frac{2}{12} = \frac{1}{6}$ — There are **2** cards with an 8 on them and **12** cards altogether.

c $\frac{5}{12}$ — There are **5** even numbers (6, 8, 14, 2 and 8) out of **12** cards.

d $\frac{7}{12}$ — There are 7 odd numbers (13, 5, 17, 19, 9, 7 and 11) out of 12 cards (or 1 − **c**).

e $\frac{7}{12}$ — There are 7 prime numbers (13, 5, 17, 2, 19, 7 and 11) out of 12 cards.

f $\frac{1}{12}$ — There is 1 square number (9) out of 12 cards.

g $\frac{5}{12}$ — (1 − **d**)

h $\frac{5}{12}$ — (1 − **e**)

i $\frac{11}{12}$ — (1 − **f**)

Test yourself answers

6 55% (100% − 45%. You could also give the answer as 0.55 or $\frac{11}{20}$)

7 a

		Spinner			
		1	2	3	4
Coin	H	H, 1	H, 2	H, 3	H, 4
	T	T, 1	T, 2	T, 3	T, 4

b 8

c $\frac{2}{8} = \frac{1}{4}$ (H, 1 and H, 3 are the two outcomes that give a Head and an odd number.)

Chapter 12

1 a $\frac{10}{15} = \frac{2}{3}$ **b** $\frac{24}{64} = \frac{3}{8}$ **c** $\frac{32}{40} = \frac{4}{5}$

2 a $\frac{1}{3} > \frac{1}{4}$ **b** $\frac{3}{4} < \frac{4}{5}$ **c** $\frac{4}{5} > \frac{5}{7}$

3 a $1 - \frac{1}{3} - \frac{3}{5} = \frac{15}{15} - \frac{5}{15} - \frac{9}{15} = \frac{1}{15}$

  b $1 - \frac{1}{3} - \frac{2}{5} = \frac{15}{15} - \frac{5}{15} - \frac{6}{15} = \frac{4}{15}$

  c $1 - \frac{1}{3} - \frac{2}{15} = \frac{15}{15} - \frac{5}{15} - \frac{2}{15} = \frac{8}{15}$

4 a $\frac{20}{100} = \frac{1}{5}$ **b** $\frac{25}{200} = \frac{1}{8}$ **c** $\frac{600}{1000} = \frac{3}{5}$ **d** $\frac{125}{1000} = \frac{1}{8}$

5 a $\frac{1}{4} \times 280$ min = 70 minutes

  b $\frac{3}{8} \times 280$ min $280 \div 8 \times 3 = 35 \times 3 = 105$

  so Chris fields for 105 minutes

  c $\frac{1}{4} + \frac{3}{8} = \frac{2}{8} + \frac{3}{8} = \frac{5}{8}$

  Chris is watching for $1 - \frac{5}{8} = \frac{3}{8}$ of the time.

6

0   0.2   0.4   0.6   0.8   1

0   20%   40%   60%   80%   100%

0    $\frac{1}{5}$ $\frac{2}{5}$ $\frac{3}{5}$ $\frac{4}{5}$ 1

7

Fraction	$\frac{1}{2}$	$\frac{35}{100} = \frac{7}{20}$	$\frac{1}{5}$	$\frac{36}{100} = \frac{9}{25}$	$\frac{12}{100} = \frac{3}{25}$	$\frac{9}{20}$	$\frac{6}{100} = \frac{3}{50}$
Percentage	50%	35%	$\frac{1}{5} = \frac{20}{100} = 20\%$	$\frac{36}{100} = 36\%$	12%	$\frac{9}{20} = \frac{45}{100} = 45\%$	$\frac{6}{100} = 6\%$
Decimal	0.5	$\frac{35}{100} = 0.35$	$\frac{20}{100} = 0.2$	0.36	$\frac{12}{100} = 0.12$	$\frac{45}{100} = 0.45$	0.06

8 Any of these is correct.

The proportion of bad eggs $= \frac{3}{24} = \frac{1}{8} = 0.125 = 12.5\% = 12\frac{1}{2}\%$

Test yourself answers

9 The proportion of brown-eyed pupils in each of the classes is
Dave's class $\frac{9}{27} = \frac{1}{3} = \frac{25}{75}$
Krishnan's class $\frac{8}{25} = \frac{24}{75}$
$\frac{25}{75} > \frac{24}{75}$ so Dave's class has the bigger proportion of brown-eyed pupils.

Chapter 13

1 a (1) add 7 (2) 39, 46
4, 11, 18, 25, 32, **39**, **46** (+7 each)

b (1) subtract 4 (2) $-12, -16$
8, 4, 0, -4, -8, **-12**, **-16** (-4 each)

c (1) add 2 (2) 11, 13
1, 3, 5, 7, 9, **11**, **13** (+2 each)

d (1) multiply by 2 (2) 64, 128
2, 4, 8, 16, 32, **64**, **128** (×2 each)

e (1) divide by 2 (2) 5, 2.5
40, 20, 10, **5**, **2.5** (÷2 each)

f (1) multiply by 5 (2) 125, 625
1, 5, 25, **125**, **625** (×5 each)

2 a You should have copied the diagrams from the question.

b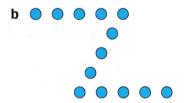

c 4, 7, 10, 13, …

d add 3   4, 7, 10, 13, … (+3 each)

e To go from one pattern to the next you add one counter to the top line of the Z, one to the bottom line and one to the sloping line.

f number of counters = 3 × **25** + 1 = 76
There are 76 counters.

3 a 17 matches   (5, 9, 13, …) (+4 each)

b $m = 4n + 1$

c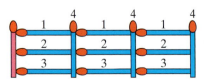

You add **4** new matches to go from one pattern to the next.
The **+1** is for the match on the left.

d No. The 12th pattern has 4 × 12 + 1 = 49 matches.
The 13th pattern has 53 matches so no pattern can have 51 matches.

4 **a** 4, 8, 12, …

b 16, 20, 24

c T(n) = 4n

d T(50) = 4 × 50 = 200. There are 200 red tiles in the 50th pattern.

5 **a** (1) T(1) = 1 + 2 = 3
T(2) = 2 + 2 = 4
T(3) = 3 + 2 = 5
T(4) = 4 + 2 = 6
T(5) = 5 + 2 = 7
(2) T(50) = 50 + 2 = 52

c (1) T(1) = 3 × 1 = 3
T(2) = 3 × 2 = 6
T(3) = 3 × 3 = 9
T(4) = 3 × 4 = 12
T(5) = 3 × 5 = 15
(2) T(50) = 3 × 50 = 150

b (1) T(1) = 2 × 1 − 1 = 1
T(2) = 2 × 2 − 1 = 3
T(3) = 2 × 3 − 1 = 5
T(4) = 2 × 4 − 1 = 7
T(5) = 2 × 5 − 1 = 9
(2) T(50) = 2 × 50 − 1 = 99

d (1) T(1) = 100 − 1 = 99
T(2) = 100 − 2 = 98
T(3) = 100 − 3 = 97
T(4) = 100 − 4 = 96
T(5) = 100 − 5 = 95
(2) T(50) = 100 − 50 = 50

6 **a** T(1) = 5 × 1 + 1 = 6
T(2) = 5 × 2 + 1 = 11
T(3) = 5 × 3 + 1 = 16
T(4) = 5 × 4 + 1 = 21
T(5) = 5 × 5 + 1 = 26

c T(1) = 7 − 4 × 1 = 3
T(2) = 7 − 4 × 2 = −1
T(3) = 7 − 4 × 3 = −5
T(4) = 7 − 4 × 4 = −9
T(5) = 7 − 4 × 5 = −13

e T(1) = 3 + 2 × 1 = 5
T(2) = 3 + 2 × 2 = 7
T(3) = 3 + 2 × 3 = 9
T(4) = 3 + 2 × 4 = 11
T(5) = 3 + 2 × 5 = 13

b T(1) = 2 × 1 − 2 = 0
T(2) = 2 × 2 − 2 = 2
T(3) = 2 × 3 − 2 = 4
T(4) = 2 × 4 − 2 = 6
T(5) = 2 × 5 − 2 = 8

d T(1) = 5 − 1 = 4
T(2) = 5 − 2 = 3
T(3) = 5 − 3 = 2
T(4) = 5 − 4 = 1
T(5) = 5 − 5 = 0

f T(1) = 4 × 1 − 11 = −7
T(2) = 4 × 2 − 11 = −3
T(3) = 4 × 3 − 11 = 1
T(4) = 4 × 4 − 11 = 5
T(5) = 4 × 5 − 11 = 9

7 **a** T(n) = 3n + 1   4, 7, 10, 13, …

b T(n) = 10n + 50   60, 70, 80, 90, …

c T(n) = 2n + 13   15, 17, 19, 21, …

Test yourself answers

8 1 and 36 (Square numbers are **1**, 4, 9, 16, 25, **36**, …
Triangular numbers are **1**, 3, 6, 10, 15, 21, 28, **36**, …)
1225 is the next number that is both square and triangular but you weren't asked to find it.

9 a $T(n) = n^2 + 2$

1, 4, 9, 16, … n^2
+2↓ +2↓ +2↓ +2↓
3, 6, 11, 18, … $n^2 + 2$

b $T(n) = n^2 - 3$

1, 4, 9, 16, … n^2
−3↓ −3↓ −3↓ −3↓
−2, 1, 6, 13, … $n^2 − 3$

c $T(n) = 3n^2$

1, 4, 9, 16, … n^2
×3↓ ×3↓ ×3↓ ×3↓
3, 12, 27, 48, … $3n^2$

d $T(n) = n^2 + 5$

1, 4, 9, 16, … n^2
+5↓ +5↓ +5↓ +5↓
6, 9, 14, 21, … $n^2 + 5$

Chapter 14

1 a

b Any triangle which has a height of 4 cm drawn using the given line as its base is correct.

2 a $12 \times 8 = 96\,cm^2$ **c** $\frac{1}{2} \times 12 \times 8 = 48\,cm^2$ **e** $\frac{1}{2}(7 + 14) \times 5 = 52.5\,cm^2$
 b $130 \times 78 = 10\,140\,cm^2$ **d** $\frac{1}{2} \times 16 \times 8.5 = 68\,mm^2$ **f** $\frac{1}{2}(4 + 15) \times 7 = 66.5\,cm^2$

3 a $22 \times 5 + 11 \times (8 − 5) = 143\,cm^2$ or $(22 − 11) \times 5 + 11 \times 8 = 143\,cm^2$

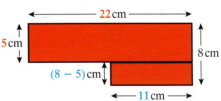

b $10 \times 7 − 5 \times 3 = 55\,cm^2$

332

Test yourself answers

4 a 160 000 m² (e.g. 800 × 100 + (500 − 100) × 100 + 200 × 200)

b

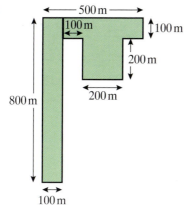

5 a 9 × 4 × 3 = 108 cm³   **b** 2 × 0.5 × 1.5 = 1.5 cm³   **c** 2 × 1.2 × 8 = 19.2 m³

6 90 litres ≈ 90 ÷ 4.5 = 20 gallons

7 a 11 yards ≈ 11 m   **d** 15 oz ≈ 15 × 30 = 450 g   **g** 12 ℓ ≈ 12 × 1.75 = 21 pints

b 108 km ≈ $\frac{108}{8}$ × 5 = 67.5 miles   **e** 101.2 lb ≈ 101.2 ÷ 2.2 = 46 kg   **h** 77 pints ≈ 77 ÷ 1.75 = 44 ℓ

c 15 miles ≈ $\frac{15}{5}$ × 8 = 24 km   **f** 5.5 kg ≈ 5.5 × 2.2 = 12.1 lb   **i** 7 gallons ≈ 7 × 4.5 = 31.5 ℓ

8 a 5.6 × 10 000 = 56 000 cm²   **c** 250 ÷ 100 = 2.5 cm²
    b 12.05 × 10 000 = 120 500 cm²   **d** 834 ÷ 100 = 8.34 cm²

Chapter 15

1 360° ÷ 45 = 8° per person

Breakfast	Cereal	Toast	Cooked	Nothing	Total
Number of people	11	21	5	8	45
Working	11 × 8°	21 × 8°	5 × 8°	8 × 8°	
Angle	88°	168°	40°	64°	360°

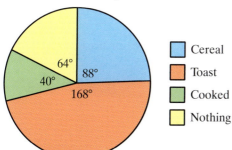

Breakfast Survey

333

Test yourself answers

2 360° ÷ 100% = 3.6° per 1%

Country	Percentage of population	Angle to 1 d.p.	Angle to nearest 1°
England	83%	298.8°	299°
Scotland	9%	32.4°	32°
Wales	5%	18.0°	18°
Northern Ireland	3%	10.8°	11°

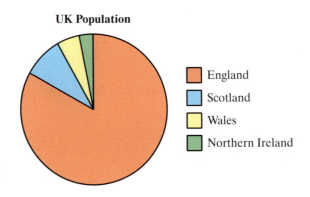

3 a

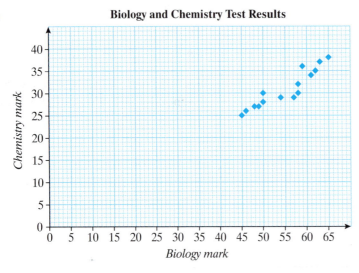

b Yes, pupils who do well in biology also do well in chemistry. The points lie within a strip which slopes upwards from left to right.

c Positive correlation

4 a Secondary   **b** Primary   **c** Experimental

5 a Open
b Closed
c Closed (It only allows you to say yes or no.)
d Closed

Test yourself answers

6 All of these are examples of what you may have written.
You should have definite options for the person answering the questions to choose from in each part.

1. How old are you? Please circle your age.
   under 13   13   14   15   16   17   18   over 18

2. How many cigarettes do you smoke on average each week? Please tick.
   None ☐
   1–10 ☐
   11–20 ☐
   21–30 ☐
   31–40 ☐
   41 or more ☐

3. How many hours a week do you exercise on average? Please tick.
   Less than 2 ☐
   At least 2 but less than 4 ☐
   At least 4 but less than 6 ☐
   At least 6 but less than 8 ☐
   At least 8 ☐

4. On average how many times a week do you visit a gym? Please tick.
   Never ☐
   1–3 ☐
   4–6 ☐
   7 or more ☐

5. How many different types of fruit and veg do you eat each day? Please tick.
   0–2 ☐
   3–5 ☐
   6–8 ☐
   9 or more ☐

6. Do you take part in any of the following school sports activities?
   Please tick all that apply.
   Football ☐
   Netball ☐
   Hockey ☐
   Rounders ☐
   Swimming ☐
   Other   Please state _____

7. How many sports teams are you a member of in school or out of school? Please tick.
   None ☐
   1 ☐
   2 ☐
   3 ☐
   4 or more ☐

7 **a** and **b**

Can you swim?	Tally	Frequency
Girl Can Swim	卌 I	6
Girl Cannot Swim	卌 I	6
Boy Can Swim	卌 III	8
Boy Cannot Swim	卌	5

Test yourself answers

c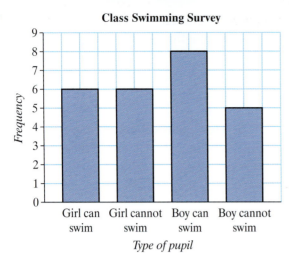

Chapter 16

1 a $\frac{21}{150} = \frac{7}{50}$ **b** $\frac{12}{150} \times 100\% = 8\%$

2 a 2 eggs make 4 pancakes ÷2 → 1 egg makes 2 pancakes ÷2, ×3 → 3 eggs make 6 pancakes ×3

b 6 dessertspoons of flour make 4 pancakes ÷2 → 3 dessertspoons of flour make 2 pancakes ÷2, ×5 → 15 dessertspoons of flour make 10 pancakes ×5

3 a $6 \times 2.54 = 15.24$ cm
 b $15 \times 2.54 = 38.1$ cm
 c $100 \times 2.54 = 254$ cm

4 £9.30 ÷ 30 × 100 = £31

5 £23 175 ÷ 103 × 100 = £22 500

6 a Divide by 130 and multiply by 100 (or divide by 1.3)
 b Divide by 70 and multiply by 100 (or divide by 0.7)

7 a 16 : 28 ÷4 → 4 : 7 ÷4
 b 3 m = 3 × 100 cm
 3 m : 20 cm = 300 cm : 20 cm = 15 : 1

8 This coffee is made from 3 + 7 = 10 parts altogether.
 a $\frac{3}{10} = 0.3 = 30\%$ of the coffee comes from Java
 b $\frac{7}{10}$ of the coffee comes from Columbia

Test yourself answers

9 The gym membership is made from 2 + 1 = **3** parts altogether.
3231 ÷ 3 = **1077**
2 × **1077** = 2154 males

10 a Altogether there are 1 + 2 + 5 = **8** parts
£16 000 ÷ **8** = **£2000**

1 × **£2000** = £2000
2 × **£2000** = £4000
5 × **£2000** = £10 000

Required shares are £2000, £4000 and £10 000.

b Altogether there are 2 + 3 + 4 = **9** parts
£58 500 ÷ **9** = **£6500**

2 × £6500 = £13 000
3 × £6500 = £19 500
4 × £6500 = £26 000

Required shares are £13 000, £19 500 and £26 000.

11 a One part = 80 kg
So nine parts = 80 kg × 9 = 720 kg, which is the mass of copper

b Total mass = 720 kg + 80 kg = 800 kg

Chapter 17

1 a (1, 3)   **b** (3, 9)   **c** (4, 12)   **d** (−6, −18)   **e** (4.5, 13.5)

2 a (1, 3)   **b** (5, 11)   **c** (−2, −3)   **d** (2.5, 6)   **e** (7, 15)

3 a

x	1	2	3	4
y	5	7	9	11

b, c, d

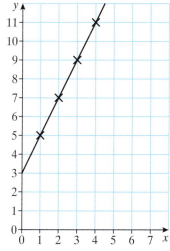

Test yourself answers

4 a

Number of sessions	0	10	20	30
Total cost (£)	0	24	**48**	**72**

b, d

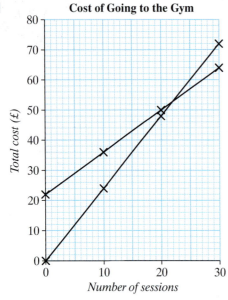

c

Number of sessions	0	10	20	30
Total cost (£)	22	36	**50**	**64**

e 22 sessions

5 a $x \mapsto 4x + 2$
(or $y = 4x + 2$)

b $x \mapsto x + 5$
(or $y = x + 5$)

c $x \mapsto 2x - 1$
(or $y = 2x - 1$)

6 a Ground floor (you can have floor 0) and floor 12

b 75 seconds − 10 seconds − 5 seconds = 60 seconds

c

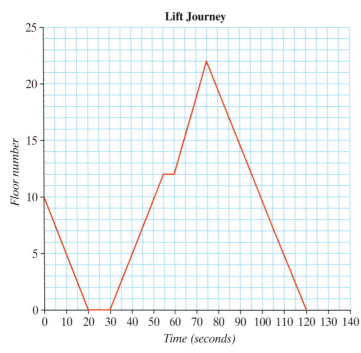

Chapter 18

1 a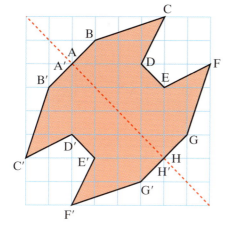

b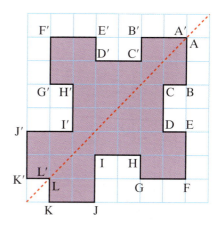

2 a, b, c, d

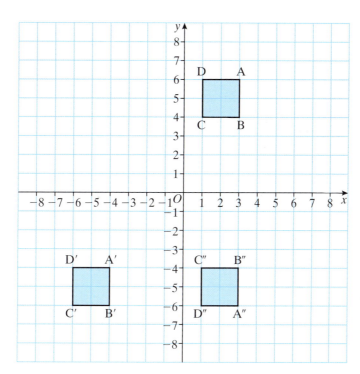

You should check carefully that your labelling of each shape is correct.

Test yourself answers

3 a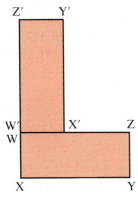

c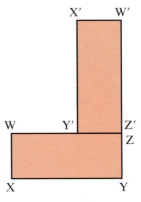

b (figure)

d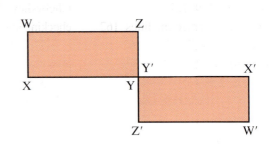

4
  a A translation of 3 right and 4 down
  b A translation of 2 left and 3 up
  c A reflection in the *x*-axis
  d A reflection in the *y*-axis
  e A rotation of 90° anticlockwise about (0, 0) or a rotation of 270° clockwise about (0, 0)
  f A rotation of 180° about (0, 0)

5 a, b, c, d, e

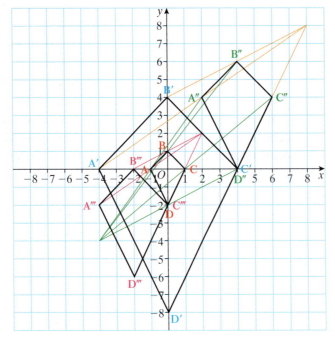

  f translation 6 to the right and 6 up
  g scale factor 2, centre of enlargement (8, 8)

Index

adding 62, 68, 191, 200
algebraic notation 2, 14
angle measurer (protractor) 154, 155, 170
angles 154-5
  acute 153
  alternate 162, 170
  calculating 155, 159, 162, 166
  corresponding 162, 170
  on a line 159, 162
  between intersecting lines 162
  between parallel lines 162
  measuring 154, 168, 170
  obtuse 153, 168
  at a point 155, 159, 170
  in quadrilaterals 164, 166
  reflex 47, 153, 155, 166
  right 153
  straight 153
  in a triangle 159, 166
  vertically opposite 162, 170
approximations 19, 21, 118, 125, 127
area 90, 203, 221, 222, 224, 236
arrowheads 47, 52, 164
artists 305
Aryabhata 90
averages 70, 74, 237
  see also mean, median, mode

balance diagrams 145, 192
bar charts, drawing 69
bias 74, 182, 250
biased questions 245, 246, 252
BODMAS 28, 30, 34, 137
  in algebra 94, 100
brackets 5, 10, 14, 28, 34
  on calculators 30
bus timetables 314-15
buses, London 229

calculators, using 30
capacity, estimating 26
capacity, units of 24, 34, 231, 236

carrying numbers (multiplication) 19, 125
Celsius, Anders 149
centilitres (cℓ) 24, 34
centimetres (cm) 24, 34, 233
  cubic 227
  square 222
century 24
certain 171, 172, 173, 186
Chebyshev's theory 58
checking answers by estimating 19, 21, 118, 125, 127
classification diagrams 48, 49, 51, 167
coins, tossing 173, 179, 186
collecting like terms 7, 10, 14, 148
common denominator 190, 202
common factors 55
common multiples 54
cones 101
congruent 297, 301
conversion graphs 281, 282
converting big/small 32
coordinates 35, 36, 39, 52, 273, 289
  negative 36, 38, 274
correlation 243, 252
counters in shapes 208
cube numbers 16, 28, 30, 34
  algebraic 3
cube roots 16, 34
cubes (shapes) 101, 104, 225, 227, 236
cubic centimetres 227
cuboids 101, 102, 104, 105
  nets 225, 228
  surface area 225, 236
  volume 227, 236
cylinders 101

data 237, 249
  analysis 249
  continuous 80, 82, 86

discrete 80, 82
experimental 244, 252
grouping 69
primary and secondary 244, 252
days 24
decades 24
decagons 101
decimal number system 23
decimal numbers 121
  dividing 120, 122, 127
  equivalent 171, 196, 202
  multiplying 120, 122, 125, 134
  negative numbers 64, 68
  rounding 116, 125, 127
decimal place 116
decimal point, alternatives 121
decimals to percentages 202, 254
denominator 28, 129, 134, 187-8, 191
  common 190, 202
diagonals 41, 47, 50
dice 175, 180, 181, 182, 186
difference patterns 204, 214, 215
dinosaurs 230
directed numbers 60, 62, 64, 68
discount 131
dividend 21
dividing 17, 21, 64, 120, 127
  decimals 120, 122, 127
  directed numbers 64, 68
  mentally 17, 32, 122
  written methods 15, 21
divisibility tests 56
divisor 21
doubling 15, 20, 34, 122
doubt 171
dust mites 121

e 116
edges 102, 112
Egyptian multiplication 20
elevation, front and side 110, 114
emirp numbers 57

Index

enlargement 234, 301, 304, 308
   centre of 301, 304, 305, 308
equal chance 175, 179, 186
equals signs 2, 140
equations 2, 144, 146, 148
   function machines solving 142, 143, 150
Eratosthenes, sieve of 58
estimating
   answers 19, 21, 118, 125, 127
   height 229, 230, 236
   measures 26
Euler's rule 104
euros 256
even chance 171, 172, 173
even numbers 58, 89, 220
events 172, 175
experimental data 244, 252
experiments, probability 181-3, 186
expressions 2, 7, 10, 87, 203
   evaluating 88, 100
   linked to n 2, 14, 87
   substituting into 88, 100

faces 102, 112
factor loops 55
factor pairs 53
factor trees 59, 66, 68
factors 16, 53, 55, 57, 59, 68
   common 55
factory line 183
facts to figure 20, 23, 58, 91, 121, 180, 189, 216, 217, 224, 230, 285, 305
Fahrenheit, Daniel 149
feet 189, 231, 236
Fibonacci's sequence 217
fifty-fifty chance 171
first term 204, 212
flags 253
flow charts 206
formulae 90, 92
   area 222, 236
   sequences 208, 214, 216
   substituting into 90, 98, 100
   temperature conversion 149

volume of cuboids 227
fraction wall 190
fractions 21, 28, 187
   3-digit 189
   adding 191, 200, 202
   of an amount 129, 134, 194
   cancelling 188, 202, 253
   comparing 190, 202
   to decimals 171, 196
   equivalent 188, 196
   lowest terms 188, 202
   simplifying 188, 202
   subtracting 191, 200, 202
   unit 193, 196
frequency diagrams 82, 86, 237
frequency tables 69
   to find the mean 72, 84, 86
fruit and veg survey 248-9
function machines 138, 140, 152
   solving equations 142, 143, 150
   inverse 140, 142
functions 276, 279, 288

gallons 231, 236
games 180, 182
Goldbach's conjecture 58
good chance 171
grams (g) 24, 34
graphs 276, 288
   conversion 281, 282
   real-life 281, 282, 284
   scales on 286
   scatter 241, 243, 252
   straight-line 77, 276, 281, 284
   time-series 79
grid, points in 35

halving 15, 20, 34, 122
hemispheres 101
hexagons 101, 209
Highest Common Factor (HCF) 55, 68, 260
hours 24
hundredths column 116

icons v
image 290, 294, 297, 301

imperial units 231, 236
imperial/metric
   approximations 231, 232, 235, 236
impossible 171, 172, 173, 186
inches 231, 236
input (function machines) 138, 140, 152
input (mapping) 279
integers 53, 59
inverse operations 21, 96, 118, 144
isometric paper, dotty 92, 105, 112, 303
isometric paper with grids 105, 106

kilograms (kg) 24, 34
kilometres (km) 24, 34, 233
kites 47, 52, 164, 168

length, estimating 26
length, units of 24, 189, 221, 231
like terms, collecting 7, 10, 14, 148
likely 171, 172
line graphs 77, 276, 281, 284
line symmetry 42, 43
lines, intersecting 162, 170
lines, measuring 153
lines, parallel 162, 170, 305
lines of symmetry 35, 41, 45, 47, 50, 290
   diagonal 290, 306
litres (ℓ) 24, 34
long multiplication 19, 34, 125
Lowest Common Multiple (LCM) 54, 68, 190
lowest terms 188, 202

magic squares 63
mapping diagrams 279, 288
maps 60, 230
mass, units of 24, 26, 231, 236
mathematicians 58, 91, 180, 193
   Aryabhata 91
   Euler 104

Index

Gauss, Carl 216
Napier, John 121
Pick, Georg Alexander 224
Toscanelli 305
maths in the real world 309-15
mean 71, 72, 74, 86, 237
   from frequency tables 72, 84, 86
median 70, 74, 86, 237
metres (m) 24, 34, 233
   square 222
metric conversions 24, 233, 236
metric units 24, 34
metric/imperial conversion 232, 282
mid-point of a line 39
miles 231, 236
millennium 24
milligrams (mg) 24, 34
millilitres (ml) 24, 34
millimetres (mm) 24, 34, 233
   square 222
minutes 24
mirror lines 35, 41, 45, 47, 50, 290
   diagonal 290, 306
mode (modal value) 69, 70, 74, 237
modelling 183
money, 'old' 257
months 24
MORI 247
multiples 53, 54, 68
   common 54
multiplication tables 1, 15, 53
multiplying 10, 16, 17, 64, 120
   carrying numbers 19, 125
   decimals 120, 122, 125, 134
   directed numbers 64, 68
   Egyptian method 20
   mentally 16-17, 115, 122
   negative numbers 64, 68
   Russian method 20
   written methods 15, 115
music notes 193

n 1, 2, 87, 88, 140, 148

National Lottery 245
negative numbers 53, 60, 62, 64, 68
Nelson's Column 230
nets 107, 109, 113, 158
no chance 171
nth term rule 214, 216, 220
number lines 60, 66, 68
number systems 23
numbers
   cube 16, 28, 34
   directed 60, 62, 64, 68
   emirp 57
   even 58, 89, 220
   larger 21
   negative 53, 60, 62, 64, 68
   prime 57, 58, 59, 68
   rectangular 217
   splitting up 15, 16, 34, 122
   square 16, 34, 216, 220
   triangular 215, 216
   whole 53, 59
numerator 28, 129, 134, 187, 188, 193

object 290, 294, 297, 301, 308
octagons 101
octahedrons 109
operations, inverse 21, 96, 118, 144
order of operations 28, 34, 137
   algebraic 5, 14, 94, 203
order of rotational symmetry 43, 45, 47, 289
ounces (oz) 231, 236
outcome 173, 175, 179, 186
output (function machines) 138, 140
output (mapping) 279

paper shapes 42
parallel lines 162, 170, 305
parallelograms 41, 47, 164, 222
partitioning 15, 16, 34, 122
pentagons 101, 209
percentages 187
   of an amount 131, 134, 199
   to decimals 131, 196
   decrease 131, 136
   equivalent 196, 202
   to fractions 196, 202
   increase 131, 136
perimeter 90, 221, 224
perspective 305
pi (π) 116
picker/guesser experiment 181
Pick's theorem 224
pie charts 77, 79, 238, 240, 252
pints 231, 236
plan view 110, 114
planes of symmetry 102, 109, 114
Playfair, William 284
playing cards 178, 186
plotting graphs 276, 288
points, generating 274
points in a grid 35
polygons 101
position-to-term formula 212
positive numbers 60, 62, 64
possible 171
pounds (lb) 231, 236
powers (indices) 3, 28
prime factor decomposition 59, 66
prime factors 59
prime numbers 57, 58, 59
prisms 101, 103, 104, 112
probability 171, 172, 173
   estimating 173
   experiments 181-3, 186
   fractional 173, 175, 178
   scale 172, 173
product 16
production line simulation 183
proportion 187, 194, 256
   comparing 254, 270
proportional change 258
protractors 154, 155, 170
pyramids 101, 104, 106, 112

quadrants, four 36, 38, 52
quadrilaterals 47, 52, 164
   angles in 164, 166
questionnaires 244, 245

Index

questions 245, 246, 252
quotient 21

random 178, 183, 186
range 69, 74, 237
Rangoli patterns 42
ratio 260, 262, 266, 268, 272
   dividing in 264, 270
recipes 256, 257, 271
rectangles 41, 43, 47, 50, 164
   area 90, 203, 221
   perimeter 90
rectangular numbers 217
reflection 35, 52, 290, 297
   symmetry 290
remainder 17, 21
revision 1, 15, 35, 53, 69, 87, 101, 115, 137, 153, 171, 187, 203, 221, 237, 253, 273, 289
rhombus 47, 52, 164
rotation 297, 298, 299
rotational symmetry 43, 45, 47, 50, 289
rounding numbers 21, 115, 118
   decimals 116, 125, 127
   sensibly 117
rules 64, 68, 208, 220
Russian multiplication 20

sale reductions 258, 272
sample space diagrams 179, 186
samples 247, 250
scale drawings 261
scale factor 301, 304, 308
scales on graphs 286
scatter graphs 241, 243, 252
seconds 24
sequence of points 274, 276
sequences 203, 204, 220
   difference patterns 204, 214, 215
   Fibonacci's 217
   generating 206, 212, 216
   linear and non-linear 204, 215, 216
   quadratic 216, 220
   finding terms 204, 214, 216

shapes, 2-D 41, 43, 45, 47, 50, 289
shapes, 3-D 101, 102, 112, 114
   2-D representation 105, 114
   surface area 225
shapes, complicated 222
shapes, concave 47, 52, 164
shares 264, 266, 268, 270
sieve of Eratosthenes 58
simulation 183
sketches 105, 106, 114
spheres 101
spinners 173, 184
splitting up numbers 15, 16, 34, 122
square centimetres 222
square metres 222
square millimetres 222
square numbers 16, 28, 34, 216, 220
   algebraic 2
square roots 16, 34, 30, 96
squares (shapes) 41, 43, 47, 164, 234
statistics project 248-9
statistics, using 244
straight-line graphs 77, 276, 281, 284
substituting into
   expressions 88, 100
   formulae 90, 98, 100
subtracting 62, 68
   directed numbers 62
   fractions 191, 200
summaries 14, 34, 52, 68, 86, 100, 114, 136, 152, 170, 186, 202, 220, 236, 252, 272, 288, 308
surface area 225, 236
survey, fruit and veg 248-9
Swedenborg 23
symbols, mathematical 82, 146
symmetry 41, 290
   planes of 102, 109, 114
   rotational 43, 45, 47, 50, 289

table of values 274
tally marks 69

tap flowing 284
temperature 53, 60, 62
   conversion 149, 281
   scales 149
term numbers $T(n)$ 212, 214, 216
terms in a sequence 204
terms 2, 204, 208
   like 7
   collecting 7, 10, 14, 148
   lowest 188, 202
term-to-term rules 204, 212, 218
test yourself 12-13, 32-3, 50-1, 66-7, 84-5, 98-9, 112-13, 134-5, 150-1, 168-9, 184-5, 200-1, 218-19, 234-5, 250-1, 270-1, 286-7, 306-7
tetrahedrons 101, 102, 104
thousandths column 116
thumb 189
time, units of 24, 32
time-series graphs, drawing 79
times tables 1, 15, 53
tonnes 24, 34
Towers 230
transformations 290, 306
translation 294, 297, 308
trapeziums 47, 92, 164, 222
trend 79
triangles 45, 166
   angles in 159, 166
   area 90, 222
   drawing 157
   equilateral 43, 45
   isosceles 45, 47, 52
   perimeter 148, 150
   right-angled 45
   scalene 45, 52
triangular numbers 215, 216
twin primes 58
unfair 171
unitary method 256, 258
unknowns 1, 87, 140, 146
unlikely 171, 172

vanishing point 305
variables 2, 88, 92
vegetable growing 312-13

Index

vertices 35, 102, 112, 306
volume 227

water use 310-11
weeks 24
whole numbers 53, 59
working backwards problems 258

x-axis 36
x-coordinates 39, 274

yards 231, 236
y-axis 36
y-coordinates 39, 274
years 24

zero 60